THE MEDIUM-SIZED BOOK OF
ZIM SCRIPTS
VOL. 1: PIGS 'N' WAFFLES

**The Stories
and the Stories Behind the Stories
of Your Favorite Invader**

by ERIC TRUEHEART
Art by Aaron Alexovich and Rikki Simons

The Medium-Sized Book of ZIM Scripts vol 1: Pigs 'n' Waffles

The Stories and the Stories Behind the Stories of Your Favorite Invader

Eric Trueheart

ISBN (Print Edition): 978-1-73469-250-1

ISBN (eBook Edition): 978-1-73469-251-8

TABLE OF CONTENTS

I just wanted something to sign at conventions.

This is what happened.

DEDICATION

To mutants everywhere, without whom evolution would never move forward. To my beloved Sammi, for believing in me. To Andrea Turner, Erica Katzenjammer, and Captain Sodium for lending their eyes. And to Richard, Andy, Rikki, Melissa, Roger, Lucille, Wally, Kevin, and of course Jhonen V., for all making something so special and weird people still wonder just how the hell it happened.

FOREWORD
by Rikki Simons

Eric Trueheart Asked Me to Write this Foreword Because He Knows I Have Insomnia

"Strike me down and my massive jugs will only get more swol, bro!" - Sir Alec Guinness as Obi Wan Kenobi ripping off his brown robe and white shirt and flexing his totally cut pecs. (This scene was in the original 1977 version of A New Hope, before George Lucas changed it in the Special Edition(s).)

I first met Eric Trueheart in an abattoir. Okay, that's not true. But there was a lot of panicked mooing.

I first met Eric Trueheart in 1997 at San Diego Comic Con, a place so crowded that if you collapsed from heart failure you would either end up crowd surfing all the way to the first aid station or end up being scooped into one of those mystery boxes they sell. This is an appropriate metaphor because Eric Trueheart is himself a sort of mystery box of a man. When you open him up, you never know what you'll find inside. I mean, I'm not a medical professional. I literally have no idea what's inside the human body.

I could say that I met Eric about three years before I was meant to. Timing is everything in animation and in this Eric is usually on the mark, except for our first encounter where he decided, unbeknownst to him, to arrive three years early to our introduction. I will explain if you want.

Okay.

I was consternated on that first encounter. I wasn't consternated with Eric. I was just very distracted with consternation because it's an unwieldy word with too many syllables. I was at San Diego Comic Con occupying a free space with my beloved spouse and art partner Tavisha in a Japanese toy booth called Kimono My House that had been secured by our friend Taliesin Jaffe. At this booth, Tavisha and I hawked whatever comic book we were producing at the time that contained a cat in it (because all of our books have cats in them). We were sitting there catching our breath after vigorously refusing to do a commission for an unsavory fanboy in a pith helmet who had a sexual monomania for muscle women in bikinis with large feet. I was just starting to calm down when our friend Michele Takahashi walked up to our table with a blondish, square-jawed man in optional non-standard sideburns. Michele was a college student studying screenwriting at USC, whom Tavisha and I met at a 10,000 square foot craft mall I used to manage for my father. This craft mall was the sort of place where you rented out spaces to people who basically tried to convince you that the potato with googly eyes they were selling was patented and under no circumstances was I to allow anyone else to sell a any other ocular-bedecked spuds. Michele had also been a crafter at this mall. She sold clay Frankenstein earrings.

So, I was sitting there at the Kimono My House booth, calming down from our encounter with the pith-helmeted pervert when Michele showed up. I looked at her and immediately had flashbacks to potato people patents. She then introduced me to her sideburn-emblazoned friend as one Eric Trueheart, a fellow USC student. Eric had recently written a comic book about a ninja office worker and he was asking for advice on publishing. I think I looked at the comic and muttered something along the lines of "Ah." I didn't mean to be rude, I was just reeling from the pith helmet encounter and the Michele-activated potato memory. Also, I was confused because Michele told me that Eric was a screen writing major. I never went to college, so I didn't know they had military rankings.

The conversation between Eric and I went on a bit longer than that of course, and after I finished gathering my composure I found Eric to be very funny and charming. He knew so much about science fiction books and movies and TV shows of the 70s and was the first person I met who deeply understood the importance of the shift in tempo in the opening theme music from season one to season two of Space: 1999. Once more, he was really cool, like all the explosions edited out of old Looney Tunes cartoons contained only by the sheer masculine superstructure of two optional non-standard sideburns.

Nothing came of that first encounter, but over the next few years Michele kept us abreast of Eric's progress at USC as he worked on different comedy writing projects (do yourself a favor and look up "Weird TV"). Then something really strange happened. I started working on *Invader ZIM*. I landed the role of GIR in November of 1998, but the pilot wasn't green lit for series until the end of 1999. I'd have two jobs on the show: GIR of course (voice over wouldn't begin until March of 2000), and then background color, which wouldn't start until August of 2000. This meant that I was unaware of the day-to-day goings on of the show until my body was needed on site. Jhonen has always been a very private man, so private that, back then, he wouldn't even refer to mutual friends by name, so you never knew who he was talking about when he said he was out with "my friend" or that he would be coming to dinner with "my friend," until he actually came to the event and you saw that the "my friend" was someone he knew you were already acquainted with. Whew.

In the spring of 2000 Jhonen invited Tavisha and I to see an amazing play called *Shockheaded Peter* based on the 150 year old book, *The Struwwelpeter*, by lunatic asylum medical professional Dr. Heinrich Hoffmann, which was about the destruction of a variety of naughty children. It was performed by

Julian Crouch and sung by my soon-to-be-favorite murder ballad anachronistically anarchical cabaret post punk trio, *The Tiger Lillies*. Jhonen said he was bringing "his friend" to see the play, which I knew could be anyone from a stranger to my own freshly cloned doppelgänger which he built out of hot dogs and ennui — but this time he said he wanted me to meet a new amazing writer he had hired who knew his way around space and time and comedy and pigs. When we all gathered at the entrance to the theater, this mysterious purveyor of tales of time traveling pig turned out to be Eric Trueheart. This was an utter coincidence. I knew Jhonen since 1995 and I had never mentioned Eric to him before. We greeted each other warmly and immediately began catching up. It was the first time I ever saw Jhonen look surprised.

Like all of my ZIM family members (even Jhonen!) I have grown to cherish my friendship with Eric. Over the last twenty years I've looked forward to hearing him talk about not only the stories he writes, but also the stories of his doings, whether it be him installing a giant jar of mayonnaise with a FREE MAYO sign in the desert at Burning Man (look up "free mayo Burning Man" in Google Images), dressing up as a corporate hippo at a full-sized office building art installation at the Coachella Valley Music and Arts Festival (look up "corporate hippos Coachella"), or just hanging out with The Humungus at Wasteland Weekend (need I say what to do?), Eric is always doing something weird and interesting as part of his nature, which made him perfect for *Invader ZIM* (When my father passed away, he very graciously accepted a invitation to his wake, even though it was all the way out in Yucca Valley, but after the ceremony he took us to a park he discovered called *Desert Christ Park* that contained a vast collection of plaster and rebar religious statues that looked like some kind of cursed gorgon battlefield — it cheered us up immensely). This praise will make him very embarrassed and it's about time, dammit. There's only so many times you watch someone join an organization like *The Ministry of Unknown Science* and film themselves invading the sun with a clone army and not expect them to someday feel self conscious about it. Take it down a peg, Eric! Save some stampeding lepre-chauns for the rest of us!

Anyways, I've gone on too long. You must read this book for two rea-sons. One: because it is sharp and humble and funny, and not only gives you a ringside seat to the production of *Invader ZIM* but also a vivid insight into the terrible hot dog factory that is the animation industry — and two: because you bought it (or stole it) and you might as well give it a go.

-Rikki Simons

INTRODUCTION:
ENTER THE NICKELODEOUS

The Sun is Pink and a Madman Laughs.

It's my first time setting foot into the realm of Nickelodeon, an unassuming building in the less-fashionable realms of Burbank, CA. The green slime-shaped sign hanging off the roof is one of the few hints of what goes on inside this edifice. That, and the huge sign that reads "Nickelodeon" in large, kid-friendly letters. All right, upon re-examination, the building isn't particularly unassuming at all. But nestled as it is down the block from a 7-11, across the street from an RV dealership, and a stone's throw from a municipal power plant, it's hardly glamorous.

I am there to meet Mary Harrington, semi-legendary producer in the cartoon world, and executive in charge of a show called *Invader: ZIM*. (Yes, the title had a colon back then)

Back in its early days as a newly-acquired network under the MTV Networks banner, Mary was one of the people responsible for defining what would become Nickelodeon's cartoon "brand." She was one of the people whose stewardship brought both *Ren & Stimpy* and *Rugrats* to life, and as a result had a reputation for championing off-beat projects at a network that was, at the time I show up, most famous for thinking dumping green slime on a child's head is the height of cultural rebellion.

Mary is tall, blonde, with a sophisticated East coast air about her, and doesn't at all seem like a killer robot secretly programmed to destroy the human race with eye lasers.*

*This is because she isn't

This is my first attempt at landing a job in the much coveted TV world, a world that seems like a magical land on the other side of an invisible fence, because basically it is. At least the invisible fence part is true. The barriers to entry in the TV business are many and varied, and usually not obvious until you've bumped your head against them more than once. So today I'm trying to be both impressive and casual at the same time. Making small talk. Trying to look both professional and nonchalant as I look in awe at the offices and cubicles lined majestically with toys, movie paraphernalia, and drawings bursting with inside jokes. Can grown-ups really make a living like this?

I had recently graduated with a Masters degree from the screenwriting program at USC. Pro tip: You do *not* need an MFA to write cartoons about pigs, but it can't hurt. The program was an intensive hodgepodge designed to force you to make five years of screenwriting mistakes over the course of two. I'd graduated somehow with both a lawyer and agent to my name — a rarity in those circles — and a spec episode of South Park that features Cartman forming a cult around pork products and some other plot points I've now forgotten. I wouldn't find out until later that pork jokes were probably what landed me this interview.

A week or two before stepping foot onto the Nickelodeon compound — past the heavily-armed security robots and the dogs trained to sniff for Disney paraphernalia — my agent had tipped me off that there was a job opening on a new animated series. Thr creator was a guy named Jhonen Vasqez, a comic book author responsible for creating Batman back in 1924 before Bob Kane was even alive to rip off Milton Finger.

That last part is not true.

Jhonen, as you all probably know, got his start creating comic books like *Johnny the Homicidal Manical* and *Squee*; comics that redefined the notion of laughing out loud at horrible things. How a man famous for blood, murder, and pig jokes got a gig at Nickelodeon is not a question I'd asked myself at the time. Back then I fancied myself as someone who was going to redefine the entire notion of something in the film business. This is how a lot of film-school grads think. They're going to redefine *something*, even if they don't know what it is yet.

So I went to my local comic shop — the legendary Golden Apple, back when it was settled at the ugly end of Melrose Ave. next to a Doc Marten's shop — and picked up a trade collection of *Johnny* and *Squee* before I went on a short trip to visit my family in the Bay Area, not all that far from where Jhonen had grown up..

"Kid's show? HA!" I had thought quietly to myself when I was offered the interview. (Yes, I said "HA!" in my own head. I really did. Check the tapes to prove it.) But as I sat outside a hippie ice cream shop in Berkeley and flipped through these comic book pages, my mind began to shift. Whoever wrote this was going to create a kids' show for the ages. Or get cancelled after one and a half seasons. Foolishly, I never considered "both" as a possible answer.

Now here I was in Burbank, California, at the headquarters of Nickelodeon Animation Studios, talking to an executive who had been willing to put up with John Krickfalusi in the 90s to get *Ren & Stimpy* on the air. It was impressive. It was intimidating.

Oh, and the whole area was turning pink.

Really, the light was changing color. It was a shade slightly fuchsia, one that put your mind somewhere between Easter and the make-up your grandma probably wore in the 1970s.

I looked up to see workmen installing red gels over the skylights that overlooked the main work area of the *ZIM* wing — an area of hundreds of square feet composed of open cubicles and the production's TV lounge. But the gels weren't turning the place the spooky red I assumed they were intended to. They were turning the whole office pink.

And there was a thin man dressed all in black with — if I remember correctly — some kind of high-laced leather boots that would look dangerous on anyone that wasn't him, laughing at the complete train wreck happening above him. This madman, I would soon discover, was Jhonen Vasquez.

This laugh was the sort of uncomfortable kind I would come to recognize over the next couple of years. It was a combination of a spontaneous outburst over things going comically, horribly wrong, coupled with the embarrassment that he was somehow responsible for it, even if he wasn't.

In his inimitable style, Jhonen had wanted to turn the offices blood red, and instead had turned them Easter pink.

And before you jump to any conclusion, this pink is *not* the metaphor for what happens when an author of murder comics is subsumed by the world's second-cuddliest children's network. No, the metaphor is the laughing. Laughing when things go wrong. Laughing when your brain is also horrified at the mess that will need cleaning up. Laughing to keep the horror at bay.

This, gentle readers, is a metaphor for the experience of being in the trenches of *Invader ZIM*.

If you've never heard of *Invader ZIM*... Why the hell are you buying this book? Of all the obscure things you could be spending your money on, it seems particularly boneheaded to buy an account of the making of a show you've never even watched.

Still, let me bring you up to speed. *Invader ZIM* is a show that ran on Nickelodeon for about one and a half seasons back in 2000, and, like a virus hiding on your hard drive, has somehow managed to stay in the consciousness of the subculture ever since.

It's the story of an Invader from the plant Irk sent to take over the earth, and the young paranormal investigator who has to stop him.

That's how the situations seems on the surface, anyway. The truth is the invader — that's ZIM — is so irritating and destructive that his superiors — the Almighty Tallest — have sent him on a fool's mission to conquer Earth just to get him out of the way. They honestly don't care one way or the other whether he breaks the Earth over his Mighty Irken Will, just so long as he stops bothering them. Meanwhile Dib — the paranormal investigator — is a kid with a big head, both literally and figuratively, whose mission may be noble, but his smug sense of superiority somehow dooms him to failure at every turn. ZIM is assisted by a small robot named GIR who is hopelessly broken. Dib is assisted by… well, nobody, but he has a sister named Gaz who really wishes he'd stop being so annoying, and a father, Professor Membrane, who looks down on Dib's paranormal investigations as pseudo science.

That's it in a nutshell. And if that description seems to leave out the fundamental insanity at the heart of the show, that's probably how the Nickelodeon executives felt when they green-lit the thing.

Roughly twenty years later, at the time of writing this, it's amazing to think this little oddball show keeps getting new fans every year. This mutant flipper baby* of a cartoon has resisted all attempts to toss it in the dumpster of pop culture history where it would rest with hundreds of other cancelled series that today couldn't even breathe the air on Hulu-plus.

*No offense meant to any mutant flipper babies reading this.

A brief aside here to speak to the fickle and ephemeral nature of television: If you've ever worked at Titmouse animation studios in Hollywood, first, you should make sure your shots are up to date. And second, you may have noticed they have a fascinating collection of magazines in their bathrooms.

Did I say fascinating? I meant historic. When I was there working on some show or another for DreamWorks, one of the bathrooms sported a People magazine from about ten years earlier, which was an amazing feat.

Most people can't resist tossing People magazine into the nearest disposal unit when it's current, much less when it's that old.

Reading that magazine was like taking a time tunnel back to an era no one cared about. It was like an alien race giving me a chance to see anywhere into our nation's past, and I happened to end up looking not at the first Constitutional Congress or Nikola Tesla's lab, but a flea circus in Des Moines Iowa in 1979, and backstage, too, where I only saw the fleas smoking tiny flea cigarettes waiting to go on. The article I most remember was something along the line of "The New Shows Coming This Season to the Networks You Can Watch as They're Broadcast Through the Air in Real Time!" This piece listed every series you absolutely must see because goddamnit, you're going to miss out on the next cultural tsunami if you miss one minute of this heartwarming show about a family of orphans adopted by a lovable blind oral surgeon and… You get it.

Out of that glorious parade of television hope, only one show had made it. It was a sit-com I never even watched, but at least I remembered the title. (At the time, anyway. Now I've completely forgotten it. So it just goes to show. "Laugh upon my works, ye mighty, and despair.") Everything else had been cancelled in its first season. A dozen shows costing millions of dollars consigned to the trash-burner of pop culture history, and taking the show-biz hopes and dreams of actors, writers, directors, and executives with them.

The human tragedy involved is best swept under the rug: Writers who ended up defaulting on mortgages and losing their homes. Actors whose big break was hopelessly blown, thus starting a slide into despair, drug addiction, and the inevitable bus ticket back home to work at dad's plumbing supplies business. Executives who somehow managed to fail upward into better jobs, because that's what executives do.

Better not to think about it.

But I mention it only for one reason: It's amazing that a show about a green-skinned alien and the pain-in-the-ass kid who wants to expose him has lasted this long. Beyond the toys, the Hot Topic t-shirts, the fan fiction, and the permanent niche on streaming services, *Invader ZIM* still gets new fans every year. It's astounding. It defies all logic. Statistically speaking, nothing we did should have lasted, and yet it did.

Theories as to why shall be explored later in this book full of scripts and the stories behind them.

Yes, scripts. I've found over the years that people have a strange fascination with the words that somehow end up creating the things they fall in love with on the screen. Maybe they're trying to find the "essence" of the story, maybe they're just fascinated with what things looked like before they turned all pretty and such. But when I was a kid I chased after TV scripts like a trained pig chased after truffles, and maybe this book can spread a little of that pig dirt to the next generation.

If we're lucky.

But first...

a WORD
aBOUT SCREENPLAYS

Or How a Bill Becomes a Law.

You may notice, gentle reader, that some of the scripts in this book don't match exactly with what appeared on the screen in the final episode. This is because a script is basically a map for everyone else to follow, and what follows doesn't always follow the map. There's a long road between the script and the screen, and that road is full of little bumps, detours, rest stops, and jokes that turned out to be just plain funnier than what was in the original script. Yeah, I abandoned the metaphor in that last sentence in favor of clarity. Fortunately, my high school English teacher will never read this.

The production of a cartoon — circa the year 2000 when *ZIM* was made — goes something like this:

First someone like me writes a script.

This one sentence makes this part sound incredibly simple. It isn't. It involves some steps baked into the process like pitching the premise and writing the outline, each of which includes feedback and approval from the network side. There's also the part where the writer goes into a dark office and stares at the blank page until he or she thinks of what the hell to write next. This part happens for many pages, and takes longer than people think it ought to.

Once the script is done, the voice recording begins. The cast is brought into the recording studio, put in front of microphones, and they read their lines in character, often to each other. You know, like actors do. They act. They wave their arms. They talk in silly voices and make strange grunting noises. On *ZIM*, there was always a fair amount of screaming, usually by Richard Horvitz.

During this phase, the actors or the voice director -- in our case Jhonen himself -- sometimes come up with funny bits to add to the script. *ZIM*'s famous near-45 second "My Tallest!" rant at the top of "Backseat Drivers From Beyond the Stars" happened because Richard was told to "give us a few'" and he just kept going. Apparently he was waiting for Jhonen to stop him. Apparently Jhonen was waiting for him to finish. The final result was used almost in its entirety.

From the voice recording session, the best takes are assembled into an audio edit called an EMR. I have at this point completely forgotten what EMR stands for, and I am too lazy to look it up. I can guarantee it doesn't stand for Emergency Medical Raccoon, or Every Man's Rhubarb, but it's basically a rough edit of just the voice lines from the episode that the storyboard artists use when crafting the character acting in the storyboards. And speaking of that...

The next step is the storyboards. A storyboard is where an artist draws on paper every last shot, every last camera angle, every last action, every last... well... pretty much everything that will visually go into the cartoon. This is usually under the supervision of the show's director, and in our case that was Steve Ressel. The storyboard doesn't map out every frame, but it does map out every major shot, character pose, and change in motion that the animators down the line will use to lay out every frame of animation.

The storyboard phase is another place where talented and funny people add jokes, mostly visual gags in *ZIM*'s case, though some shows like *Spongebob Squarepants* are what they call "board-driven," meaning the actual dialogue is hashed out by the board artists, and then recorded later. Our board artists were extremely talented and funny, even by talented-and-funny standards, and many, many gags were added in this phase that may not have even been mentioned in the script. For example, the sequence in "Door to Door" where the neighbors experience rising terror as the kids spread out over the neighborhood to sell their candy was something added in the storyboard stage. Or almost any time GIR fell over trying to do something really simple.

At the same time, a series of artists are busy drawing up the backgrounds, new character and props for the episode. You know, so if, say, there's a scene where Mortos der Soulstealer demands Dib take him to a pet store and buy a puppy from Maurice the Puppy Man (yes, that was his name in the script,) Maurice, the puppy, the store, and Mortos himself all have to be drawn up by artists so everyone else in the production knows just what the hell they look like.

During this time, the color artists are also busy assigning colors for these things, though this info won't be needed for the next stage: the animatic! (Ooooo! Say it with me! *The Animatic!*)

The animatic is where the storyboard is married with the audio track to create a rough animation of what the episode will look like. Usually black and white, and only "animated" in the most basic sense, it looks something like a motion comic but more detailed. Here is a where the director and the showrunner can really start to see how the episode is taking place. How does the pacing work? Do the drawn expressions on the characters' faces match the emotions of the actors' voices? Can some things be cut, fine-tuned, or made better? Have we all been wasting our time since art school? The usual.

As you might expect, this is also a place where the show can deviate from the original script. Once the story is "on its feet," jokes start jumping out of the woodwork, or things that seemed great on paper suddenly don't seem so great any more. I can't remember ever working on a cartoon where the show didn't change during the animatic at least a little bit, and usually more than a little bit. Scenes are tweaked, gags added, and new lines written that will be recorded later in pick-up sessions.

This is also where the episode is generally cut down for time. For whatever reason, it seems a universal human phenomenon that people tend to go long on whatever their creative brief might be. Or as the old saying goes, "I'm sorry this letter is so long, I didn't have time to make it shorter." There's always something they to cut from an animatic to get it to length. That's just science.

When the animatic is locked — that is to say it's decided that there will be no more changes, not that it's put behind bars — a group of timers go through the episode and break down frame by frame just what's going to move when and for how long. If ZIM waves his hand while making an over-dramatic pronouncement, the timers determine just how many frames of animation it will take between his hand starting at his side and extending upward toward the heavens. Every last thing you see move on the screen was at some point timed-out by a timer. This always struck me as a harrowing process, and my hat was always off to these people, though my head being hatless never seems to help their job in the least. Let it never be said that I didn't try.

Everything up until this point has been done inside the orange walls of the Nickelodeon studios, by good old-fashioned Burbank-dwelling people. Soon that will all change, when every last piece of physical material -- the storyboards, the character designs, the backgrounds, the timing sheets, color sheets, audio cassettes of the EMR, video cassettes of the animatic -- are packed up into a box and shipped off to the animation studio, who will do all of the final physical animation. More often than not, this studio is in a foreign country where the living wage for someone whose job it is to sit at a desk and draw frame after frame of cartoon joy is much less than it would be in America.

And yes, I said shipped off in a box. An actual box. Well, at least back in the cartoon dark ages it was. Back before high speed internet connections, the fastest way to get this stuff to the people who needed it was to simply put it in a box and overnight ship it to a far off land. In fact, my first job in the animation business involved packing up and shipping the episodes as a production assistant on *The Wild Thornberries*. Ship days were always late nights, as I and one other trusty production assistant stayed deep into the wee hours long after the building had emptied and filled that magic cardboard box with everything the studio needed to make a cartoon. There was a lot of photocopying involved. A lot. Storyborads, timing sheets, scripts, character turnarounds, backgrounds, all had to be copied and packed into a box that ended up weighing what seemed like a ton. It was a long night punctuated by the smell of toner and the eye-grating glow of fluorescent office lights. Also, my fellow P.A. on *Thornberries* was a big fan of Pat Benatar, and played her Pat Benatar tapes more often than most sane people could tolerate.

Animation, like love, is a battlefield.

(That's a Pat Benatar joke.)

On *ZIM*, the studio was Sun Woo studios in South Korea, and there were four separate teams assigned to *Invader ZIM* episodes. It seems working on *ZIM* was a badge of both honor and suffering, our show being far more complicated than your average episode of *Hey Arnold*, and we got word that teams were routinely working long, long hours, late, late into the wee hours of the morning to meet their deadlines. That always made me feel a little bad. I hope we didn't break up any Korean marriages over it. I don't know how I could have made it any easier for them in my scripts. Maybe I should have put things like "Dib stares unmoving for thirty full seconds while the world freezes around him," though I doubt it would have survived the first round of notes.

There are a number of steps after this one. Let's step through them just for completeness' sake, shall we? Completeness will really appreciate the effort.

A number of weeks later, the animated scenes start to come back from the overseas studios. Sometimes these turned out spot-on, other times they need tweaking, and re-takes are called. Then the show is edited together on video, sent to the composer for scoring, color-balanced, audio-mixed, and finally pronounced ready to go on the air by a team of Nobel prize-winning scientists who, through many years of extensive training, have developed the skills necessary -- like a rabbi versed in the Talmudic laws of kosher hot dogs -- to declare a cartoon to be well and truly finished.

Sometimes later, a version of the script called "the conformed draft" is written-up by the script assistant, changing whatever was on the page to match what ended up on the screen after all the changes that happened during this long process. The conformed draft is largely designed so the studio can have a written record of the episode, but it also has the added value of making it look like the writers knew *exactly* what they were doing from the very beginning.

Many writers are happy to keep this illusion alive.

In the case of this book, there are no conformed drafts. The scripts presented here are the versions that flew out of the nest of the writing department off to their new life in production. Many things changed between the last words I wrote and what the world finally saw on the screen, and I hope the differences are a matter of interest for you.

If they are actually a matter of annoyance, there's nothing I can do about it now, and you already paid for the book, so you may as well suffer through reading them. There's far, far greater suffering in this world.

Also, note that some script text is presented **in bold**, with *asterisks* along the edge of the page. This is the screenwriting convention for marking text that has been revised since the previous draft so members of the crew don't have to painstakingly compare two different drafts to figure out what has changed.

So there's nothing special about bold text and little stars on the edge of the screen, but if it makes reading them more interesting, feel free to imagine they're secret coded messages to undercover agents in the field, or clues to revealing the hidden burial place of the only existing copy of the animatic for *ZIM*'s lost dog show episode "Best in Show."

First person to find it wins a bejeweled gold pig.

a LITTLE HISTORY

An Alien is Born Screaming unto an Unsuspecting Network.

So you've learned how a bill becomes a law, but just how did *ZIM* go from a strange mutant idea in the back of the brain of a comic book artist into a full-fledged, honest-to-Skooge big-time TV-cartoon series production brouhaha?

Let's return now to Nickelodeon of yesteryear, wind the footage back past the pink-lit offices and cackling creators, back to how *Invader ZIM* came into being long before I ever got there. (I will confess, the reality of this tales flies right in the face of my theory that nothing exists when I'm not actually there looking at it, but everything is, in fact, taken apart and reassembled by a group of discrete and talented Reality Gnomes who work very hard to maintain an illusion of a "real world" for my benefit. Turns out the gnomes lied to me. Stoopid gnomes.)

ZIM was first a glint in the eye of the cartoon gods when Mary Harrington met Jhonen Vasquez on a trip up to San Jose. Part of Mary's job involves scouting the world for artists with interesting points of view, and Jhonen certainly qualified, so she went up to his home town to sit down with this strange artist face to face. Mary says she remembers meeting him in a cargo van behind the parking lot behind a pancake restaurant, and thinking he was like a young Benjamin Franklin, but with hair.*

*None of this is true, I just can't remember the real story, and Mary won't return my calls. If this story is still in the final version of this book, just assume Mary hid under her desk until I went away.

What is undeniable truth is that Mary had been impressed with Jhonen's comic book work. It had a quality that was unquestionably demented, but on some level a little bit adorable. So she met with Jhonen, and asked him if he had any ideas for an animated show, and if he did, he should pitch them to her. A few minutes later -- OK, far, far longer than that— Jhonen came up with *Invader ZIM*.

Writer Rob Hummel got involved around this point. Rob was a friend and aspiring screenwriter from Jhonen's home town who eventually followed him down to Burbank be "the writer" on the project. Fun fact for those outside the animation business: Most animated shows are bought on the basis of the artwork and the concept, but most artists aren't always the most accomplished screenwriters. Thank God for that, otherwise people like me would be out of a job. However, because of that inconvenient fact, a network will usually hire a writer to help shape the artist's ideas into a form that will play as a story on the screen. Jhonen had a good sense of story on his own, but you know, tradition is tradition.

Here's the condensed version of what happens next: Rob and Jhonen write a pitch for the network. The network buys it. Then they write a show bible that fleshes out the fictional world. That also gets approved. They write a pilot script. Approved! Jhonen makes tons of art. People record actors' voices. Artists draw storyboards. Storyboard get animated. Eventually they have a "pilot" episode of *Invader ZIM* ready to be focus tested in front groups of random children.

As a side note: along the way, the voice of ZIM changed a few times. The first version was voiced by Mark "Luke SkyJoker" Hamill, whose interpretation was manic and fabulous, but somehow missed the ZIMness Jhonen was looking for. The pilot was then re-dubbed with Billy West doing the voice of ZIM, which was also quite good, but not quite right for the series. Richard Horvitz -- the final voice of ZIM, and a man we have come to know and love despite his unfortunate facial tics, questionable haircuts, and bad habit of randomly sucker-punching members of the clergy -- didn't come in until after the show was green-lit.

The pilot itself was a short little story that involved Dib challenging ZIM to a food fight in the cafeteria, and ZIM arming himself with an advanced tech battle suit that shot burritos but somehow ended up malfunctioning and... well... Things go horribly wrong.

When the network people saw it, they were, in a word, confused. In four words, they "didn't really get it." It was weird, it wasn't heartwarming at all, and... OK, it was funny, sure, but it didn't have the familiar loveable-yet-flawed-go-get-'em-style kids that Nickelodeon had built their reputation on from the dawn of *Rugrats*.

(For a particularly awkward example of this kind of character, go watch an old episode of an old Nickelodeon show called *Rocket Powered*. It's a hangnail from that painful time in the 90s when every kid on TV had to ride a skateboard to telegraph to the audience that they were "radical," and wear helmets and knee pads to ensure that parents couldn't sue the network if their own kid broke their neck skateboarding. I mean, because these Rocket-Powered Kids were safety-conscious, and *being safety-conscious is radical!*)

Fortunately for *ZIM*, real kids knew better. The pilot tested through the roof.

"Tested" means shown to test audiences consisting of small groups of kids who were asked to give their opinions of what they just saw. The *ZIM* pilot had a massively high approval rating. Like, unnaturally high. Like, the sort of shining beacon of success that most animation executives only dream of after long nights of drinking in seedy Burbank bar wondering just what they can do to keep their jobs for one more year.

So *Invader ZIM* was green-lit and put into production. Artists and crewfolk of varying descriptions were hired, office space was secured for the express purpose of being colored pink. Scripts were put in the pipeline. And I found myself in Jhonen's office pitching my first round of stories.

THE FOLLOWING IS A COMPLETELY FICTIONAL ACCOUNT OF MY FIRST MEETING WITH JHONEN VASQUEZ.

The only true detail I remember is that his office was dark and covered with posters, including one for Johnny the Homicidal Maniac, and another for Ridley Scott's *Alien*. Everything else is entirely fictional.

TRANSCRIPTION FOLLOWS.

Me: Hey, do you mind if I record this for a book I'm going to write about 20 years from now?

JV: Go right ahead. Humanity will have degenerated into a slime-based hive creature by then, but it's important that we have hope.

Me: Nice office, by the way.

JV: Thanks. Do you like the bowl of still-beating human hearts?

Me: I do. Feast on them often?

JV: Only when The Feastening Time calls.

Me: So, I have some ideas for stories.

JV: This is unfortunate. But I suppose sacrifices must be made.

Me: The first one is ZIM wants to build a monorail for Springfield, but Mr. Burns won't allow it.

JV: Is that an episode of *The Simpsons*?

Me: Yeah, but nobody's heard of that show.

JV: Pass.

(Sounds of low growling and grate rattling.)

JV: Sorry, they built my office over a gateway to hell. I put an iron grate over it, but the Cursed Ones still crawl up from time to time.

ET: Yeah, I have the same problem at home. The next pitch is about a talking burrito.

JV: Interesting. Is there a story?

ET: No. It just talks for eleven straight minutes as the camera slowly pushes in on its face. The audience starts to realize the burrito lives in a constant state of existential terror because it knows it's an animated cartoon, and it will cease to exist when the cartoon is over, only to be reborn when it's watched again, but just as helpless to change its fate.

JV: Save it for season three.

ET: Will there be a season three?

JV: There will be HUNDREDS OF SEASONS! (Laughter for a long time, possibly ironic, possibly not.)

ET: OK, so in this one, ZIM makes a time machine, and he wants to go back in time and stop Dib as an infant, kind of Terminator-style...

JV: Won't we get sued by Harlan Ellison? He sued over the original *Terminator*.

ET: You aren't being sued by Harlan Ellison already? I assumed everyone in Hollywood is in a constant state of being sued by Harlan Ellison. It's, like, a rite of passage in this business.

JV: Fair enough. Continue...

ET: But ZIM screws up and instead of sending a killer robot back to kill Dib, he accidentally sends a toy rubber pig. But the pig messes with Dib's past in a way that causes him to be debilitated in the future, so ZIM keeps going. He keeps sending pigs back in time, each time making Dib a little weaker in the present. But just as it looks like ZIM is going to win, Dib is pushed into such a weakened state that Professor Membrane builds him a weaponized exo-skeleton and he uses it to start a grunge band. The end.

JV: I'm sorry, I wasn't listening. I was feeding hearts to the souls of past cartoon writers stuck in hell. Could you start over?

ET: Probably not.

JV: Fine. Just change the grunge band to an attack on ZIM's base, push the reset button at the end, and go for it.

ET: Awesome!

END TRANSCRIPTION.

None of that actually happened. But the script is in the next chapter.

BAD, BAD RUBBER PIGGY

In Which the Writer Drops a Time-Travel Paradox on a Nation of Unsuspecting Children, and Nobody Bats an Eye.

Years after it aired, a friend of mine who'd never seen a single episode of *Invader ZIM* decided he wanted to watch something I'd written, and he stumbled across "Bad, Bad Rubber Piggy." His e-mail to me after the fact contained a sentence like, "So it's the first script you write for Nickelodeon, and you shove a time-travel paradox on these unsuspecting children?"

I suppose he had a point.

Bad, Bad Rubber Piggy" wasn't the first script I wrote for *Invader ZIM*. Before that, I'd co-written with Rob Hummell on DARK HARVEST, being brought in to help get a nearly-late script across the finish line on time by co-writing it with Rob. Writing that was a good time, and I will forever be nostalgic for the sound of a moo-can and the name "Torque Smackey" because of it.

"Piggy" was my first solo script, the first thing I'd ever written for broadcast -- OK, cable -- television, and I was itching to prove myself.*

*That sentence is poorly worded. It sounds like it could mean I was scratching myself all over my body in an attempt to prove something. If that's what you envisioned, take the other, more obvious meaning.

I'm going to assume if you bought this book, you've probably seen Bad, Bad Rubber Piggy more than once, but to refresh your memory, it's the story of ZIM messing with Dib's past by using a time machine, and doing it so badly that his plan eventually backfires, and Dib takes revenge inside a giant battle suit built to compensate for all the physical damage he suffered at ZIM's hands in his past. Or rather, at ZIM's piggies. See, because ZIM can't send a killer robot back to do the job, he sends rubber pig toys to strategic moments in Dib's past with the design of eliminating him completely.

I will confess that, like most writers writing their first script, I wanted to prove I was brilliant as the brightest sun in the galaxy. (Memo to first-time cartoon writers: You only have to prove you're bright enough that they didn't make a mistake in hiring you.) I wanted to bring all of my science-fiction influences to the fore, and focus them into an idea so mind-blowing and cool it would impress both the Saturn and Hugo committees, who had never considered 11-minute cartoons to be worthy before. Fueled by an abiding love of science-fiction influences that included *Star Trek's* hard science, *Doctor Who's* wild imagination, *The Twilight Zone's* dark irony, and Harlan Ellison's willingness to sue emotional bite,* I set out to break Nickelodeon's ceiling of normalcy.

*I make jokes about Harlan Ellsion, but he really is one of my literary heroes. I survived my high school emotional hellscape in no small part because of his work. Thanks, Harlan! Please don't sue me in the afterlife.

Unfortunately -- or fortunately -- I was also cursed with comedy instincts that leaned as much toward "stoopid" as they did "sophisticated," and "*really* stoopid" won out. The twist of rubber pigs being the vehicle for Dib's demise was something out of my own moronic playbook, even if the detail of "pig" was right out of Jhonen's proverbial wheelhouse. (NOTE: Jhonen did not at the time, nor has he ever to my knowledge, owned or spent time in an actual wheelhouse.)

I approached the writing with the usual novice combination of hubris and terror. I was dead sure this idea was so amazing, nobody could possibly object to anything about it, even if I knew it's time travel paradox was not out of your typical episode of *Rugrats*. I think I spent long hours in my office laboring over the outline, or rather, long hours biting my lips, wringing my hands, and going over the outline *one more time* to make sure I was doing the thing properly, while occasionally bouncing over to playing Diablo on the other computer I had to one side of my desk just for distracting myself with games.

Back then I had bad writing habits, and would often stay late, late into the night wracking my brain for the perfect next sentence rather than writing a rough draft full of imperfect next sentences that I could go back and fix later when my critical brain could see exactly what wasn't working.

But see for yourself how it turned out. The Outline is here.

```
INVADER ZIM
Outline
BAD, BAD RUBBER PIGGY
07/14/00
```

We open with an episode of "Ask Professor Membrane." Membrane is explaining how time travel into the past can alter the present. (And it's clear, concise, funny, and we can show it to you if you don't believe us.) He finishes his explanation by saying, "Of course, no one would ever attempt to alter the past. The consequences are just too unpredictable and dangerous."

CLICK — The screen goes black. Pull back to reveal ZIM, who has been watching the Membrane show on his screen. ZIM turns to the camera and flashes his eyebrows. He has an idea.

ZIM'S MAKING STUFF ROOM: ZIM puts the finishing touches on his Time/Matter Displacement Device. It consists of a transport chamber and a screen that can look into the past. On the time projector's target screen is a scene from Dib's childhood. His plan is to send a hunter-killer robot into a crucial point in Dib's past, thus dispatching his enemy before they even meet.

As ZIM works, GIR bombards him with some incredibly astute, very un-GIR-like questions: Why not send a robot over to get him now? If you stop Dib in the past so you never meet, would you then never have to send the robot into the past in the first place? So then you would meet -- ZIM silences him.

On the screen, ZIM hones in on a moment in Dib's past: A bunch of kids are sitting around punching a little rubber alien inflatable punching bag. A three-year-old Dib rides up on a tricycle. "An alien! I will save you!" The kids roll their eyes. A target locks on to Dib's tricycle, and the scene pauses.

ZIM brings out an evil giant robot with a horrible collection of weapons, and it lumbers onto the transfer pad. ZIM readies the machine, things hum and whine, the light lights up green and… Nothing. The machine is unable to send the robot back in time due to problems with its "Temporal Stability Field." (i.e. it's just too damn big.)

ZIM tries smaller and smaller robots. Each one fails. Finally we see him with a collection of killer cyborgs piled up to one side. ZIM tries to send ANYTHING through the portal, but still no luck. Everything just keeps getting spit back out. All but defeated, he tries GIR's rubber piggy toy. It works. The machine sends out a tricycle, as it has been replaced by the pig in the past.

On the screen the Dib scene plays out again. "An alien! I will save you!" ZAP! Suddenly the tricycle is replaced with the small rubber pig. Dib takes a tumble.

ZIM watches a "Dib's Life Timeline" screen and watches the events roll over and change after this traumatic blow to Dib's life. ZIM rubs his hands together. Zim muses, "Excellent. Although the piggy does not attack Dib the way the robot would have, it is still capable of replacing inanimate objects.

While it can't make things all explodey, it is effective none the less."

Meanwhile, in Dib's living room, Gaz watches TV. Dib is putting the finishing touches on his latest plan to get ZIM. Suddenly… ffzzzzap… Dib transforms. He looks weaker, and his glasses are even thicker. When he speaks, he speaks with a lisp.

He looks up, somehow noticing something's wrong. "Gath," he says, "Haff I Alwayth thpoken like thith? "Tricycle accident when you were three, don't you remember? You messed your teeth up." she replies. "Oh yeah," says Dib, thinking this odd. A pig appears on TV. Dib flinches — WHAA! — then recovers himself. Again, he thinks this is odd.

ZIM demands another pig, and GIR gets one from his stash. Then ZIM looks over Dib's timeline again, and finds another point to focus on…

Dib is at a lake vacation, looking for the mysterious Giant Lake Sloth of Canandagua. He gets a few feet out and starts going under, too weak to handle the water. Someone throws him a life preserver. He reaches out to grab it… ZAP! A small rubber piggy appears in its place. Dib goes under, clutching the small useless toy.

THE PRESENT: Dib and Gaz casing ZIM's house. Gaz eats an ice cream pop. When suddenly… ffzzppp! The scene morphs and now Dib carries a large piece of respiratory machinery on his back. "Gaz, have I always had an artificial lung attached to my body?" "Drowning accident when you were four. Don't you remember?" She offers him a lick of a pig-shaped ice cream pop. He screams in horror. "And was I always afraid of pigs?" He looks over at ZIM's house, curious. "Hmmmm…" Dib is becoming more and more suspicious of these events.

After throwing the life preserver on the pile of accumulated objects, ZIM finds another point in Dib's past.

Dib is chasing a hairy kid through the playground with a video camera. "He's a Bigfoot baby! I know it!" The kid just wants to be left alone, and runs and jumps over playground equipment. Looking through the view-finder, Dib follows him and jumps as best he can with the respirator on his back. ZAP! The video camera is replaced with a rubber pig, which Dib can't see through. He crashes head-first into a jungle gym, and his respirator shorts out, electrocuting him. Again, ZIM laughs, with much more evil though. SOON, Dib will be a jelly-like mess of nerves, barely strong enough to lift a finger, let alone stand in ZIM's way ever again.

Outside, Dib sneaks closer to ZIM's house, but ZAP! He changes again. Now his hair is white and he jerks with nervous twitches. He rounds a corner and sees GIR playing with a rubber pig. He screams. GIR screams. GIR runs inside, but Dib's eyes narrow.

Downstairs, ZIM is interrupted by a banging on the front door. It's Dib. "I know you're behind the pigs, ZIM! I don't know how, but I know it's you!" He's pounding on the door, trying to get in.

ZIM flashes his eyebrows. He goes to the machine and looks into the past. He finds Dib just after the last accident, surrounded by EMT's. "Maybe we can save him!" The EMT reaches for the defibrillator paddles. ZAP! Two rubber piggies appear in their place. He beats on Dib's chest with the useless rubber toys. "Why, Why? He's so young!!"

ZIM laughs harder to himself and turns off the machine, his work done. He goes to the kitchen for a bowl of space cereal. Suddenly there's a terrible RENDING AND CRASHING, like the house is being torn apart. He is distracted by the sound of the timeline changing on the screen. He watches with amusement, and then horror as the Dib timeline shows a feeble Dib being rebuilt by his father. Rebuilt, as a giant, cyborg superbeing. News clips of press conferences show Membrane discussing the daring new experimental operation he has given his son.

ZIM is distracted from the monitors by the sudden rumbling of his house.

OUTSIDE is Dib, now in a gigantic robotic exo-skeleton. And what do you know, he IS tearing the house apart. "You'll pay for this, ZIM! You will pay!"

Upstairs, Dib is ripping down the side of the house to get in.

ZIM starts randomly sending piggies back as quickly as he can, desperate to destroy his newly enhanced enemy.

With each pig sent back in time, Dib's armor becomes more fearsome and laden with horrible weapons. He cuts holes through ZIM's living room with laser beams. GIR tries throwing a small rubber pig at him. Dib brushes it off. "Exposure to so many

pigs has only turned my fear to rage!" GIR disappears down into the basement, and Dib begins pounding on the floor, trying to get down.

Debris falls from the ceiling in ZIM's lab as the whole room shakes. GIR huddles at ZIM's feet. ZIM is at his wit's end and down to his last pig. He pounds his head against the machine. "We're doomed!" But wait.

ZIM, in a panic, comes up with a new plan. If he can send a pig back into his OWN recent past, perhaps he can alter his initial plan to destroy Dib with pigs in the first place! It just might work. He decides to send the final pig back. This HAS to work.

Suddenly, there's a flash, and the pig is gone. It has apparently displaced a brain, as that is exactly what pops out of the portal. Now there's a normal, every-day un-debilitated Dib, standing outside ZIM's house. He's about to ring the doorbell, when he stops, and looks around confused. "Did something just happen?"

Down in ZIM's lab, GIR is also confused. "What did you do?" ZIM just grins.

CAPTION: "ONE HOUR EARLIER." In ZIM's lab, ZIM is just about to send the first pig back in time. He reaches for the lever to start the machine. ZAP!

ZIM begins to drool immediately, and smiles like a
moron. The camera pushes into to his drooling head,
and goes into his skull, where a piggy has replaced
his brain.

END.

Surprisingly, when I submitted my outline, I got little push back from
on high. I do remember standing in an office explaining how time travel
works in this particular story, and how the repeated process of messing with
Dib's past would lead to his slow debilitation in the present, which would get
worse with each new pig. Seeing these words typed out twenty years later, it
still seems even more incredible to me that they went with it, but they went
with it. I even dug up the notes on the outline at the time. See for yourself.

INVADER ZIM
BAD, BAD RUBBER PIGGY
Outline Notes
7/19/00

The outline needs to be sent to standards but otherwise it's very good.

Because, Dibs increasing debilitation may be con-
strued as making fun of handicapped kids, his weak-
nesses should be silly.

At the beginning of the story, Dib puts the final
touches on his plan for ZIM. This is good and should
be emphasized as it highlights that Dib is a threat
to ZIM.

A point to look out for in terms of clarity is when
Membrane's actions alter the timeline. Also, we
can't rely on characters reading to explain what's
going on. They can watch old news video or anything
else visual. (This is because of foreign markets and
kids too young to read and because this is such a
key story point.)

This episode requires more visual and camera description written into the script than normal for the
story board artists.

> Make sure not to tip the ending that ZIM is going into his own past.
>
> **Go to script** but bare in mind that some things might need to be changed after we get the notes from Standards.

"This episode requires more visual and camera description written into the script than normal for the story board artists."

I took it as "You're just so goddamn sophisticated, Trueheart! The whole solar system must orbit around your amazing brain, changing the direction water swirls down the drain when you're too close to the sink." Or something.

The point is, I let it go to my head, which means I put even more pressure on myself when writing the script. I filled the rough draft with a lot of unnecessary jokes that were cut later; some by me, and some by Jhonen, who really didn't like my joke involving John Denver. (In fairness, I didn't really like my joke involving John Denver, either.) But hours of pounding away at the formica desk of my office, surrounded by the formica walls, and lit only by the light of a novelty green lightbulb covered in silicone spines that I bought at an oddball hipster gift shop in Burbank produced something I was actually proud of. It was a story that was at once funny, sophisticated, stupid, and weirdly heartfelt. Who figured that would happen with a script about a time-traveling rubber pig?

Even if it leads with the high concept, at the heart of BAD, BAD RUBBERY PIGGY lurks an old familiar emotional core. On some level, it's the story of what happens when a bullied kid gets pushed too far. Dib's Megaboy 3000 suit is probably a dream come true for all of us who got pushed around when we were small, the ultimate manifestation of nerd-rage revenge. And how many of us have felt like someone was targeting our lives on a cosmic level to make things terrible for us at every turn? Sadly for most human beings, that's just the normal bumper car existence of life itself.

There isn't a green alien secretly messing things up for us behind the scenes -- particularly not one voiced by Richard Horvitz. But wouldn't it be nice if we could have someone to blame for all of our setbacks and problems other than circumstances? And wouldn't it be nicer to unleash a rocket attack on them? F—- you, fate.

Sadly, just a few months later, the massacre at Columbine High School would cement the image of nerds in black trench coats seeking revenge into the minds of the public in a very bad way. As I type this near the end of 2019, the rise of crazy white people shooting up public places in the name of revenge has become too common to ignore. I'm not crazy enough to think most kids can't tell the difference between cartoons and reality, but it has made me wonder whether the intellectual nuance of revenge tales like these gets lost on certain people looking for someone to blame for their problems. Our pop culture is saturated in tales of good vs. evil, and some people out there really do see the world in those black and white tones. Though I do hope most of those people were not raised on Nickelodeon cartoons.

The script was shockingly well received. In fact, these were the main notes:

```
BAD, BAD RUBBER PIGGY
SCRIPT NOTES
8/14/00

• Clarify that ZIM can see all of time including the
  present, so that it makes sense that he can see how
  Dib is changed in the present.

• Might want to tone down the heart attack business.
  (wait for standards notes)

• Add a second time when GIR questions ZIM's logic.
  (per Jhonen)
```

Yes, there were a few changes for practical concerns, but I thought, "Wow, my script sailed through, and they liked it! They really liked it!" This one will be easy, right?

No. The opposite of right.

The production revealed just how complicated a tale I was telling, and just how much the details hadn't really been "beated-out" in the script. "Beat" is a verb that writers and directors use to describe any moment in drama. The term can change in scope depending on context, and can be as large as "the beat where she holds up a convenience store" or as small as "the beat when he notices his watch is on the wrong hand." When a writer says she's "beating" a scene, she's not taking it out in the parking lot and hitting it with a crowbar, she's planning out how each moment leads from one to the other.

"Piggy" had a lot to get across to the audience. It opened by introducing the viewer to the whole idea of time travel using Professor Membrane's show as the vehicle. Then we jump straight into ZIM with a time machine of his very own, first not working as intended, then working with the unintended rubber pigs. ZIM, of course, jumps on the failure as a new plan. Then we have to keep track of what we're seeing in the past vs. what we're seeing in the future, and how one is affecting the other. The idea that rubber pigs replace random objects and then change Dib's life up until the present moment isn't exactly obvious to the average viewer at first.

It was obvious to *me,* of course. I was an uber-nerd who had the advantage of not only being familiar with a host of time-travel movies and TV shows, I'd also written the damn script so I made the rules. But it seemed they weren't quite as obvious to the rest of humanity. There was definitely some concern higher ups that this piggy was bouncing around too fast and too crazy for your common kid.

This is where the people on the production side started working what I call "their magic," what our bosses called "their jobs," and what they called "their long hours." In fairness to the "Piggy," the hours for this story were not particularly longer than any other, but still the number and subtlety of the details they added to clear up the confusing piggy mass was very impressive.

One of the biggest changes you might notice between the script and the screen is the addition of Professor Membrane's narration over the explanation of how time travel works. These were added in ADR -- the industry way of saying "Additional Dialogue Replacement" -- after the animation returned. Roger Bumpass was brought in to record some explanatory dialogue over the finished sequence, so there'd be no question that everybody knew just what the hell they were looking at and why. Whether his asides like "I guess he worked in a garbage dump or something" and "Oh, look, he's happy!" were improvised in the booth or suggested by Jhonen during the record is a fact lost to history.

You may also notice the captions on various screens letting us know what time period we're looking at. These were added in post-production, after the animated scenes came back from Korea, so no, they weren't in the original storyboards. While one could argue that they aren't strictly "necessary," they sure as hell don't hurt while sorting out this temporal boondoggle. Even if the average viewer isn't strictly reading them, they do telegraph to the unconscious mind just where the heck these scenes are taking place, planting the idea early so the viewer can sit back and just enjoy the story once they've gotten the hang of what's going on. My personal favorite is the caption of "TOKYO: PRESENT" over the giant fish in the bear suit rampaging through the streets. Where else would a giant fish in a bear suit rampage?

An additional moment of drama that wasn't in the script is playing out the moment of Dib's "death." In the original script, Dib never even makes it to the point of flatlining. In the final, the director (Steve Ressel) and the board artists (Chris Graham, Ian Graham, and Dave Krocker) turned the drama of the scene up as we see Dib's vitals go outright dead and ZIM casually sipping a beverage as he takes the elevator back upstairs, his work done. It was both one of those many moments when the crew made me look smarter than I was.

It was also one of those moments that gave Standards and Practices a heart attack. We were actually showing a lead character dying -- *dying!!* -- on screen. The fact that strictly speaking, he was dying off-screen and all we showed on screen were his vital signs going flat didn't seem to sway them. What did sway them was the counterpoint that his "death" lasted literally only a few seconds, and that he came back even more powerful than before, and everyone was just back to normal and happy as clams by the time it was all over.

Oh, TV reset button, is there no problem you can't fix? I wasn't in on the back-and-forth between the production team and the people over at Standards and Practices, but they either finally convinced them that it would all be OK, or they just slipped the episode through when no one was looking. It was probably the former.

As hard as it is tracking the time travel on screen, it's just as hard keeping the order of events straight as I look back at this. All of this final on-screen tweaking didn't happen until months after I turned in the script, after the boards had been drawn and the animation finally returned. At the time, when I was dusting my hands clean and congratulating myself on a script well done, things looked bright. My script was nuts, yet it had been approved by the higher-ups with little head-bashing, teeth-gnashing, or check-cashing. (This third thing is added only because it rhymes.)

I thought this bode well for the future. I thought the network could see what we were doing and loved it. I thought they were unequivocally on our side, standing on the sidelines waving pom-poms as we ran this cartoon across the goal line of the sports metaphor.

I took it as a sign that there would be nothing but smooth sailing from here on out.

I couldn't have been more wrong. Unless I had taken it as a sign that my legs were going to turn into two fighting mountain goats, -- one named "Chet" and the other named "Goatpheus" -- who would battle each other for the fate of the lost continent of Atlantis when I went to sleep at night. That would have been more wrong.

Regardless, here is the scripted piggy in its entirety:

SCRIPT: BaD, BaD RUBBER PIGGY

illustration by Rikki Simons

Eric Trueheart

"INVADER ZIM"   09/19/00

            "BAD, BAD RUBBER PIGGY" #7b

                    2.1

TITLE - "POKING THE MEMBRANE OF SCIENCE".

The "Poking the Membrane of Science!" logo appears on the
screen: Professor Membrane looking powerful in front of a
double helix (or some such thing).

                    ANNOUNCER
            And now more adventures in science with
            Professor Membrane! Professor...?

INT. TV STUDIO.

KIDS CHEER like crazed maniacs. Women pull at their clothing
and swoon. Men punch themselves in the head. PROF. MEMBRANE
stands in front of a table full of indecipherable scientific
equipment -- the set for the show.

                    PROF MEMBRANE
            Thanks again to Dr. Falkie and his
            miserably failed attempt at a better cold
            fusion. Now let's take a question from
            the audience.

IN THE AUDIENCE, a MELVIN-LIKE KID speaks into a microphone
held by a robot arm.

                    MELVIN-LIKE KID
            My mom makes me eat Breakfast Chunks for
            breakfast. But I hate them. I hate them
            so much. Could I go back in time and
            stop them from ever being invented?

                    PROF MEMBRANE
            I'm glad you asked that. Altering the
            past to affect the present is
            theoretically possible.

A screen hovers in next to him. A scene appears on the
screen of a KID at a table, scowling over a single large
cinnamon raisin breakfast chunk.

                    prof membrane (CONT'D)
            You could prevent Ralston Chunkie from
            ever inventing Breakfast Chunks by using
            Temporal Object Replacement Technology.

                                        (CONTINUED)

CONTINUED:

CAPTION: "25 YEARS AGO." A young RALSTON CHUNKIE eats from a
burlap sack marked "BRAN" while working crushing cars in a
metal compactor. He looks down at the compactor, thinking.

             PROF MEMBRANE (CONT'D)
        Using a space-time transfer device, you
        replace an object in the past with an
        object from the present, and stop this
        moment from ever happening.

He reaches for the sack, but it is suddenly replaced with a
GIANT SQUID. Ralston SCREAMS. The squid wraps it's
tentacles around him. PULL BACK to see a bunch of SCIENTISTS
watching this on a SCREEN. Next to them is a TEMPORAL OBJECT
REPLACEMENT MACHINE. The outline of a squid sparkles away on
the pad, and the bag of bran appears in its place. A
computer screen shows an icon of a squid moving over a time
line. The two scientists look at each other and nod.

             PROF MEMBRANE (CONT'D)
        But be careful. If the breakfast cube
        was never invented, Tasty Breakfast
        Squids would sweep the nation.

SHOT of the same kid, sulking over his breakfast cube. The
cube fades out. The kid CHEERS. A horrible squid appears in
the bowl, and attaches to the child's face. The kid CRIES.

             PROF MEMBRANE (v.o.) (CONT'D)
        Further unpredictable effects would arise
        as a result of mankind's foolish altering
        of the timeline.

SHOT of enormous fish people stomping through the city,
wearing gigantic bear suits. Humans cower.

             PROF MEMBRANE (CONT'D)
        The consequences would be disastrous.

RETURN TO THE MEMBRANE STUDIO, where Membrane wraps it up.

             PROF MEMBRANE (CONT'D)
        So, despite the temptation, altering the
        time line more foolish than productive.
        Any such attempts would be the folly of a
        true moron... moron... moron...

CLICK. The show switches off. Membrane's voice echoes as we
realize we've been watching this on TV. We are in...

INT. ZIM's MAKING STUFF ROOM - day.

ZIM turns from a TV screen nodding and looking all evil. He is standing in front of a TEMPORAL OBJECT REPLACEMENT MACHINE of his own. It's a large cluster of odd electronics with at least four screens: One with a graphic readout, one showing the present, one showing the past, one for cable TV. There's also a "beam-out pad" surrounded by electrodes and other pointy electronic things, and a control panel at ZIM height.

ZIM puts the finishing touches on the machine. GIR runs around the room, playing with his RUBBER PIGGY as if it were a jet plane.

ZIM presses a button, and a scene from Dib's childhood appears on the screen.

EXT. suburban street - day.

A couple of kids play, punching a little alien-shaped knock-down punching bag. A large tree looms nearby.

A THREE-YEAR-OLD DIB appears on the horizon, dramatically riding his tricycle.

                    DIB
          An alien!! Stand back! I'll get it!

A Two-YEAR OLD GAZ watches from beside the tree.

                    GAZ
                (with contempt)
          Not again.

                    ZIM (v.o.)
          THERE! Dib in the past. So unknowing,
          so unprepared. Back before he was ever a
          threat to our mission, GIR.

The picture freezes on Dib in mid-pedal.

ZIM GRINS. He targets the tricycle in the scene from Dib's past. He presses another button, and a hatch opens in the wall behind GIR, revealing a BIG NASTY ROBOT.

                    GIR
          Ooh!

                    ZIM
          A Hunter-Destroyer machine. Programmed
          to target the earth boy in the past to
          ensure that he will not be a problem to
          us in the present!

                                        (CONTINUED)

46

4.

CONTINUED:

While speaking, a monitor displays a graphic of ZIM and Dib
fighting in the present. The hunter robot appears with
little Dib in the past, enveloping him in doom. The Dib in
the present vanishes, leaving a victorious ZIM.

                    GIR (thinking intensely)
               Wait..if you destroy Dib in the past,
               then he won't ever be your enemy, then
               you won't have to send a robot back to
               destroy him, so then he... WILL be your
               enemy, so then you WILL have to send a
               robot back...

BOOM. GIR's head explodes in a shower of sparks. The Hunter-
Killer cyborg lumbers onto the transport pad. On the screen,
a pair of cross-hairs target Dib's tricycle.

                    ZIM
               Now to unleash screaming temporal doom!

He pushes the Destroyer into the time portal, and after a
beat, it is spat right back out.

                    COMPUTER VOICE
               Object not compatible with temporal
               field.

                    ZIM
               Arrgh! Not compatible? Is this thing
               just completely useless!? Not
               compatible!

In a wailing fit, ZIM snatches up GIR's rubber piggy and
throws it at the machine. It enters portal, makes an amazing
flash, and does not return.

                    COMPUTER VOICE
               Object accepted. Temporal displacement
               in process.

                    ZIM
               Huh?

The portal fluctuates, sparking, and shoots bolts of energy.

EXT. suburban street - day.

The kids play with the blow-up alien toy again. Dib comes
over the horizon on his tricycle.

                    DIB
               An alien! Stand back! I'll get it!

                                        (CONTINUED)

CONTINUED:

Dib bears down on the rubber toy. Suddenly there's a high-pitched whine, and his tricycle start to glow.

>   DIB (CONT'D)
>   Beware, alien! I'm gonna...

ZAP! The trike is replaced with GIR's piggy. Dib sails through the air, riding the pig where his trike used to be. He looks down for an incredulous moment, then looks up. WHAAA! He SPLATS sidelong into a tree.

>   DIB (CONT'D)
>   (barely conscious)
>   Take that.

int. DIB'S LIVING ROOM - Present day

Dib walks into the living room, where Gaz is watching TV. Dib holds up an empty box of Coco Splodees. He looks irritated.

>   DIB
>   Hey, GAZ? Did you eat all the cereal? I
>   was gonna have this for breakfast
>   tomorrow, you know?

>   GAZ
>   You think you own ALL the cereal. Well
>   you know what, Dib? You don't. You just
>   don't.

>   DIB
>   Look, all I'm saying is if you're--

FZZZZZRPP. The scene shifts. Everything is in the same place, but DIB looks skinnier, he has dark circles under his eyes, he's missing a tooth, and he has a metal claw where his hand should be. He drops the box of cereal. When he speaks, he speaks his voice just sounds... goofier. He also seems somehow MORE DEPRESSED, as if a spark has gone out of him.

>   DIB (CONT'D)
>   --what was I saying?

He stops. Something's wrong. He can't put his finger on it.

>   DIB (CONT'D)
>   Gaz, have I always sounded this funny?

>   GAZ
>   Long as I've known you.

He holds up his withered arm.

>   (CONTINUED)

CONTINUED:

> DIB
> And have I always had this claw for a
> hand?

> GAZ
> Tricycle accident when you were three.
> Don't you remember?

> DIB
> Now that you mention it, I do.

She changes the channel. The TV now shows a commercial for
Bloaty's Pizza Hog. Bloaty in his pig suit yells at kids.

> BLOATY
> Ayyy... You eat some pizza!!

Dib is visibly disturbed, and looks frightened.

> DIB
> The pig. It haunts me.

INT. ZIM's MAKING STUFF ROOM.

ZIM turns from the screen at looks at GIR, his eyes filled
with new possibilities. Dib's tricycle sits on the launch
pad, crackling with electrons.

> ZIM
> Fascinating! Not the same as the hunter
> destroyer plan but I might be able to rid
> myself of Dib after all.

GIR looks down at his empty hands, horrified.

> GIR
> WHYYYY!??? WHY MY PIGGY!!! I LOVEDED YOU
> PIGGY!! I LOVEDED YOOOOOOOOOOOOOU!!!

On a television nearby, a news broadcast is airing.

> TV ANNOUNCER
> ...and in other news, giant fish people
> are rampaging through the city.

EXT. MEMBRANE HOME - THE PAST - DAY.

6 year old Dib and 5 year old Gaz are in the backyard. Dib
is putting a strange looking hat-like device on his head,
held in place with a chin strap. (Note: This Dib has the
claw hand he got at age three, as well as the missing tooth.)

(CONTINUED)

CONTINUED:

>   GAZ
>   You're gonna get in trouble as soon as
>   Dad finds out you took his hover helmet.

>   DIB
>   I'll put it right back. I just wanna see
>   if I can make it into space with this
>   thing.

He cinches the chin strap tightly, and activates the helmet.
It yanks him up by the head, and he begins to fly up in to
the air.

INT. ZIM'S MAKING STUFF ROOM

ZIM watches the flying Dib scene happen on a monitor, and
smiles. GIR enters an elaborately long code on a floating
control panel. A slot opens in the floor and a new rubber
piggy pops up. He sits down next to ZIM and starts to play.

>   ZIM
>   GIR! Another pig!

GIR sadly relinquishes the pig.

EXT. MEMBRANE HOME - THE PAST - DAY

Dib is way up in the sky. Gaz is a tiny dot on the ground.

>   DIB
>   WOW! I can spy on that family of
>   Nosferatu's that moved in down the
>   street!

Suddenly, a flash, and the helmet becomes a little rubber
piggy, strapped tightly to Dib's head. Dib falls.

Gaz tracks the fall with her head. She unwraps a chew bar
and gnaws on it, her attention held by the falling Dib. O.S,
her brother lets out a squeal of impact, and a deeply distant
SPLASH. The little piggy rolls over to Gaz's feet.

>   GAZ (chewing)
>   Wow.

INT. MEMBRANE LIVING ROOM - PRESENT DAY

Gaz is just trying to watch a a nature documentary about
bats. A LOLLIPOP STICK sticks out of her mouth. Dib's head
enters. He's wearing a CLOAKING JACKET, so the space where
his body should be looks like the distorted transparent
cloaking device in "Predator".

>   (CONTINUED)

8.

CONTINUED:

                    DIB
          So anyhow, I was thinking I'd try out one
          of dad's old cloaking jackets to go spy
          on ZIM's house...

                    GAZ
          Dib, SHHHH!! They're gonna show the bats
          eating a cow!

He holds up a small video camera.

                    DIB
          Whatever. I'm gonna sneak up past those
          giant gnomes and...

FZZZZZP. The scene shifts again. Now DIB has a LARGE
RESPIRATION DEVICE strapped to his back, with tubes leading
into his neck. The camera has changed to a piece of paper.

                 DIB (CONT'D)
          -- and leaving a nasty note on his door.

Dib is shaken again... something is wrong. He now seems even
MORE DEPRESSED than his depressed self.

                 DIB (CONT'D)
          Gaz, have I always had these tubes in my
          neck?

                    Gaz
          Hover helmet accident when you were six.
          Punched a hole through to the sewer
          system. Don't you remember?

                    Dib
          And have my plans always been this lame?

He holds up the piece of paper.

                    GAZ
          Ohhhhh yeah.

                 DIB (strained)
          And these visions of pigs...in my head!
          What's with the pigs?

INT. ZIM's making stuff room.

ZIM is searching the room. The helmet lies on the pad.

                    ZIM
          More piggies, GIR. I demand piggies!

                        (CONTINUED)

CONTINUED:

GIR pulls a pig from behind his back and hands it over. ZIM
snatches it, then holds his hand out again as if to say, "All
of them." GIR presses a button. A hatch in the floor opens
and a box slides up, pops open, and dozens of rubber pigs
bounce out. GIR begins to play.

                         ZIM (CONT'D)
                 No! These are for science. Science!
                     (off GIR's sad look)
                 OK...

He hands him one pig. GIR takes it and smiles. His smile
turns suspicious, as he shoots ZIM a wary look. He protects
his only piggy, and skulks away.

ZIM hunkers down in front of the screen. He leans in close.

                         ZIM (CONT'D)
                 Now...

EXT. PLAYGROUND - DAY.

POV SHOT through a video camera. A HAIRY KID is being chased
through the playground by the owner of the camera.

                         DIB
                 It's a bigfoot baby! I know it!

WIDE TO REVEAL: A SIX-YEAR OLD DIB (with gnome arm and
respiratory device) chasing the kid through the playground.

                         HAIRY KID
                 Leave me alone!

                         DIB
                 Nobody has ever gotten footage this close
                 before.

POV SHOT. The kid scrambles over a a jungle gym.

                         HAIRY KID
                 I'm a regular kid! I just want to eat
                 grubs!

ZAP! The Camera POV is replaced by a RUBBER PIG FACE!

WIDE to see Dib's camera has been replaced by yet another
rubber piggy. Of course, he can't see through a rubber pig,
and he goes crashing headlong into the jungle gym.

                         Dib
                 Eat your grubs, Sasquatch! -- yeeieerg!

                                        (CONTINUED)

10.

CONTINUED:

The respirator smashes open and sends electrical charges all over poor Dib.

EXT. ZIM'S HOUSE - DAY.

Dib is sneaking up the side of ZIM's house to the front gate with the note. Suddenly... FZZZZZP. He shifts again. Now in addition to everything else he has white hair, is terribly enfeebled, and shakes. He stops, noticing something is wrong again.

Just then, GIR skips around the corner, Rubber Piggy in hand. Dib sees the pig and SCREAMS! GIR SCREAMS back! Dib SCREAMS again! GIR runs away, leaving the pig on the ground. Dib picks the pig up, a new-found look of anger on his face.

                    Dib
          Hrmmmm....

He runs through the front gate, past the SECURITY GNOMES, which come to life just too slowly to catch him.

int. ZIM's making stuff room.

ZIM at the controls, when he hears a banging from upstairs.

                    Dib (o.s.)
          ZIM! ZIM!

EXT. ZIM'S FRONT DOOR - DAY.

Dib bangs on the front door, as hard as his little arms will allow. GIR peeks out the window at him.

                    DIB
          I know you're behind the piggies, ZIM! I
          don't know how, but I know it's you!
          Rubber piggies have ruined my life and
          it's all been you!

INT. ZIM's MAKING STUFF ROOM

ZIM chuckles and leans over the screen again. It shows the continuation of the same playground scene.

                    ZIM
          So close to victory...

EXT. PLAYGROUND - DAY.

An AMBULANCE has pulled up to the fallen little DIB. A small crowd has gathered. A pair of PARAMEDICS bend over him. One of them has the defibrillation paddles.

                              (CONTINUED)

Eric Trueheart

CONTINUED:

> PARAMEDIC ONE
> Come on, kid! If I lose one more patient
> today I'm going to get a written warning!

The paddles charge up. POV from DIB, the PARAMEDIC bends
over him, and slams the paddles down on his chest. ZAP!

> PARAMEDIC TWO
> CLEAR!

> PARAMEDIC ONE
> Come on, kid!

> PARAMEDIC TWO
> CLEAR!

FZZAP! The paddles change to two rubber pigs. He smashes
them down repeatedly on Dib's chest.

> PaRAMEDIC ONE
> Stay with me! STAY WITH ME!

INT. ZIM's MAKING STUFF ROOM.

Dib's pounding stops. ZIM switches off the screen and dusts
off his hands, his work done. A cool beverage descends from
the ceiling on a cable. ZIM takes a sip.

> ZIM
> Ah! Foolish earth creature. Your feeble
> earth doings are no match for my --

THUMP. THUMP. ZIM stops. The room shakes. RUMBLE...
CRASH! A horrible RENDING is heard from upstairs.

INT. ZIM'S LIVING ROOM - day.

GIR looks up in horror. A shaft of light appears on his
face. REVERSE ANGLE TO SEE: DIB - now inside a GIANT ROBOT
EXO-SKELETON - ripping open the front of ZIM's house.

> DIB
> You will pay for ruining my childhood,
> ZIM! YOU WILL PAY!

INT. ZIM'S MAKING STUFF ROOM

ZIM turns from a security monitor showing the destruction
upstairs back to the machine.

> ZIM
> That last piggy should have reduced him
> to nothing! What happened? Where did
> history go wrong?

(CONTINUED)

54

CONTINUED:

He frantically runs the machine over DIB's time-line. It
stop's at a flashing red point. He calls it up:

INT. CONFERENCE ROOM - DAY.

Prof. Membrane stands before a collection of microphones,
giving a press conference.

> pROF MEMBRANE
> Since my son's skeleton was accidentally
> crushed by a paramedic in a freak piggy
> accident, I have created the new Megulese-
> 3000 fusion-powered titanium exoskeleton.
> It will give him the strength of ten
> thousand little boys!

INT. ZIM'S MAKING STUFF ROOM

> ZIM
> Ten thousand Dibs?

INT. ZIM'S LIVING ROOM

Dib has completely ripped off the front of the house and
comes crashing through the living room, tearing down walls
with his mighty fists.

> DIB
> My whole life has been a miserable pig-
> filled ordeal because of YOU! You can
> hide, ZIM, but you can't... hide!

GIR scurries around underfoot. He finds his little rubber
piggy on the ground and scoops it up.

INT. ZIM's MAKING STUFF ROOM.

ZIM now frantically throws rubber pigs into the machine,
sending them back one after another. A collection of misc.
Dib junk piles up to one side. ZAP! ZAP! ZAP!

> ZIM
> There must be some way of stopping him!
> Some point in history where he's still
> vulnerable to the piggy!

INT. ZIM's LIVING ROOM - DAY.

ZAP! ZAP! ZAP! With each pig sent back in time, DIB's
exoskeleton becomes more fearsome and even begins to sprout
lasers, rockets, and other weapons.

                              (CONTINUED)

13.

CONTINUED:

                    DIB
          ZIM! I've got a thermonuclear ZIM-
          seeking missile with your name on it!

A barrage of rockets cuts down the wall leading to the
kitchen. A wall crumbles, revealing GIR, cowering down low.
He throws his little piggy at Dib. Dib brushes it off.

                    GIR
          Boo!

                    DIB
          Fool! Exposure to so many piggies has
          hardened my fear into piggy rage!

                    GIR
          Doop! I have to go now!

INT. ZIM'S KITCHEN - DAY.

GIR scurries down the shaft to ZIM's lab. Dib stomps up to
it and begins blasting chunks in the floor.

INT. ZIM's MAKING STUFF ROOM.

ZIM is still sending pigs back one by one. Huge chunks of
debris fall from the ceiling. The room shakes with every
blast. GIR runs to his feet and cowers. ZAP! ZAP! ZIM
reaches for another pig, and... There's only ONE LEFT!

                    ZIM
          Only one left! Noooooo!

He pounds his head on the machine.

                    GIR
              (with child-like curiosity)
          YAY!! WE'RE DOOMED!!

                    ZIM
              (he stops)
          Wait! There may be one last chance.

On the screen he targets an image of HIMSELF at the same time
machine... He sets the pig in the chamber, and...

INT. TUNNEL TO ZIM'S LAB.

Dib is blasting throw layers and layers of ZIM house. He
finally makes it through to ZIM's lab.

                                        (CONTINUED)

14.

CONTINUED:

                    DIB
          And now, ZIM! This is for tampering with
          the past!! This is for the pigs! Enjoy
          your last moments...

He pulls back his arm and... FFZZZZZ...

EXT. ZIM'S FRONT DOOR - DAY.

ZZAP! Dib - regular old every day Dib - reaches out and
places the little camera next to ZIM's door. He is now back
to how he was at the beginning of the story. He stops.

                    Dib
          ...of privacy! Soon the world will see--
          Wait a minute. Have I always been like
          this? Yes, I have, haven't I! My whole
          life! Good ol' Dib-like Dib -- Whaaaa!

The Security Gnomes grab him and drag him away.

INT. ZIM's MAKING STUFF ROOM.

The whole place is back to normal. GIR looks up at ZIM.

                    GIR
          It's like none of it ever happened.
          Where did the last piggy go?

ZIM just smiles a really, really, dopey smile. In his hand
he holds up a brain.

INT. ZIM's MAKING STUFF ROOM - EARLIER.

CAPTION: "ONE HOUR EARLIER"

ZIM is preparing to send the first robot back in time.

                    zim
          Now to unleash screaming temporal doom!

The machine whirrs to life... when suddenly... FZZAP! ZIM's
head flashes. He turns to the camera and begins to drool.

PUSH IN to the inside of ZIM's head. His brain has been
replaced with a small rubber piggy. On the piggy is a note:

"ZIM, DON'T USE THE TIME MACHINE. LOVE, ZIM." SQUEAK!

                              FADE OUT.

STRAY PIGGY OBSERVATIONS

- The Breakfast Orbs joke originally featured a Navy ship on the high seas rolling back and forth, causing the breakfast to roll off the table. It was cut just because there was so damn much going on already.

- This first script is probably my longest, as we were put under very sensible pressure to scale our scripts down. Well, it was sensible at first. Our original mandate was to deliver a script about 15 pages long, and of course, being writers, we tended to let it bleed a little onto page sixteen. Unfortunately, this meant the original animatic was always too long, and things the board artists had spent long hours on were trimmed to fit the show to length. Soon Steve Ressell was asking us to trim the scripts down to 14 pages to save the poor storyboarders from spending late nights on sequences that would never be used. Fair enough. Later we got a request to trim the scripts down to "about 12 pages," so the board artists had some room to expand the visual gags. I winced at the reduced size, but couldn't argue with them throwing more jokes in. A few weeks later this was reduced to "11 pages tops.". When it literally hit "10 and a half pages, and no more," I officially protested. We prided our stories on being on some level sophisticated. A weird ride like "Rubbe Piggy" could never, ever be told in 10 and a half pages. It's why by the time we were cancelled, I was feeling like the stories weren't quite as complex as they'd been in the past.

- An earlier draft of the script featured a *much longer* Professor Membrane segment explaining the repercussions of time travel. In it was a joke about killing John Denver. It was the first and absolute last time I proposed a joke about John Denver in any *ZIM*-related media, or indeed, in any media at all

- The Fish in a Bear Suit was Jhonen's idea. At the time I wasn't sure I liked how random it was. Now I love how random it was.

- Even though this was my first solo script, the episode is listed later in the run after "Hamstergeddon," though it aired before. I'm sure there was a reason for this, but it's lost in time due to how boring the reason was.

- The *Invader ZIM* fandom wiki claims, "Walton Chunky's name is similar to that of Milton Bradley." Is it really? Any more than it's similar to, say, Winston Churchill, on whom the character is based not at all? Or maybe it's closer to "Ralston Purina," which is what I was thinking when trying to come up with the name of a fictional breakfast cereal inventor. I was *not* thinking of a guy famous for making board games.

- Corollary observation: The *Invader ZIM* fandom wiki is a wonderful labor of love by some very dedicated people, but it's wrong at least 25% of the time. There's so much misinformation about the show already, it makes me crazy to see things that are outright wrong posted as stone-cold internet fact. So look forward to a "THINGS THE ZIM WIKI GETS WRONG" section in every script from now on.

In fact, let's start that now:

(OTHER) THINGS THE ZIM WIKI GETS WRONG.

- "The shot where a giant fish in a bear costume is destroying the city is a reference to the Stay Puft Marshmallow Man from *Ghostbusters*."

No it isn't. It's just Jhonen being weird. If anything, it's a reference to classic Kaiju movies like Godzilla, as tipped off by the news caption that reads "TOKYO." And while the framing of the shot may vaguely invoke *Ghostbusters*, I can reassure you it was nobody's intention to simply drop an unadulterated *Ghostbusters* reference into the show. So there.

- "During Bad, Bad Rubber Piggy's commentary on the DVD Doom Doom Doom, Jhonen states that the original idea was for Zim to kill Dib permanently in this episode. After Dib's death, he wanted to replace Dib with a joke character Louie. Suee was also supposed to be an option. Nickelodeon didn't allow killing in a children's show, though."

Not true, I'm afraid. This was a joke Jhonen made on the commentaries. Jhonen at no point thought he would actually kill off one of the lead characters in the series. This should be obvious.

*A brief side note on scripts for animated series: Contrary to popular belief, writers get no residuals for most animated shows. I'll say this again in all caps. ANIMATION WRITERS GET NO RESIDUALS. The exceptions are the high-profile broadcast network shows like *Family Guy* or *Bob's Burgers* because they're covered by the highly-respected Writers Guild of America. The WGA has a reputation for being so hot-headed they'll strike and shut down the industry just to get back at every asshole exec who ever turned a writer down because his script was "too smart," demanded unpaid rewrites, or didn't know what *Roshomon* was. This reputation is not completely warranted, because the WGA has never struck without a completely batshit-crazy goal like the financial survival of their members, or getting residuals from digital downloads. (This is sarcasm.)

Most animation writers, however, are members of The Animator's Guild, a union that has never struck in recent memory. Seriously, when's the last time you heard of an animator's strike? 1946? As a result, we work for about a third of what WGA members get paid. Hooray. At least this ensures people who go into animation do it for the love of cartoons, and not such craven urges as earning enough money to buy a home somewhere in Los Angeles county.

THE ZIM OFFICES

An Immature Wonderland for Overgrown Twelve-Year Olds, and More Glory to It.

ZIM was a fun place to work.

Yeah, let's start with that sentence. It's simple, short, and probably something you had guessed already. It's also naive enough to conveniently sweep the miserable, long hours of hard work under the rug, and shove the strained interpersonal conflicts way behind the curtains where no one can see them.

And for the first time in my career, I had an office. A whole stinkin' office to myself, gawshdarnit! It was facing the main lounge area in the *ZIM* pit, and to one side was Rob Hummel's office, to the other was Roman Dirge's. Roman was there part time to come up with stories, and I'm not spending another word on him, no matter how interesting he may be, because this is all about *my office, dammit!* I'd seen a lot of offices in my lifetime -- austere, staid, professional places lined with useful furniture and maybe a photo of the owner's family making painfully happy faces for the camera. But settling in at Nickelodeon made me realize that an office in the cartoon business was another thing entirely.

I mean, if you think the *Invader ZIM* offices looked like what would happen if a twelve-year-old got an adult-sized salary and a free ride to every comic book and toy store in town, well, that's more or less what happened.

Yes, every office was something out of an amazing, immature wonderland. Everyone -- from the lowliest assistant to the highest-ranking director -- had a glorious collection of toys, models, action figures, etc. perched on their desk, on the shelves, or on the circular window sills that faced into the main space. Every office looked like a little pop culture museum curated to the exacting taste of the person who put their butt in that chair.

I learned about a lot of anime shows I'd never heard of from just some of the imported toys people left lying around their desks. Had it not been for these bits of plastic, I would have never learned about Cowboy Bebop, Evangelion, FLCL, and God knows how many strange Japanese imports. The phrase "Crush them now, Giant Robo!" was shouted by grown adults more times than most sensible people would be proud of. (It's from the show *Giant Robo*. Duh.)

So I set about furnishing my little space with posters, photos, postcards, and toys. Oh yes, the toys... I had a lot of them. Robots, demons, and tiny space ships. In that first year, I was a nerd child empowered to irresponsible elevens by a steady paycheck and the complete lack of a family to support.

At one point my desk was festooned with a collection of approximately fourteen small stuffed hamsters I'd bought at Ikea. Why? I have no idea! There's no explanation that could possibly justify. But there was something absurdly wonderful about a mass of these rather plain and innocuous toys piled in one place for no reason. It was a statement, and that statement was, "I have no idea what this is stating." This fact is *totally unrelated* to the fact that I wrote a story about a giant hamster terrorizing a city. Totally. Unrelated.

I also had a large-scale action figure of *Star Trek's* Mr. Chekov placed in my interior window directly across from the cubicle of our script coordinator, Danielle Koenig. Danielle was the daughter of Walter Koenig, the actor who played Pavel Chekov on the original series, so I figured it was a particularly annoying move to put a plastic replica of her dad in exactly the right location to stare at her every time she looked out of her cubicle. This move would later backfire on me the day Walter himself came into the office to meet Danielle for lunch. I looked up from my keyboard to find a full-sized Mr. Chekov staring at me, pointing at the small plastic replica of himself, and then at me. My head did, in fact, explode. To this day, I have no head.

And the art… There was art on every goddamn surface of every goddamn wall, door, and sometimes window. A large percentage of it was commercially-printed. Movie posters. Comic book covers. Band fliers. etc. But another, more interesting percentage were drawn by the artists themselves. There was a lot of that. The artists had a tendency to channel their ids into images that would never see the light of day on respectable kids' TV. Sketches of GIR eating human flesh, or a massive airship made of Dib's head destroying a city were not uncommon.

The cluster of offices that housed the storyboard artists started two doors down from my own, and I spent a fair amount of time hanging out with Chris and Ian Graham (no relation, despite being tagged as "The Graham Brothers" in the credits) talking about one brilliantly stupid thing or another. Like where to place a vaguely suggestive image in a scene where no one would find it. Or whether the video game "Star Wars Super Bombad Racing" was canon.

The infamous "Bloody GIR" -- a single-frame image of GIR covered in blood that was inserted into "Bad, Bad, Rubber Piggy" as well as (allegedly) fourteen other stories -- was Chris' doing. That sick bastard.

I bring up "hanging with the artists" not in a hopeless attempt to make me look "cool," "hip," "with it," "rad," or even "fly." I mention it because apparently, it's unusual in animation for the artist and writers to work in such close physical proximity to each other. On long-running shows like *The Simpsons*, the artists aren't even in the same building as the people who write the stories. Why? Nobody knows. It's a weird fact of the business that both sides seem to have shrugged their shoulders at this as "the way it is." Artists and Writers shall not meet except in designated meeting areas. And they must never intermarry. What would the neighbors think?

Personally, I find this unfathomable.

The idea that the guy making the words and the guy making the pictures shouldn't be in constant communication is ridiculous, and in my humble opinion has led to a strange rift of animosity existing between the two parts of the production team. Maybe it's a secret capitalist plot by the executives to divide and conquer us, enacted under the theory that if the writers and artists start talking too much, they'll realize they can make the show without them, and everyone will start to wonder just what those suits are contributing in the first place.

If any of the artists had a question about something particularly ridiculous or indecipherable I'd written, they could walk a few feet down the hall and ask me directly just what in God's name was I thinking. And some of the best bits of my scripts came out because I knew the board artist who'd be drawing it, and I wanted to give him something he'd at least be laughing at as he stayed in the office until 3:00AM to get it done. Sometimes I was still in the office, too, cursing myself for not writing better and faster when the sun had been up.

It was one of those late nights when Chris Graham mentioned one of the things he liked about *Invader ZIM*. "It's like we're making mini movies," he said, referring to the tendency of the show not only to go to epic scale while other shows usually kept things small, but the sheer glee that we had bending classic sci-fi and horror tropes into the mold of our show. "Game Slave 2" is a take on slasher movies, with Gaz standing in for the hockey-masked psycho when she decides to enact justice on the kid who stole her slot in the line to get the last new Game Slave. And of course the kaiju roots of "Hamerstergeddon" will be discussed later in this book.

"Mini-Movies" was a term that would stick in my head later. I hadn't really categorized what I thought I was doing with my stories, but that was damn close.

See what happens when artists and writers hang out?

THE NOTEMARE BEGINS

A Big Little Detour to Gaze in Wonder at ZIM's Reputation as a Problem Child.

Before I dive into another script, let me take a moment to talk about feedback from the network, or as it was lovingly called, "Notes." As in "Nice script. But we have a few notes..." Oh yes. They always have a few notes.

Notes are a fact of life in the television business, and every screenwriter knows they'll get them. Seriously, no writer just walks in, slaps the script on the executive's desk and declares, "Every last word is perfect, my friend. To alter a single vowel would be an artistic offense against the buttocks of God himself, buttocks you see in every sunrise, in the smile of every child. You can reach me on my private island should you need to praise me again. You're welcome!"

All screenwriters know that when a company is going to spend hundreds of thousands of dollars to produce something as inherently frivolous as animation, they tend to want a say in how the money is spent. From one perspective, this is understandable. It would be bad business -- nay, irresponsible! -- to leave a multi-million dollar production unattended. (I mean, if cartoons were left in the hands of mere professional artists, who knows what could happen?)

Another perspective says this attitude is stark raving bullshit, the mad rules of a control freak culture that's fallen so deeply into neuroticism that it can't let the tiniest detail pass without company approval. Why do the goddamn Suits always have to step on the necks of real artists trying to share their vision with the world, huh? *Huh??*

Reality lies somewhere in between. The truth is, it's always nice to have a second set of eyes to see if you've written something completely insane, or forgot that you killed Dib in the first scene but have him show up again two scenes later with a live sloth on his head. And not all notes are bad. On most animated series, the show's director will give notes on things that he thinks won't translate to the screen very well, or chip in ideas to make the show funnier. And, of course, the show's creator usually has a thing or two to add, since the show is their creative voice, after all.

So network notes are as inevitable as the sunrise, and an unhappy percentage of a writer's job is figuring out how to wrestle with notes that he or she knows on a gut level are bad for the script. When the notes come from other creative-types, it's usually an easy conversation. With executives, it can be a simple, rational discussion between professional adults. Or it can be a process as miserable as chewing on hot tinfoil.

Invader ZIM had a famously rocky relationship with the higher-ups assigned to oversee us. This doesn't make us terribly unique. The old tale of "the bourgeois network ass-monkeys made us change it!" has been spun around every show successful enough to have people who want to hear tales about it. Think *South Park*. Think *Saturday Night Live*. Think even *I Love Lucy*, if you want to go that far back. (But really, you don't. It was a horrible time when married people on TV slept in separate beds three feet apart, and a redhead wed to a musician from Cuba was considered an "interracial marriage.")

I'll dive a little bit deeper into theories of "why" a little later, but long story short, the notes meetings on *ZIM* got ugly. There were fights over tone. There were fights over whether the show was "too mean." There were sometimes fights over the tiniest joke, and having done some sketch comedy, there's nothing worse than being an adult caught in a debate over whether a moose is funnier than a pig.

In the light of hindsight, the executive assigned by Nickelodeon to oversee our show -- who was, and still is a decent guy, by the way -- probably felt like he had to keep a lid on an inexperienced show creator, and as a result clamped down harder than he should have. Jhonen, for his part, came from a background of comics, where the entire process was between him and the page, and he could decide for himself what was working and what wasn't. It wasn't a recipe for success, even if it wasn't particularly anyone's "fault."

As for myself, I didn't have the thickest skin back then. Sure, I was cocky, but somewhere deep in the back of my mind I held the secret fear that everything I did was going to be met with scorn, derision, and… a third thing I can't think of at the moment that's like scorn and derision, and please don't scorn or deride me for not thinking of it.

Some people suggest a cantankerous relationship can be good for the creativity of a show, that fighting with the network can force you to come up with even more creative solutions that only make the final product better.

Those people should have been forced to sit in on the *ZIM* meetings.

After "Bad, Bad Rubber Piggy" was so well received, I had gotten the feeling that this job was going to be, as they say in yacht rock, "smooth sailing." Or perhaps "smooth as whale shit off an ice floe" as someone who I never want to hear speak again once said. (I managed to blot everything about that person out of my mind except that one sentence. I hate myself for even bringing that sentence back. It's their anonymous revenge on me, getting their stupid phrase into my book. Unless I delete it. Maybe I will delete it. If you just read that phrase, you know that somehow I have lost this battle, and may yet lose the war.)

"Piggy" had gone through the system with little trouble. People liked how the script turned out, and I was actually pleased with what would turn out to be my first solo writing credit on a produced piece of television. I felt this could be the beginning of a trend.

It was, in a word, "not."

Which brings me to "Battle-Dib."

"Battle-Dib" was the next story I worked on with Jhonen. (I'm not including it in this volume simply because I'm limiting myself to scripts I wrote myself. Maybe if this book is successful, I'll release a sequel with scripts I co-wrote with others. So if you ever want to see the script for "Tak the Hideous New Girl" in print, you'd better buy a copy of this volume for everyone you know, and some people you don't.)

I had recently worked with Jhonen on "Attack of the Saucer Morons," and it turned out great. Having ZIM disguise the space ships retrieval unit as a pig was Jhonen's idea, but I'm very pleased that "GIR! Ride the pig!" was my line. It's very strange seeing random things you write catch on and end up on t-shirts and lunch boxes.

OK, in all honesty, that line wasn't random. I was proud of it, and I still am. It's weird and vaguely unsettling while at the same time something one could shout with life-affirming zeal. Do it now. Do it! See how good you feel? And isn't it great that the other people in the coffee shop are looking at you differently?

But back to "Battle-Dib." Why mention it? It's probably not anyone's favorite story. And as the first experiment in a Dib-centric ZIM-free episode, it wasn't terribly well-received by the viewing public. Apparently Nickelodeon got actual complaints that ZIM wasn't even in it. Whether these complaints came via e-mail, postal mail, or delivered in person by children with tear-stained faces who'd walked to Burbank on shoeless, bloody feet for that very purpose, I don't know.

I mention it because "Battle-Dib" was my first real head-on encounter with the Executive Note Tsunami that plagued our show.

It was the first time the wave of network notes hit me square in the face, bent my neck back ninety degrees, and knocked me across the parking lot, leaving me stunned, face-hit, and bent-necked. A man broken and in need of a neck doctor where there was no neck doctor to be found. The bent neck screams a silent, bent scream but there's no one to hear it. Oh, the bent anguish of a neck that can no longer-- I'll stop now.

I'll emphasize that I don't want to complain too much. I'm not the sort of writer who thinks every word and punctuation mark that hits the page has been channeled from a divine source through my unicorn-colored imagination straight to my rainbow-scented fingertips.

I also don't want to pour fuel on the raging inferno of fan hatred toward the mythical "executive." The indignant legends of how those damn eight-eyed slime-dripping suit-demons had the nerve to tell the creatives that they couldn't actually behead that kid on children's TV! Where do they get off telling the only people who make this horrible life worth living how to practice their craft at a level of genius found only in cartoon monasteries nestled in the remote mountaintops of Tibet?

Not only are these wild-eyed stories often exaggerated, unfair, or just plain inaccurate, they're the source of way too much fanboy glee to make me comfortable. We live in a world where looking for people to vilify and demonize has somehow become a hobby everyone practices at an expert level. I blame the Internet. It's a villain and a demon.

At Nickelodeon, the people giving us notes were just doing their jobs the best they knew how, no malice intended. But I don't think I'm too out of line in saying that the relationship between Nickelodeon and *Invader ZIM* was, unfortunately, kind of dysfunctional. On later show I would see examples of how show runners and executives could work together without driving each other completely crazy. Sadly, not on *ZIM*. It's not that our executive was a bad person with evil intent. He wasn't at all. It's not that Jhonen was a foot-stomping diva who couldn't stand to have the tiniest corner of his vision crimped. He absolutely wasn't. There was just a conflict in personalities, intentions, and modus operandi. It was a cross-purpose exchange of--

Oh hell, it was an unlucky mismatch. The wrong show with the wrong guy. He would have been great on some other series — in fact, he went on to be exactly that after *ZIM* ended — and we probably would have worked just peachy with someone else giving us feedback. The reality was just not a great fit, and yes, it was a problem.

We got a lot of notes.

A *lot* of notes.

Like, way more than most shows got.

And the minutiae of the points addressed was, in retrospect, bordering on maniacal. "This joke doesn't work, here's a paragraph explaining why." "We still don't know what Dib's motivation is, and rather than trying to figure out a solution, we're going to spend the next few sentences lambasting you about it."

On top of it, yes, the notes meetings were brutal. At least that's what I heard. Jhonen and Mary deliberately kept the writers out of them because, in Jhonen's opinion, the madness of having to fight for every line was more than anyone should have to endure. The one time I did attend, I remember an exchange over one dumb joke or another getting so heated the executive shouted "This just doesn't work," and I shouted back, "I'm sorry you feel that way!"

Adults shouting at each other over jokes. This is one of the stupid facts of the business of making children laugh. And I'm not proud of my behavior in that meeting.

Ironically, years later I heard second-hand that our executive -- no, I'm still not naming him in case some crazy out there decides he wants to mail him a dead beaver or something -- felt the same dread toward us. The quote I heard was that he felt like he was "facing down a firing squad every week." Well, I suppose it didn't have to be that way, but at the time, neither side could have told you how.

But getting back to the notes. If only I had a record of what those notes were.

Oh wait, I do.

I found these notes on the second draft of "Battle-Dib" lurking in an old folder buried deep my hard drive. But before I share them with you, know that I thought long and hard about whether it was fair to drag these notes out into the light. Is this somehow violating an unspoken code of silence between executives and production staff, passed down for decades through secret rituals held in subterranean caves under Burbank? Is this like showing private e-mails between friends who never expected anyone else to see them?

After a lot of thought, I've decided to release them for two reasons.

The first is that these were never private communications, but open memos that a lot of studio employees saw. After twenty years, I think nobody has any personal stake in this any more. Nobody's career is on the line, nobody has anything to be ashamed of. None of us are the people we were back then. Also, I'm offering up my far-from-perfect scripts to this project, so I think a little peek into the other side is perfectly fair.

The other reasons is that when I was a kid, one of my favorite tomes was David Gerrold's book on the making of the *Star Trek* episode "The Trouble With Tribbles." For the wide-eyed nine-year-old that I was, it was the most astounding inside look at the process of writing and producing TV I could have ever imagined. I spent hours in my bedroom beneath a hand-drawn poster of the USS Enterprise — looking exactly as wonky and bent as you would expect a nine-year-old with markers would draw it — eating up every word, every photo, and even every internal memo. My journey into a career in television was launched at least partly by this paper rocket.

That book didn't shy away from printing network notes, so I won't, either. I think I would be doing the future TV writers of America a disservice if I did, too. You're welcome.

So without further ado, the notes on draft two of "Battle Dib!"

```
Date: 8/9/00
Subject:        Invader Zim - "Battle Dib" 2nd Draft
```

```
Overall:
```

Unfortunately the same concerns still exist regarding the character development throughout the story. Most notably, Dib's motivation still does not come across clearly enough for us to identify with or care about his story.

Dib's conflict still seems unclear. What drives him? Losing his presentation spot? Appearing to be a flake? Saving the planet? Proving his worth? Each one of these goals is suggested, but none is established powerfully enough to drive the story (the new lines on p. 2 just don't seem to be convincing enough). It remains unclear what will really be the big deal if he misses the meeting. What specifically is at stake for him? It's hard to root for him if we don't feel for him.

Also, we discussed this story as an opportunity to highlight Dib's character in a way that's been impossible in other 'Zim-centric' stories. But in this story Dib comes across as surprisingly clueless (p.3 he doesn't know Dad isn't home even though his show is on TV and he already went to the signature machine; p.6 he doesn't get Gaz's obvious sarcasm; p.12 he's in a battle dome wearing battle gear and just fought an opponent in "Battle One," yet thinks "Battle Two" may be a chemistry exam; etc. etc.). Individually these points are insignificant, but collectively they present Dib as a somewhat ineffective character who's just bounced through his own story. This seems to be contrary to his usual depiction as 'smart but often frustrated or foiled by everyone else's cluelessness.'

Gaz -- two problems still persist. First, her motivation still is not established clearly enough. While the 'pizza' additions help greatly, we need to understand why this is such a big deal to her (p.6 if she's really hungry, why not just eat something else? why is this pizza so special?). Second, her relationship with Dib does not come across. We've discussed several times Dib 'stepping on her toes' several times in the opening before she swears vengeance. This would convey what their day-to-day interaction is like, and would also strengthen the set-up for her anger. Furthermore, their interaction throughout the rest of the story doesn't leave a strong enough impression.

The battle beats in the middle (p. 10-15) still feel too long and somewhat repetitive. By this point we've lost track of Dib's real mission -- giving his presentation that is so important to him (for reasons that will be better set up). Do we really need 3 battles here?

The conclusion -- there seems to be no pay off to Dib's mission (to give his presentation). On p. 18 he says "I did it" yet we're left with the feeling that in fact he will not do it -- we've seen an auditorium of people waiting for him to start and here he is stumbling around outside somewhere. The cutaway to the auditorium helps build the tension, though, so let's discuss a possible final scene (he gets up to give his presentation and it's gone? replaced with a pizza crust -- Gaz's final vengeance?) It feels like it needs something.

Specifics:

Page 2 - Need to clarify/strengthen Dib's motivation in his speech at the top of the page. What's at stake for him? What is he about to expose, or what will happen if he doesn't show it? etc. etc.

Page 2 - Does Dib need a permission slip to give a presentation, or just to attend a meeting? Seems like he'd know about this if he's already a member of the organization.

Page 3 - For consistency, can we make sure we spell out "Prof." in Membrane's Signature Machine line (like it's spelled out in TV Announcer's line)?

Can we eliminate Dib's line, "Where's dad! He's got to be here!"? Wouldn't he know he's not home if he already attempted the signature machine? Rather, can we emphasize his urgency (and show that he knows his Dad is gone) with something like "I need the phone! I need to call Dad" etc.

Page 4 - Can we amp up Gaz's excitement about ordering her pizza here? Why is this particular type of pizza so special to her? Can't she just get something else to eat?

Page 5 - To build Gaz's frustration, perhaps the Pizza Man should disconnect her in mid-sentence from the phone, instead of her hanging up the phone.

Page 6 - To increase Gaz's role in the story, perhaps she should be more actively scheming here (instead of merely sarcastic). As is, her dialogue feels a bit forced ("You're REALLY going?")

Also, can we rework her line, "Wait up!" at the bottom of the page? Gaz should seem active in her plan, rather than coming off as a follower.

Page 11 - "Gaz GRRRRs. She can't let this happen." This implies she has a plan that isn't working, but what is that plan? Is it just vaguely to ruin Dib's day? Her specific goal needs to be more clear throughout the story.

Page 12 - As mentioned before, Dib seems too oblivious when he says, "Pyro-Chaos? Maybe it's a chemistry exam." esp. since the announcer just mentioned they will be doing two of three battles.

Perhaps we should get a Gaz reaction of pleasure after Shunk knocks the eyedropper from his hands? We want to make sure we keep her constantly mindful of her mission/plan to foil Dib.

Page 13 - Again, by this point in the story we are very removed from the Swollen Eyeball Network and Dib's mission. Can we make sure we keep this alive somehow?

Can Gaz do something a little more active to rival up Shunk? We felt her telling him more insults was coming off as a double beat.

Page 14 - "Do spiders have robots?" Seems like an odd line, but we assume it's just meant to show his state of confusion/disorientation?

During the battle, perhaps Gaz should do something active to throw off Dib's concentration during this fight scene, i.e. make a faces at him through the dome, etc.? Once again, we want to keep her as active as possible.

Page 15 - "The earth depends on it!!" -- we've totally lost this sense of danger/purpose in the story. Need to consider how to build this tension/ motivation more clearly throughout.

Page 18 - As mentioned in the Overall notes, we need more of a pay off to Dib's presentation/mission. He still feels so far away from showing his presentation at this point. We need to finish his story more effectively.

Looking back, some of these were probably fair points. It's not like we thought the draft was perfect. We had written the best script we could to meet the deadline, a script I thought was funny, engaging, and on the whole worked. The problem was that every note seemed to boil down to one thought: "You're doing it wrong."

Why was there such a disconnect? Why did they never seem to "get" the show we were trying to make, and always try to school us on that fact?

I keep coming back to what I've come to call "The *Rugrats* Theory."

It's an old adage in the entertainment business that "nobody knows anything." It's a short-hand way of saying nobody can really predict which show or movie is going to take off like a rocket, and which is going to fizzle out on the launch pad. Everyone approaches this business with their own personal tastes front-and-center. If you read the first *Twilight* book and thought it was indulgent, regressive garbage — you know, like most rational people did — you probably wouldn't have predicted the movie would be so damn popular, and if you were the executive who passed on it, you'd probably have that career stigma tattooed on your forehead.

This is the curse of being an executive: you come armed only with your own tastes, but your job is to second-guess the tastes of a nation. Your role is not to recognize the things that you like, but to look at something and try to evaluate if everyone else is going to like it.

During that period, Nickelodeon's biggest hit had been *Rugrats*. It was one of the shows green-lit in the 90s that just kept enduring. Every year a new generation of kids got old enough to watch it, so every year dozens of old episodes suddenly became new to a whole new audience, and its success rolled on.

It wouldn't be surprising, then, that Nickelodeon probably looked to *Rugrats* as a model of what a cartoon should be. It should be friendly. It should be on some level heartwarming. It should be full of kid-relatable characters dealing with kid-relatable challenges. The stories should be motivated by personal issues, and the characters should grow a little from them. Everything should be just a little bit adorable.

Invader ZIM was none of these things.

In that light, it makes complete sense that we broke Nickelodeon's collective brain. Everyone up the Nick ladder knew *Rugrats* worked. It was successful, and it just kept on being successful. They had come to decide -- consciously or not -- that *Rugrats* was the round hole that every Nickelodeon cartoon should fit into.

ZIM was not just a square peg, it was a rhombus-shaped peg with spikes sticking out of it and a tiny screaming monkey head on the top.

In that light, it's no wonder the higher-ups kept telling us, "You're doing it wrong!"

and a note
on psychology

The Battle-Dib Conversation Won't Leave,
Like a Hobo Sleeping on your Back Porch.

Before we move on from "Battle-Dib," there's one other little thing I'd like to mention, something that the aspiring writers out there might find interesting, even if the rest of you will want to move on to that story where GIR goes nuts and kills people.

"Battle-Dib" was the first time I seriously tried to wrap my head around the psychology of the regular characters.

Who these people were -- the human people, not the single-minded ZIM -- wasn't completely obvious at first. Just what kind of relationship did Dib have with his dad, anyway? Apparently it was pretty dysfunctional, but did Dib realize it? And what's Gaz's motivation in this dysfunctional family besides simply driving Dib crazy?

I remember over-thinking it a lot, and it culminated with a discussion with Rob Hummel, Mary Harrington and me in Mary's office as I insisted that the reason Gaz was so angry all the time, and so focused on her games to the exclusion of all else was that she actually realized her father would never really care about them. He was emotionally cut-off and so wrapped up in himself he'll never give the kids any kind of love their whole lives, and so why not just bury yourself in games and hope the world goes away?

"Well," Mary said, "I can see you've thought a lot about this."

Yeah, I'd probably thought about it a bit too much. In a very early draft, I even gave Gaz a line near the end where she tries to tell Dib to just go home, because Dad will never care about them more than his work. "Don't you get it??" Jhonen cut that line.

It was probably an object lesson in just how deep you can usefully explore the psychology of a cartoon character in a children's show, and the practical answer to that is, "It depends."

One one level, the answer is "not beyond what makes it funny." As long as what the character does makes a certain sense on the screen, why go deeper? Do we really need to know the details of his childhood to know why Ren hit Stimpy?

Gaz likes what Gaz likes, and simply has no patience for anyone who gets between her and whatever that is at the time. And her penchant for making Dib's life miserable stems from a desire to get back at him for all the times his self-important missions to "save the world" got in her way. It works. You could psychoanalyze it, but that analysis might stand between you and the laughs.

Interestingly though, when we went on to write the comic series years later, and then when the show was revived in the *Enter the Florpus* movie, Jhonen decided he wanted more nuance in the characters. They would have at least some layers of compassion underneath the horrible screaming. These days, *Rick and Morty* is wonderfully adept at telling stories both emotionally complex and fantastically stupid. Back when we were doing *ZIM*, we were on the network that gave the world a show with a lead character that was a dog on one end and a cat on the other, so depth wasn't strictly a mandate.

One last thing about "Battle-Dib" before I move on. This is the last one, I promise.

Years later, at a New Year's eve party with a bunch of my friends, after drinking more than I should have and being handed something to smoke that at the time probably wasn't strictly legal, I found myself wandering into a dark, dank-smelling room where someone had set up a TV playing nothing but old episodes of *Invader ZIM*. Usually when I re-watch any cartoon I worked on, my brain torments me with everything I wish I'd done differently. "Aw, that joke could have been better. Maybe I should have started that scene stronger. Why isn't GIR blowing pig-shaped bubbles out of a hole in his bellybutton, FFS?" That night, probably because my brain was insulated in a layer of legal and semi-legal intoxicants, I could actually look at the cartoon as just something to be enjoyed.

And I actually loved it.

Not just because it was funny, and the animation was incredible, but because I was just so happy that we'd managed to do something this weird and ridiculous and get it on TV. I think it's some kind of mark of achievement to work very hard to produce something with no practical value except to be inherently ridiculous. It's kind of humanity's finest achievement.

That is, beyond the wheel, flush toilets, sandwiches, and figuring out that boiling water before drinking it can keep diseases from killing you.

HAMSTERGEDDON

A Hamster Rises, Buildings Fall, a Network Says "Too Soon."

Trivia: This one aired after "Piggy," so it's listed before it in most *ZIM* episode guides but it was written afterward. The production order and the air order are often much, much different. More interesting: "Hamstergeddon" very nearly became a lost episode; eleven *ZIM* minutes Nickelodeon nearly pulled from the air forever.

"Hamstergeddon" -- for those of you who have forgotten, or who have a post-hypnotic block implanted in your subconscious that prevents you from just Googling shit -- is the story of Ultra-Peepi, the cutest hamster in school, and his kaiju rampage through the city. When ZIM discovers that humans are hypnotized by how adorable the class pet hamster is, he attempts to harness that cuteness for his own evil ends, and of course, it spirals out of control, like all perversions of science must in a rational universe.*

*This last part isn't really true.

It's also, if you look carefully, it's the story of a small farm family struggling to survive during the dust bowl of America's Great Depression. But you have to look *very* carefully to see that. Like, I think maybe Farmer Miles P. Heartweather can be seen poking an arm from behind a car in exactly one frame. So in retrospect, it's almost not about that at all. The story of the Heartweather struggle may never truly be told.

Where was I?

Yes, "Hamstergeddon."

As I mentioned earlier, storyboard artist Chris Graham remarked that at this point in the show, we were making "mini-movies." This was definitely an element of my approach, though I wasn't overtly thinking it at the time. In retrospect, I was taking what Russell T. Davies -- the writer/producer who rebooted *Doctor Who* in 2005 -- called "the one with..." philosophy. (Point of fact, this was pioneered by the title of every *Friends* episode ever. You know, "The one where Joey Eats Garbage" or "The One Where Phoebe Beheads Some Guy" or whatever.)

I grew up as a big fan of science fiction shows that told self-contained stories with some kind of distinguishing "thing" as part of them. *Star Trek, Doctor Who, Space: 1999*, all forged their stories from a memorable central concept that drove everything. In the 80s, they started calling this approach "high concept," not because the concept at the center is particularly lofty, but because the story leads with the concept rather than the characters. It's about, say, an alien planet that's patterned itself after Nazi Germany, rather than, say, a young girl trying to find herself as she comes of age in a small New England town, or anything starring Emma Thompson in the 90's.

In the days before the internet gave viewers instant access to detailed episode guides, most viewers remembered episodes of these series as "the one with..." "The one with the living plastic," "The one with the evil Spock," "The one with the silver robots stomping through London," "The one with the fuzzy purring balls that get in everything," etc.

It's not to hard to see that Hamstergeddon is "The one where ZIM questions the very foundations of his existence, staring into a personal abyss that even Neitzsche himself would--" I'm kidding. It's obviously "The one with the Godzilla-sized hamster that's too cute to kill."

Maybe there's some deeper meaning in the story of ZIM giving a cute hamster an implant so he can use its cuteness against the humans, and I could probably tease something out related to humanity's relationship to civilization vs. their inner primitive mammalian nature or something, but that would get very pretentious very fast.

I think ultimately I wanted to see how our production would handle a Kaiju story, and I thought doing it with one of the tiniest animals found in an average American classroom would be funny. That's almost a mathematical formula, right? Tiny cute thing gets huge and everyone's scared of it. I wouldn't discover until years later that the 1970s UK comedy show *The Goodies* had done something similar in an episode called "Kitten Kong." Honestly, I never saw an episode of *The Goodies* until about 2005, and if any one of the Goodies themselves ever saw "Hamstergeddon," they never wrote me to complain. There was no "Crazy Bucket" in theirs, though.* I think this gives the ZIM version its clear edge.

*There was no "Crazy Bucket" in the original script, as you'll soon see. It was a gag added in the storyboard phase. To this day, I am jealous.

This is also the one where I tried to subvert as many giant monster movie tropes as possible, or at least as many as I thought would be funny. Dib as the scientist running in to the room of generals with the secret to the monster... only to reveal that he has no idea how to defeat him. ZIM's "keep watching the skies" speech at the end that goes nowhere. Peepi eating a vehicle only to have it get stuck in his teeth. And everyone who flees in terror stopping at least once to adore just how cute that oversized monster is.

Despite how purposefully obvious it all is, I actually had trouble hammering the structure together. Quick tip for you aspiring screenwriting people out there: Drama is what happens when a character wants something and has trouble getting it. ZIM wants to use Peepi to ride to victory over humanity, and midway through the story, while he doesn't quite get exactly what he wanted, he decides it's good enough and walks away. At that point,

ZIM's story of perverting hamsters for conquest looks more or less over, and I was left wondering just what would happen next. This is a very mild case of what writers call "writing yourself into a corner." It's no wonder that I decided to switch the narrative to Dib and the military, who both wanted to stop that giant hamster very, very badly. And it's a good thing I had the old monster movie tropes to fall back on to kickstart that into gear.

Still, knowing I had to get ZIM back in the game, I had to threaten him with the destruction of his base to get him off his alien butt. ZIM is nothing if not self-interested, as evidenced by he and GIR passively watching the *Angry Monkey* show (a.k.a. *The Scary Monkey Show* in another episode) while the sound of the city being stomped by a monstrous rodent seeps in through the living room walls.

When it was done, I was enormously happy. This little 11-minute mutant kaiju tale turned out shockingly well, and everyone seems pleased.

But...

Okay, this is the point in the narrative when I have to mention why "Hamstergeddon" nearly became a lost episode, and if I were a more portentous writer, I'd have a particularly poignant paragraph here that would sound just heartbreaking if it were read by Morgan Freeman or even Jeff Goldblum. I don't have that. I thought about it, but I decided in a book like this, there's no way I could pull that off without driving off a cliff into into a canyon of unbearable maudlin cheese. (Yes, those canyons exists.) So I'll just lay it down as a simple fact.

Shortly after first air date of "Hamstergeddon," the World Trade Center was attacked by terrorists flying two planes into the buildings on the day history has now short-handed as "9-11."

I should follow this with the personal story about how I hadn't been listening to the radio as I drove to an early doctor appointment, so I had no idea the attack had happened until the doctor told me in her office. And then maybe tell about driving to the studio to find most everyone had gone home, but just a few crew members were clustered around the big-screen TV in the little couch pit at the center of the *ZIM* offices, watching the footage play over and over again on the news. And how surreal it all was, and nobody knew what to feel besides shock and horror. Unsurprisingly, the studio closed for the day, and everyone went home to try to grapple with just what the hell had happened, and how things were about to get a whole lot worse for everyone.

Since that event, probably millions of words have been written by people with more interesting, harrowing, miraculous, or tragic experiences than I had, as well as about the ugly turn history took later when the US went storming into a country that hadn't actually staged the attacks. (Does history also tell you at least half of everyone in the country could see in advance that we were invading the wrong people? We tried to say something to stop them. We really did.)

As a result of these attacks, security was reinforced at the studio with an iron fist. We all had to check in at the front, the number of guards was doubled, visitors had to be escorted through the building... Despite the fact that we obviously knew that the last thing the terrorists were coming for was our cartoons. They may have hated us for our freedom, as George W. told the crowds, but it was a good bet they didn't hate us for *Doug*.

Also as a result, "Hamstergeddon" was yanked from rotation and put on indefinite hold. I got an e-mail from Standards and Practices saying they were pulling it because they thought the sight of falling buildings might not go over well with sensitive viewers. It had aired once, but it might never air again.

At the time — in my uppity late-20s, — I was angry. Surely the kids of America were smart enough to know in their bones the difference between a two-dimensionally drawn cartoon hamster wrecking fake cartoon buildings. What is wrong with you people?!

These days I can see their point. I can appreciate the value of being cautious over being horribly tone deaf. Look, yeah, most kids absolutely *can* tell the difference, but it doesn't hurt to teach them what constitutes an appropriate amount of respect, and in the big picture what's the loss of one cartoon versus some common respect during a tragedy?

Nickelodeon didn't give us a new air date, and given the state of the country, I had a feeling it could be lost forever. So I retired to my office, shut the door, and sat there once again silently cursing "the suits" for not trusting the children of American to handle even the slightest— blah blah... You know, the usual stuff.

Fortunately, I was wrong. I don't know the exact date when "Hamstergeddon" went back into rotation, but yes, eventually the nation decided it was safe to show falling buildings as entertainment again, because if there's one thing America hates, it's letting disaster stand in the way of the status quo.

So yes, Ultra-Peepi lives on. Out there. On streaming services.

SCRIPT: HAMSTERGEDDON

illustration: Aaron Alexovich

```
INVADER: ZIM                                    11/28/00
                       "Hamstergeddon"
                          Draft 3a
                      (Revised 11/28/00)                    *

INT. MISS BITTERS CLASSROOM - DAY.

EXTREME CLOSE UPS of different parts of a big, scary metal   *
box.  Black rivets, LED's, explosive bolts, a "Danger"      *
sign, etc.  MISS BITTERS reaches up a finger and presses a  *
button.  The box bursts open to reveal...                   *

A HAMSTER.  A standard-issue hamster.  Sitting in a cage.
Chewing cedar chips.  There's a wheel, a water bottle, the
whole standard hamster bit.  And damn if this hamster isn't
just the cutest thing.

                          KIDS
                OOOOOOOOOOOOOOOOOOOOOH!

Miss Bitters reads the invoice that came with the box as
the two men turn and leave.

                       MISS BITTERS
                    (military-like)
                By order of the school board's program
                to reduce misery among school children,
                this class is issued one classroom pet,
                hamster-class.  Name: Peepi.

AT THE CAGE, a group of KIDS gather around to OOH and AHH.
They're enraptured by the little fuzzball.                   *

                          ZITA
                Oh, Peepi is so cute!

                          MOGNO
                Look at his little Peepi face!

                          MELVIN
                He's like a little fuzzy Peepi person.

The Hamster bends over and nibbles his own butt.

                          ALL
                Awwwwwww.

PAN ACROSS a row of wide-eyed kids to find ZIM, looking at
the little thing with fear and loathing.  PEEPI runs across
the cage, by coincidence, toward ZIM.  ZIM recoils and
SCREECHES in horror.  He nearly collides with DIB.


                                        (CONTINUED)
```

Eric Trueheart

```
                                                    2.
    CONTINUED:
                        DIB
            Do I even have to say anything at this
            point?

                        ZIM
            If you are referring to my reaction to
            that hair... monster, I can assure you
            that like the other normal children I
            find it... er...

                        DIB
            Cute!  The word is "Cute," ZIM.  Humans
            think hamsters are cute!

                        ZIM
            Yes.  This "cuteness" has a curious
            effect on human beings.  Makes
            them...weak.

                                            DISSOLVE TO:

    EXT. CITY STREET - ZIM'S FANTASY - DAY.

    ZIM rides through the streets atop a giant ten-foot
    hamster.  People line the sidewalks, adoringly loving
    Peepi!

                        ZIM
            People of earth!  Can you resist the
            hypnotic power of Peepi?

                        CROWD
            Awwwwwwww!

                        ZIM
            Now... Kneel before ZIM!

    INT. MISS BITTERS CLASSROOM - RETURN.

    Peepi runs in his wheel as the kids ooh and ahh.        *

                        MISS BITTERS                        *
            Take a good look, children.  It will            *
            prepare you for your adult lives in our         *
            nightmarish corporate system.                   *

    ZIM is lost in thought.                                 *

                        ZIM
            Hmmmmm... Yesss... it just might work.

    Dib looks suspiciously at ZIM.                          *

                                            DISSOLVE TO:
```

90

3.

INT. MISS BITTERS CLASSROOM - NIGHT.

Peepi sleeps in his wheel, cuter than ever. Suddenly a
powerful beam of LIGHT shines sideways through the window
into his cage. **A ZIM-shaped shadow falls on him...**   *

INT. MISS BITTERS CLASSROOM - DAY.

The next day. A girl sits upsidedown on a chair. Bitters
hovers over her with a watch.

                    MISS BITTERS
          Minute 26. If you're determined to let
          the blood rush to your head, you'd
          better have trained for it --

                    DIB
          Miss Bitters? Have you noticed
          anything strange about the hamster?

SHOT OF Peepi, sitting in his cage, now easily three times
his size, and no less cute.

                    DIB (CONT'D)
          He's three times his size and he has
          that hideous, throbbing alien device on
          his back!

Peepi turns to reveal a Borg-like device grafted onto his
back. Peepi BURPS, and begins eating the floor of his
cage.   *

ZIM starts to look nervous. He fingers a small   *
communicator/controller looking thing on his wrist.

                    ZIM
               (to himself)
          The earth boy is trying to interfere.
          Now's the time to use the Peepi
          creature's "cuteness" to divert
          attention.

He's about to press a button on the communicator, when
CRASH! All attention in the room turns to Peepi's cage,
which has fallen on the floor.

There's a loud CHEWING SOUND. Pan across the class as one
by one the kids' chairs drop to the ground as the legs are
eaten out from the under them. When we reach the outer
wall, the sound CHEWS it's way through.

                    ZIM (CONT'D)
          This is a little ahead of schedule.   *

Eric Trueheart

INT. SKOOL HALLWAY - DAY.

ZIM steps through the hole and watches as the back of a
hamster runs across the Skool Grounds. It eats a hole
through the fence, and GROWS immediately. It escapes
across the street and into the city. HORNS HONK and PEOPLE
YELL.

                    ZIM
          Yes, my creation! Grow! Grow!
               (into his communicator)
          Now, Peepi! Come to your master!
               (nothing)
          Peepi?
               (nothing)
          PEEPI? Obey me! PEEPI!

He looks on as Peepi disappears into the distance. PAN UP
with the sounds of the chaos to the NUCLEAR POWER PLANT on
the horizon. Silence. The SIRENS go off and RED LIGHTS
flash on the plant. AN EXPLOSION rocks one of the towers.

Then... above the wreckage of the nuclear power plant rises
ULTRA-PEEPI! He's two-hundred feet high, crisscrossed with
Borg-like technology, but still CUTE AS THE DICKENS! In
the distance, we hear the crowd:

                    CROWD
          Look out! Look out! Awwww... He's
          so CUTE!

Dib looks on from the hole. He turns to ZIM.

                    DIB
          Anything you'd like to confess?

                    ZIM
               (with false casualness)
          No. Don't be silly.

He exits.

INT. NEWS STUDIO - DAY.

A reporter reads news from his desk. A graphic in the
corner reads "ULTRA-PEEPI".

                    REPORTER #1
          Experts are still baffled over the
          origins of Ultra-Peepi, the giant
          mutant hamster now ravaging the city,
          but they all agree, he's just fuzzy
          wuzzy adorable, isn't he? He sure is!
          AAAARGH!!

                              (CONTINUED)

5.

CONTINUED:

The reporter is crushed by the ceiling as a giant hamster foot smashes through.

EXT. CITY SKYLINE - DAY.

Peepi stomps over an office building, crumbling it to the ground. He SQUEAKS and starts eating a city bus, holding it between his paws like a person would. It's just too cute.

On the ground people run in terror and SCREAM.

The bus gets stuck in his teeth. Peepi tries to pick it out by rubbing his teeth on the pointed spire of an skyscraper. It's real cute.

The people stop running and look back at the giant beast.

> WOMAN #1
> IEEEIEIEEEEIEE!
> (suddenly seeing how cute)
> Look! He's using the building like a
> tooth pick.   *

Big chunks of debris come crashing down on them.

A squadron of JET FIGHTERS come SCREAMING IN at Peepi. He
swats them out of the sky with his back feet.   *

EXT. CITY ANOTHER CITY STREET - DAY.

The flaming wreckage of a jet plane comes screaming out of the sky and crashes next to ZIM. He's looking up at Peepi, desperately yelling into his communicator.

> ZIM   *
> No, Peepi! Come here! You must obey   *
> me! I am your lord and hamstermaster!
> (to a fleeing citizen)
> No! Don't fear the Peepi! Fear me!
> FEAR ME!

ZIM looks around him at the chaos Peepi is bringing. Fires burn. Buildings crumble. Police cars are vaporized.

> ZIM (CONT'D)
> (reconsidering)
> Well... he does seem to be destroying
> the humans... and that IS good. Um...
> GOOD JOB, Peepi. I'll just wait until
> you're all done here. Carry on!

ZIM shrugs and walks off. A SCREAMING CITIZEN runs by.

(CONTINUED)

6.

CONTINUED:

                    SCREAMING CITIZEN
          HELP! HELP!
          (she looks up at Peepi)
          Awww... Wook at his widdle feet!
          ARRGH!

Peepi's giant foot stomps on him.

INT. ARMY COMMAND TENT - DAY.

A group of SOLDIERS stand around a map of the city. A
small model hamster marks Peepi's present location. The
GENERAL looks over the map.

                    GENERAL
          I don't care what the blazes it wants,
          I just want it stopped!

                    COLONEL
          But general, I couldn't fire a missile
          at that furry little face. Could you?

                    OTHER SOLDIERS
          No. Not me. (etc.)

Someone pushes his way through the soldiers. It's Dib.

                    DIB
          Wait! I have important information
          about Ultra-Peepi! You have to listen!

                    GENERAL
          Let the boy talk!

                    DIB
          He's not a normal hamster. He's been
          altered somehow through alien tampering
          Eating makes him larger. The more he
          eats, the bigger he gets.

                    GENERAL
          Good work, boy! How do we stop him?

Dib stops. He hadn't thought of this.

                    DIB (WITH CONVINCTION)
          I... don't know.

                    GENERAL
          Get him out of here.

The soldiers drag him out. The Colonel looks up from a
radio operator in the corner.

                              (CONTINUED)

7.

CONTINUED:

                    COLONEL
          General! We think we know where he's
          going!

INT. ZIM'S LIVING ROOM - DAY.

GIR sits on the couch, lazily watching TV. ZIM walks in
with a packet of Irken Licking Powder and two sticks. He
sits down on the couch and gives one stick to GIR. Outside
we can hear SCREAMS, SIRENS, THUNDERING FOOTSTEPS, ETC.
ZIM ignores them. They speak between licks.

                    ZIM
          What are you watching?

Beat.

                    GIR
          Angry Monkey.

Beat.

                    ZIM
          That... horrible monkey.

Beat.

                    GIR
          Mmm-hmm.
               (beat)
          Where's Ultra-Peepi?

Beat.

                    ZIM
          He's working.

On the screen it's the usual monkey shtick. The show is
interrupted by a "SPECIAL NEWS BULLETIN". There's already
a new anchor to replace the old one..   *

                    REPORTER #2
          Reports are now in that Ultra-Peepi is
          heading for the city's pellet plant.
          If he reaches the reserve supply of
          hamster pellets, he could grow to
          unimaginable proportions!   *

On the screen appears an overhead view of the city. A line
is drawn between Peepi and the city's pellet plant. It
crosses what is clearly ZIM's house.   *

                              (CONTINUED)

8.

CONTINUED:

                    ZIM
                (offhand)
          That path will take him right through
          this neighborhood.

BOOM! The room shakes. And shakes again. Like GIANT
FOOTSTEPS. ZIM notices the growing sound.

                    ZIM (CONT'D)
          What is that noise?

EXT. ZIM'S FRONT DOOR - DAY.

ZIM opens the front door. He looks around his front yard
for the source of the offending noise. Nothing. He turns
around and looks up to see...

ULTRA-PEEPI! Bearing down on his house, maybe just a block
away.

CLOSE ON PEEPI'S FEET as he stomps on house after house.
He stops to roll around in one.

                    ZIM
          No! You will NOT destroy your master's
          secret base! I command you to stop!
          OBEY YOUR CREATOR!!

Ultra-Peepi SQUEEEEKS! ZIM runs inside.

EXT. ZIM'S ROOF - DAY.

The roof opens up. ZIM's VOOT CRUISER rises up, and
launches into the sky.

He screams toward Ultra-Peepi, launching missiles at him.

                    ZIM
          You made me do this, Peepi. I hate to
          be the bad guy, but you must be
          disciplined or you'll never learn.

EXT.YET ANOTHER CITY STREET - DAY.

Dib looks up to see ZIM's VOOT CRUISER'S screaming attack
on the giant hamster.

                    DIB
          Never thought I'd see that.

9.

EXT. CITY SKYLINE - DAY.

Peepi is bearing down on ZIM's house, when a cluster of
Irken lasers nail him in the flank. He bucks, and turns
toward ZIM's VOOT CRUISER.

                    ZIM
          Peepi! TURN BACK NOW! DO not invoke
          the wrath of the IRKEN ELITE!!

Peepi retaliates with an adorable blast of nuclear breath.
It hits ZIM's shields, but he careens across the city and
smashes into the side of a building, then to the ground.

Ultra-Peepi picks up the cruiser, with ZIM still in it. He
chews for a bit, and then picks the cruiser out with his
pinky paw toe. He flicks it off into the city.

EXT. PARKING LOT CRASH SITE - DAY.

The cruiser lies crashed in the parking lot of a large
Hotdog-Shaped restaurant. (The famed "Delicious Weenie"
restaurant.) Smoke pours from the wrecked ship. ZIM lies
half out of the cockpit. Dib runs to his unconscious body.   *

                    DIB   *
          Wait. If I capture him now, no one
          will be able to stop the hamster. But
          if I let him go to fight Peepi, he'll
          just keep on trying to destroy mankind.
          This stinks. Okay, so if I save ZIM,
          then...

As he talks, ZIM comes to. He gets up and looks at Dib
monologizing. He thinks about saying something to him,
then stops. Instead he shrugs, and calls into his
communicator.

                    ZIM
              (behind Dib)
          GIR. Come get me.

                    GIR (O.S.)
          Yes my lord.

While Dib continues his speech, GIR zips in. ZIM hops on
his back, and takes off.

                    DIB
          ...if the hamster goes on to save
          mankind... wait.. no that's not
          right.
              (noticing ZIM is up)
              (MORE)

                                        (CONTINUED)

97

CONTINUED:

                         DIB (CONT'D)
          Wait! ZIM! Promise me you're on our
          side this time!

                         ZIM
          I know not of sides, earth stink! But
          just this once, I agree with you. The
          hamster must be stopped.

                         DIB
          NOOOO!!!! Oh, wait... yeah. Go on
          then.

ZIM flies away.

EXT. CITY PELLET PLANT - DAY.

A large electrical fence with a sign reading "CITY PELLET
PLANT." Tanks and missile launchers lined up, guns raised.
Peepi rises above the skyline, merrily galumphing toward
them. A MISSLE COMMANDER barks orders into a walkie-
talkie.

                    MISSLE COMMANDER
          Ready unit seven. Fire on my mark.
          Three... Two... Oh, just LOOK at him!

Peepi stomps on a missile launcher. His shadow looms over
the commander. Suddenly a SOUND echoes over the city.

                         ZIM
                  (thunderously booming)
          Peepi! Peeeeeepi?

Peepi stops and looks around. REVEAL ZIM's BACKUP CRUISER,
holding the giant Hotdog restaurant in the air by a tractor
beam. ZIM's voice booms from a megaphone under the ship.

                    ZIM (CONT'D)
          THE WEENIE TEMPTS YOU.

Peepi SQUEALS, changes direction and follows the weenie.
ZIM shoots off over the city. The missile commander turns
to his troops.

                    MISSLE COMMANDER
          Now we're being attacked by giant
          weenies! GET the weenie! Get it!!

The tanks begin to fire.   *

EXT. FAIR GROUNDS - DAY.

ZIM stands in front of the Weenie Stand, now resting on the
ground. We're close on ZIM's face.

                                        (CONTINUED)

CONTINUED:

> ZIM
> Yes, Ultra-Peepi... Yess...obeyyyy!

Pull back to see the weenie has been placed in the middle
of the carnival's Ferris Wheel. **ZIM presses a button and** *
two HOVER SLEDS with ROCKETS and CLAMPS on them roll up *
next to the ferris wheel. The rockets rise up, ready to *
clamp on the wheel. *

Peepi stomps over the rollercoaster and bears down on ZIM.

> ZIM (CONT'D)
> Yes... Yes... Yes...

Peepi lunges **forward... But instead of eating the hotdog,** *
he starts gnawing on the ferris wheel! *

> **ZIM (CONT'D)**
> NO! Bad Peepi! Don't eat the wheel!
> HUH?

ZIM looks over to see: *

TANKS and MISSLE LAUNCHERS rolling toward the fair grounds.
The Missle Commander barks orders from one of the tanks.

> MISSLE COMMANDER
> Okay, let's try going at the hamster
> this time. We gotta use this stuff on
> SOMETHING. *

The tanks start to fire. Peepi begins to retreat away from
the fairgrounds.

> ZIM
> AAARGH!! No time to spare!! Fine!
> Ultra-Peepi, you have this coming!

ZIM presses the button on the controller. The hover-sleds
chase after Peepi, and the rockets clamp onto Peepi
himself. ZIM presses another button and the rockets
ignite. SQUEEEEEK! Peepi launches up into the sky.
Everyone stops to watch, until the rockets are just a
single glowing point hanging high in the sky.

A SMALL CHILD tugs on ZIM's sleeve, a tear in her eye.

> SMALL CHILD
> Why?

ZIM looks around at the devastation that Peepi has wrought.
The burning city, the crumbled landscape. Dib rolls into *
frame, still encased in the bucket.

(CONTINUED)

Eric Trueheart

CONTINUED: (2)   12.

                        DIB
            Why? Because alien tampering with our
            life forms is dangerous, and ends in
            pain--

ZIM kicks the bucket away into some unseen wreckage.

                        ZIM
            Because when you create a giant monster
            of doom, no matter how "cute"... you
            have to... you have to... I just
            don't know.

A TEAR runs down the child's cheek.

                        ZIM (CONT'D)
            But stop snivelling, little worm
            monkey. Ultra-Peepi will live on, out
            there, in the stars.

As he talks, the little glowing star that is Ultra-Peepi
comes SCREAMING down to earth. Unable to make it into
orbit, it CRASHES somewhere on the horizon.

                        END

STRAY HAMSTER THOUGHTS!

- This story went through a couple of titles before we ended up with "Hamstergeddon." One of them was "ZIM vs Hamstro," but my favorite was "Hamsterdammerung," even though I knew Nickelodeon would never let us name a cartoon with a pun based on Norse mythology's apocalypse.

- The funk music behind the one shot of Ultra-Peepi grooving down the city streets -- "Yeahhhhh... Ultra-Peepeeeeee..." -- came about because of a mistake by the Korean animation company. For some reason, the first take they sent us of that scene used an odd walk cycle that seemed to make Peepi saunter down the street like he's stepped out of a 1970's *Shaft* movie. Jhonen thought it was so funny he kept it, and had composer Kevin Manthei come up with an appropriately funky theme to go over it.

- The original name for the hamster was Mr. Boodles. I'm glad we settled on a final name that sounds just a little bit like a dick joke without actually being one.

- "NO ANIMATED CHARACTERS WERE HARMED IN THE FILMING OF THIS PRODUCTION." You'll notice that little disclaimer at the end. Standards and Practices were very concerned with showing a character — any character — die on screen, so we put that at the end to calm their fears that children would be up nights weeping at the fate of "Citizen #2." You'll notice in later episodes we sometimes would add a line of dialogue to a character who seemingly met their demise. They'd shout "I'm okay!" from underneath the chunk of debris that smashed into them. These days, "I'm okay!" has become something of a running gag in the cartoon world, and you'll see it pop up a lot of shows.

- "The Crazy Bucket" wasn't in my original draft, but damn, I love it, and unbeknownst to me, it became a running gag among some of my friends. One of them even told me they brought an actual crazy bucket with them when they went to the Burning Man festival in the early 2000s, just in case they needed it.

- The show GIR calls simply *Angry Monkey*, is the same show he called *The Scary Monkey Show* the first time it appeared. It's the same show, and I don't know how I missed that. We'd been calling it *Angry Monkey* around the office, and I suspect the story where he called it *Scary Monkey* hadn't been finished yet, so we'd all forgotten. The best way to explain this inconsistency inside the show's continuity is that GIR gets a lot of things wrong, and since he didn't know what the show was really called, he simply described it. "The Scary Monkey Show" was just his term for it, just like he'd theoretically call *Star Trek: The Next Generation* "The Bald Captain Show." For all we know, the monkey show really isn't really called either title, but is named something like "Dr. Livingston's Economic Roundtable," which wouldn't explain the monkey, but might explain why GIR didn't bother to learn the real title. People who want more explanation than that should take a hard look at their priorities in life.

- *The Angry Monkey Show* actually had an in-universe backstory. Once upon a time, there had been a show featuring some scientists in an animal lab. One of the monkeys had broken out, killed its scientist masters, then spent the rest of the run of the show just staring into the camera in a murderous rage. The reason the network still aired it was because they'd contracted for a full 22-episode season, and, well, they'd already nailed down the schedule, so it was too late to back out now. In the *Truthshrieker* issue of the *Invader ZIM* comic (officially issue no. 0,) there's an ad for an *Angry Monkey* DVD season 18 set, implying that the show was such a runaway hit the network would never think of cancelling it.

- *Evangelion* was big among the crew at the time. There are quite a few homage shots in this one. See if you can spot them. Go ahead. I'll wait.

THINGS THE ZIM WIKI GETS WRONG

- "At one point, ZIM and GIR are on the couch sucking/licking on candysticks, which is a reference to *Fun Dip*."

No, ZIM wiki, it's a reference to Lik-a-Stix, DUH!!! Actually I can assure you, it's a not a "reference" to any specific candy any more than Krazy Taco is a "reference" to taco restaurants in general. Can't an alien lick some candy without people saying it's a pop-culture joke? JEEZE!

Hey, only one wrong thing? Well done, ZIM wiki! Perhaps I have misjudged you, after all.

THE DAILY JOB OF
WRITING STUFF

Or: Sending Ghosts to Arnold.

My workday on *ZIM* was a strange experience. Every day I would arrive at Nickelodeon about 9:00AM, park in the parking lot, and enter the building through the disused back entrance — located behind the second of two dumpsters — reserved for *Invader ZIM* employees. This corridor led under the building through a series of steam tunnels and past the holding cages where Nickelodeon kept those who had, in their determination, "wronged them, and brought shame upon the orange splotch." The use of this entrance was a mandate from Nickelodeon upper management so we wouldn't attract the attention of other people working at the studio who didn't know the network was producing a show as shameful as ours.

I would then enter my office, pour myself a cup of hot blood, and drive out the evil spirits that had gathered overnight while I was gone. They were often very, very unhappy to be disturbed, so I had a library of ancient magical tomes loaded with banishing rituals in arcane languages that could do the job one way or another. I remember one such spell sent the spirits over to the production of *Hey Arnold*, which for some reason then sent the spirits screaming in fear back into the dark void from whence they came. Thanks, Arnold!

Then I would start on my daily writing tasks. This was either revising a script based on notes, or writing a script based on the outline, or revising the outline based on notes, or writing the outline based on the one-page premise, or revising the one-page premise, or writing the one-page premise based on the approval of an idea pitch, or coming up with new idea pitches in the first place. The progression of the process here is easy to see. What it leaves out is the time I spent mentally either beating my head on the desk or gazing off at the horizon coming up with new ideas to pitch.

People often ask writers, "Where do you get your ideas from?" At least this is what I'm told. Nobody's ever asked me that, which leads me to believe either my ideas aren't interesting enough to care about their origins, or the origins are incredibly obvious, or people are just scared of asking me things in general. The latter is the reason most people tell me. I usually respond, "How dare you, you goddamned monster?!" and then wave a bat with nails stuck through it at them for their insolence. They never ask me anything again.

As it turns out, coming up with a lot ideas for potential episodes is a big part of what the job of a TV staff writer entails, and just given the nature of math, you come up with a lot more ideas than ever get used.

Sifting through my old notes -- by shaking my hard drive over a small pasta strainer -- I found a list of premises from what must have been the show's second season. You can see the beginnings of "The Voting of the Doomed," "Mortos der Soulstealer" and "ZIM Eats Waffles." I'll put it in the text later on.

```
INVADER ZIM
Incredible Mass of Premises
By Eric "L. Ron" Trueheart
03/12/2001


NOTE: Most of these are seeds of ideas that can be
expanded if they don't get violently shot down at
this stage.
```

SKOOL ELECTION

The Skool President has always received his orders
from an implant in his brain which links directly
to the Principal's office. (Nobody has ever seen the
principal, they just get mysterious orders from
black boxes on their desks, or, in the case of the
Skool president, from the brain implant. But this is
all background...)

When the current Skool President has her brain
implant fail, reducing her to a babbling mess, it's
time for a new election. Miss Bitters calls for can-
didates, and of course ZIM volunteers, hoping to get
inside the principal's office, the center of Supreme
Skool Power. There, he plans on introducing a brain
implant of his own into the Principal's brain, and...
you get the idea.

Dib decided to run against ZIM, but Miss Bitters
decides he's too annoying, so she appoints Willy, who
is incapable of putting together coherent sentences.
Seeing this is no competition, Dib decides he'll run
as a thrid-party candidate. The race begins. ZIM
promises to replace the kids brains with lumps of
iron, Willy jabbers incoherently, Dib has to debate
from behind a cardboard box because the Skool won't
recognize him as a legitimate candidate.

Along the way, Dib discovers that ZIM has rigged
the election so he'll win. (We'll have some really
cool technical explanation here, really.) Dib tries
to stop it, but fails. But in the end, it turns out
Willy gets elected, because the Principal has fixed
the whole thing. With his new implant, Willy is
actually really coherent, and spouts a lot of pro-
Skool rhetoric.

Both ZIM and Dib are pissed. (In a really funny way,
believe me.)

BATTLE OF THE LAWN

ZIM walks out his front door one day to find his
neighbor has placed a Lawn Hippo on his front lawn.
ZIM is outraged. It seems the Hippo is the spitting

image of a horrible war criminal from IRKEN history. (It would be the equivalent of putting a light-up Hitler on your front lawn.) Thinking this is a direct insult to him, ZIM destroys the hideous lawn ornament. The neighbor responds by building a new one, but fortified. ZIM destroys that one, too. When the neighbor realizes it's ZIM, it turns into a full-scale war of attrition - it seems the neighbor is a former member of the Navy Eels or Black Pants Berets or some similar military organization. It eventually ends with their homes reduced two smoking holes in the ground, and GIR building a scarecrow out of toilet paper rolls so there'll be at least SOMETHING on the front lawn.

TWO BAGS FOR BUCKY - A.K.A. GIR'S BIG DAY

ZIM sends GIR on a menial errand - go pick up some human so-called "Head Cheese" at the store. Along the way, he runs into a large mentally-challenged man-child named Bucky. (Like Lenny from "Of Mice and Men.") Lenny has two bags of "treasure" which he wants to hide. Together they learn the ways of love as they frolic around the city, having fun, and getting in trouble. At the end of the day, Bucky must go back to the mental hospital. It seems he escaped, but he's learned something from his little friend GIR.

When GIR gets home, he has no head cheese, but he has one of the bags Bucky took from the hospital, a bag full of medical waste. ZIM is furious. GIR, of course, doesn't care.

MORTOS - DER SOUL STEALER.

While doing research on "grave gas" in a cemetery one night, ZIM stumbles across a strange, bat-like man doing dances around the graves. He claims he is "Mortos the Soul Stealer," and that he can steal the soul of anything or any one. (He demonstrates by stealing the soul of a crispy chicken sandwich.) Dib asks Mortos if he could steal the soul of an alien. Of course Mortos can, but there will be "a price." The price, it turns out, is Dib having to follow Mortos around all day, buy him burritos, listen to his poetry, etc. When Dib threatens to leave, Mortos gets all spooky on him, telling him not to cross a soul-stealer, and that soon he will have enough "power" to steal the alien's soul, just be patient.

As the hour of midnight approaches, and Mortos enacts a ceremony on ZIM's from lawn that turns out to do nothing at all. It turns out that Mortos is a complete fraud. He's just a failed musician hoping to get a new act going. He never thought Dib would go through with all of this. His big bat-ears aren't even real. Dib gets angry pummels Mortos on ZIM's front lawn, much to ZIM's complete confusion.

ZIM EATS WAFFLES

Dib finally plants a hidden camera in Dib's house. He summons Agent Darkbootie on-line and asks him to watch at the amazing behavior of The Alien. We watch from a single security camera as ZIM eats IRKEN waffles for nine whole minutes. Meanwhile, GIR walks around in the background, doing little chores, getting the syrup, setting the base on fire, etc. In short, nothing interesting at all.

Darkbootie tells Dib to not call him again.

THE WRATH OF BOB

ZIM receives a distress signal from a freighter carrying tons of Mikesplosive. Thinking he could use this, he heads out in the Voot Cruiser to intercept. But when he gets on board, he discovers the ship is abandoned, and the cargo bays are not filled with horrible explosives, but with hundreds of Pooders, stupid sheep-like alien livestock. Suddenly a second ship de-cloaks and open fires. It's all been a trap.

His assailant reveals himself to be [either service drone bob or some random guy ZIM cut off in line years ago. "I will remember you..." he said]. Bob is going to make ZIM suffer at his hands by blasting the ship to smithereens. ZIM must fight back with the only weapon at his disposal - the Pooders.

This episode is an excuse for a big space battle in which ZIM launches stupid-looking sheep-like creatures at the enemy. Obviously.

DETENTION (A.K.A. BIG PHANTOM ZONE OF NOTHINGNESS)

ZIM and Dib get thrown into detention together. Neither one can stand being forced to sit next to each other in a big empty room with only a bloated detention monitor to watch them. ZIM tries to escape by opening up a dimensional gateway, but Dib chases after him and screws up the settings. They both end up in a big, white empty void with no laws of physics. Now they really hate each other because there's really nothing to do.

(Yes, this one is a little thin, but it's an attempt to do something cool that will go easy on the board artists and background guys. The alternate concept is that in this void there's some alien guy calling himself a "guardian," who makes them do humiliating things to escape, but he's actually just making it up.)

PANTS!

Hey, remember that alien pants episode? How about we revive it, except this time when the pants are worn by the host subject, they become all veiny and disgusting? What ya think, huh?

DIB'S SPACE SHIP ADVENTURE

Dib has just gotten his new space ship, as recovered from the other IRKEN invader. Unfortunately, it has a personality, and when he attempts to make it work, the space ship has ideas of it's own.

(If you like this concept, I can actually think about taking it somewhere.)

Obviously not every premise is gold here, and part of the process is starting with a core idea and then building a story around it. That's the process for me, anyway. There are some people out there that start with the human conflict and then work from there, like "two siblings vie for the approval of their dad," or "an evangelist and an atheist are trapped on an elevator," but not me. This is why I'll never write for that show about people of different religions trapped in an elevator every week. It's held my career back.

Listed among these premises is "Pants!," which I'll discuss in the next chapter.

Another one I should mention is "Two Bags for Bucky," which I pitched mostly because the title made me chuckle. In the description, I'm clearly struggling to come up with a way of describing this tale without playing Bucky's mental handicap for laughs. Thinking about it now, the whole endeavor was probably on some level a "dick move." Sure, *Of Mice and Men* had been a staple for parody since shortly after it was written — Looney Toons did it more than once — and back then the phrase "idiot man-child" was used in the name of comedy more often than anyone should be proud of. But can you parody Of *Mice and Men* without ending up taking cheap shots at people with mental disabilities? Maybe the more pressing question is if you're going to parody *Of Mice and Men*, shouldn't GIR be the Lennie character?

"Two Bags for Bucky" was an early stab at a story I pitched several times called "GIR's Big Day." In all versions of this tale, GIR would set out on some mission by ZIM at the top of the episode, and get nothing but distracted throughout the second act, only to circuitously end up back with his master, his mission complete by pure happenstance. I banged my head against this premise again and again throughout my time on the show, never quite cracking it, but definitely hurting my head in the process.

Years later I'd write a "GIR's Big Day" comic for Oni Press. In fact, at the time of the writing of this book, I've just finished the script for the Onifolks., and *ZIM* character designer Aaron Alexovich has started on the art. Honestly, it turned out better than anything I would have done back then. You should track it down and read it, then treasure it for the rest of your life, then hand it down to your children when you finally pass on. It's only right.

STORIES WHAT NEVER WAS: PANTS!

a.k.a. When Pants Ruled

I have a bad habit of not letting things go.

Like the time I held onto that sandwich even after it was snatched up by a giant Arctic icehawk, and I was carried to its nest in Greenland.

Sometime in the middle of *ZIM's* run, I got it in my head that I wanted to do some kind of *Invasion of the Bodysnatchers* episode. This was in no way because many members of the staff liked to suddenly stop and point at each other with their eyes rolled back into their skulls and their mouths wide open, emitting a horrible screeching sound like Donald Sutherland at the end of the 1978 movie, *Invasion of the Bodysnatchers*. No way at all.

No, I was more bothered by a recent run of fashion ads that featured people deliriously excited over some of the most boring pants in the world. For those who might only vaguely remember this time, it was a period in history when khaki trousers seemed to have gripped the public's imagination. Things called "Dockers" graced billboards and TV ads, touted as thought they were something we were meant to care about.

We all know advertising at a certain point is less about creating demand for something and more about reassuring an otherwise numb and dazed public that yes, this product is real, and you can buy it without being weird.

Everyone is doing it. Just go into a store and exchange money for it. No one will mock you. You won't be tackled by security. Really, it will be that easy. The person at the counter will intuitively understand the transaction you're there for. Then you can take the product home and wear it in public without fear of strangers singling you out for scorn in the streets, pointing with twisted looks of glee on their faces while they scream "Look at the trouser-wearing freakboy! Look at 'em! Huuuuuh?"

Buy Dockers.

Anyway, an idea drifted slowly into my head for a scenario something like *Invasion of the Bodysnatchers*, but the aliens taking over human beings were shaped like pants. They were designed to be worn by their victims, and once they had their alien form wrapped around that poor hapless person's legs, they would control their mind, slowly convincing them that these alien pants were the height of fashion, and they should track down everyone NOT wearing them and peer pressure them into putting on a pair, thus forwarding their conquest of the host world.

The main character in a story like this would naturally be Dib, and ZIM would have to be somehow in league with these alien pants, siding with them to take over the earth, but for his own gain. Somehow Dib would eventually show these alien pants that ZIM was using them, they'd turn on him, and we'd have a bombastic climax worthy of the sort of things we did on this ridiculous show.

Totally pleased with my vision, I went off to pitch it to Jhonen in his office.

He was busy altering the DNA of fly larvae to drink blood and survive in the vacuum of space, but he listened with a certain degree of interest. Then he asked me, "And what do the pants look like?"

Stuck on the horror of the kakhi slacksian menace currently ravaging America, I responded, "I dunno, like boring old Docker type things."

Immediately, his attention drifted away, ostensibly to stop one of the mutant slugs from murdering an intern. But I knew what's had happened. The boring pants had lost him. The story just wasn't... I dunno... visually weird enough.

So I filed the story back into the rusty filing cabinet of my mind and went back to my office to wrap myself in a cocoon of failure and shame, or to just play *Diablo* until my next assignment or something.

A few weeks later, it occurred to me how to make this idea more appealing, and I subtly began slipping it into the pitches I was submitting. Between the ideas about ZIM opening a diner selling the best durn pies in the county and Dib captaining an 18th century merchant sailing vessel into the heart of pirate waters to rescue the princess of Portugal, I slipped in "Oh hey, remember that pants story...?"

This time when Jhonen asked me about it, I was ready.

"What are the pants like," he asked, clearly expecting me to fall for the same trick twice.

"Like, veiny, slimy, H.R. Geiger type pants," I responded, and in that moment, I knew I had won!

Fortunately, Mary Harrington liked it, too, and armed with an "approved to outline" notice, I set about crafting this story's outline.

Unfortunately, a deep dark evil way more insidious than alien pants stopped this story in its tracks: *Jimmy Neutron: Boy Genius!*

One day we got word back from the executives that the episode would have to be cancelled.

"WHY?" we shouted in unison.

"*Jimmy Neutron* is doing a Christmas special called 'When Pants Attack.'"

"SO?" we shouted again.

"So, it's about some robotic pants that get hit with a virus and try to take over the city."

We paused briefly, assessing the situation, then answered:

"SO??"

"So, it's too close to your pants episode. This network can't have *two* cartoons about pants, by gum!"

There was a long pause, and then...

"WHY?!?" we screamed again in unison.

We tried reasoning with them. Look, we proposed, this pants episode won't be even finished for at least nine months after the *Jimmy Neutron* special aired. Surely that's enough time for America to cleanse its memory of any pants-related hijinks!

They still said no.

We tried countering again. The two shows don't even have the same audience, we pointed out, but the executive captains would not be swayed.

Jhonen also presented one of the most cogent arguments of all, "It's *Jimmy Neutron!* It's not like it's anything anyone cares about!" Curiously, this changed no one's mind.

Full disclosure: I once worked for the people who made *Jimmy Neutron* on a show that never saw the light of day called *Dirk Derby: Wonder Jockey.* They're good people, and funny, and clearly not deliberately out to stop anyone's pants ambitions. Also, *Dirk Derby* was a genuinely hilarious show that unfortunately couldn't find a home on TV, probably because it was too "out there" for kids TV. So for the record, them *Neutron* folks are all right!

That was the end of the Pants episode, one of my favorite ideas killed in its tracks by a trouser-themed Christmas special. It would have ended there, but fate intervened.

Years later, when the good people at Oni Press decided to launch a series of *Invader ZIM* comic books, I once again pitched the "Pants!" episode. Now it had the added bonus of being a "lost episode" of the series. This time good sense was on my side, and our editor Robin Herrera said yes almost immediately.

You'll find the script for this little comic epic later in this volume. Suffice to say, I was as surprised as I was happy to tie up that weird little loose end almost twenty years later.

I even got to slip in Donald Sutherland making that face.

LUNCH, DAMMIT!

A Fool's Errand and an Irish Burrito.

Yes, I'm actually going to devote valuable print space to talking about going to lunch, mostly because there's a legend about a single restaurant being the birthplace of three different stories.

Lunch was a ritual for us on the show.

While this wasn't the first job I'd ever had where I was able to set my own schedule like a goddamn grown-up, it was certainly the one where I was almost completely released on my own recognizance most of the time. Apart from meeting all of my deadlines and making the meetings, nobody really cared what I did. I could have ducked out for hours at a time to dig a secret underground tunnel that led across Burbank to Warner Brothers studios, where I would soon build my own Bat Cave, and surprise them all when I emerged as the crime fighter Burbank so desperately needed and--- I've drifted away again. Sorry.

Lunch was, in the parlance of today's youth, "a thing." It was something we wouldn't miss for the world, if the world was being offered, which it wasn't, so we never really had to make that hard choice.

The plan was always simple: We could get the hell out of the orange-walled building, go to some nearby restaurant, hit the comic book store or some similarly juvenile establishment on the way back, and if we were gone for two hours, nobody would notice. We'd just stay late to get done whatever we needed to get done. We were grown-ass adults, after all, despite spending half of our lunch time at stores designed to sell things to children. None of us had children or pets to get back to, and if we did we'd have trained them to use a can opener and feed themselves.

So every day around 12:30, a bunch of us would pile into a car and drive out of the building, past the stalwart presence of Don the security guard (the inspiration for "Old Kid" in "The Nightmare Begins") and out into the wild expanse of Burbank.

Burbank is, in a word, boring. In two words, it's not-great. In three words, it's barely-worth-discussing. In eight, it's why-are-we-spending-eight-words-on-Burbank? And, as such, the selection of restaurants wasn't particularly stellar. True, it wasn't cursed with an Applebee's or a T.G.I. Friday's, which was a blessing in itself, but... Look, I'm getting bored trying to come up with things to say about Burbank's restaurants.

But Burbank had something other municipalities didn't: a Mexican restaurant with an Irish name.

It was called Barragan's, and it sold the usual cluster of burritos, tacos, quesadillas, and other combinations of beans and tortillas. There was also the usual unending buckets of nacho chips shoveled onto the table before every meal just to make sure you were getting enough salt. Just an Irish name wouldn't be enough to deserve mention, but this restaurant is where I came up with the idea for three stories during the same lunch. "GIR Goes Crazy and Stuff," "Walk for Your Lives," and... "ZIM Eats Waffles." Though that last one had been gestating in my head for a long time

Maybe this isn't that interesting after all.

Look, we came up with a lot of ideas at lunch, okay? That was the whole point here.

Did I mention we also came up with "Deelishus Weenie" in the car one time?

Never mind.

Let's move on.

GIR GOES CRAZY
AND STUFF

Friends Become Enemies, Officers Become Squids,
Networks Become Kids with Brain Probes.

Two things had tugged at the back of my brain for a long time. One was a way to make an episode that was more GIR-centric. GIR had already proved to be tremendously popular, and that was no surprise. In a show where everything is just a little bit gross, mean, dirty, or unpleasant, GIR was the insane ray of unconditional sunshine in a world darkened by radioactive clouds of filth. (That's a metaphor, obviously. It is in no way canon that the clouds seen in the *Invader ZIM* universe were radioactive.)

But GIR was everything a network loves in a cartoon characters: cute, energetic, consistently funny, easily imitatable by children, and ripe for plush toys and T-shirts. Of course, back then nobody knew just how much GIR would come to anchor the merchandise in every Hot Topic in America. That little green and/or gray robot dog probably financed the paycheck of more depressed teenage girls than... actually, this joke can only go somewhere terrible after that set-up. Let's move on, shall we?

GIR was that rare breed of character that successfully filled the role of "comic relief" in a show that was already a comedy in the first place.

The fact that flew straight over a lot of people's heads is that GIR could also do horrible things. He was so crazy, and on some level amoral, his random antics in service of laughs sometimes went kind of dark. He could throw horrible screaming fits if he didn't get his way. In "Attack of the Idiot Dog Brain," his city-wide rampage causes untold damage. In the Halloween special, it's implied he may have actually eaten children. GIR could be on the serving end of some pretty nasty business.

I had already tried pitching an episode called simply "GIR's Big Day" with not much success. For whatever reason, telling a full 11-minute story around random craziness, calls for tacos, adorable non sequiturs and big-eyed "ooh"-ing was more difficult than it seemed. Yes, GIR is fun when he pokes in and causes some adorable trouble, but do you really want to spend a whole day with him running around like an idiot?

Still, my quest for the GIR-centric story continued, and on one of our many lunch trips out into the wilds of Burbank, I stumbled upon an idea that I thought might do it. What would GIR look like, I wondered, if he actually worked like he was supposed to? If he was the competent, able and sophisticated robot servant he was meant to be, would he realize almost immediately that ZIM is an idiot, and idiocy is detrimental to the success of the mission?

The answer in my mind was "YES!" and fortunately, the higher-ups agreed. I picked the title "Gir Goes Crazy and Stuff" as an obvious little gag based on the fact that GIR "going crazy and stuff" is pretty much all he does anyway, so building a story around it being something special would be like naming an episode "ZIM Shouts a Lot."

Ironically, in this story, it's actually GIR going sane that causes all the problems.

It all seems kind of obvious. However, in writing this account years later, I'm starting to wonder about just what motivated me to put this story together in the first place? Are there deeper strata to be mined here, O reader?

It's obviously what's driving a story like "Voting of the Doomed." The political commentary is worn right there on the sleeve of its filthy school uniform. That one is so obviously about politics like NASCAR is so obviously all about drunk people watching car crashes. There's no mystery there, pal.

But what made me think "GIR Goes Crazy and Stuff" was an idea potentially worthy enough to be turned into eleven minutes of animated television? What drove me through the writing of it beyond just wanting a paycheck so I wouldn't end up homeless? Now I address the question that was not burning at all in anyone's mind -- including my own -- until I got stuck on it thinking about this last night in a sandwich shop:

GIR GOES CRAZY AND STUFF: JUST WHAT WAS I THINKING?

Or in a big wide world of possibilities, why did I decide that this is what I would put my energies into instead of building an off-the-grid secret headquarters where I could build my army of giant robots?

PROPOSAL: Character Drama. A story is about conflict, and one of the most potent sources of conflict in a story is finding the conflict between two characters who would be otherwise friends if not for the fundamental problem the episode churns up. This is what they say, right? This is what the professors tell you in TV writing 101. This is what script gurus in expensive shirts will tell to you in a conference room at a Holiday Inn after you've spent several hundred dollars for the "Weekend Screenwriting Bootcamp Seminar and Self-Actualization Life Plan." "Find ways to put your lead characters in conflict!" they say. Put Walter White in conflict with Jessie Pinkman. Make Riker prosecuting attorney at Data's trial to be human. This is juicy* drama, people!

*And I hate applying the word "juicy" to anything that doesn't physically produce juice. Drama is not oranges or uncooked red meat. I stand by this opinion.

But really, is this it? Was I really out to create something as *dramatic* as possible? Obviously there's a certain wisdom here. GIR not going crazy but sitting around watching TV would make as tepid an episode as ZIM sitting around eating waffles and-- Let's scrap that analogy and maybe come back to it later, shall we?

I can't help but feel that's not really the whole story. That feels like a tool in the tool box, but not the grand vision of a gold-inlaid toolbox with built in smart-phone connectivity that I had in my head. So maybe there's something else here.

PROPOSAL: World-Building!

Perhaps deep down my thought was, "Let's look deeper into the *Invader ZIM* universe! A place where massive world-conquering Irken Aramadas blast their way unopposed through the galaxy, while the conquered worlds are turned into things stupid as shipping centers and food courts." The nuts and bolts of this kind of reality must be pretty fascinating. How does an empire cut a path of fire and destruction across the galaxy when it's run by a couple of flat-out idiots?

From this perspective, was I hoping to dig a little deeper into the reality of what a fully-functioning SIR unit would act like? One of the tricks of writing television comedy is to call into question certain flatly-ridiculous elements of the conceits of the show while at the same time respecting that other flatly-ridiculous elements are laws of iron-clad reality brought down from a mountain on slabs of stone. We've never seen a single bathroom in the *Star Trek* universe, but you rightfully don't build an episode around the Enterprise needing to stop at a planet so Riker can relieve himself after three pitchers of synthale. But an episode where Picard's artificial heart needs servicing seems like a nice way of peeling back the perfect veneer of Star Fleet technology. Right? (And man, Riker is turning up a lot in this section. I should write Jonathan Frakes a thank you note.)

So maybe I asked myself, just how would an actual SIR unit respond to an invader as clearly incompetent as ZIM? The Irken empire is built on brutally efficient weapons of conquest, and yet they're always wielded by idiots.

You wonder how the Tallest have conquered anything, but they have, so the people working behind the scenes must be pretty amazing, and engineering technology that's on some level pretty damn bad-ass. Maybe I wanted to take a look at the reality of the deadly competence behind the layer of incompetent bumbling we always see. Hey, even Table-Headed-Service-Drone-Bob manages to out-bet the Tallest, and he's a table-headed service drone.

Was this it? Maybe. Again, it feels like another tool in the box, another arrow in the quiver, another key on the chain, another coin in the fountain, another spot on the Dalmatian, another mint chip in the froyo, another shmippie in the zibblesquanz. Know what I mean?

PROPOSAL: America Loves GIR!

As I mentioned earlier, I'd ben trying to write a more GIR-centric story for a long time. Why? BECAUSE AMERICA LOVED GIR! And who wouldn't love that little robot scamp, with his random outbursts of joy and his dangerous leaps into mania? Deep down, we're all just pining for *The GIR Show*, so I figured, let's just give everyone what they want? Surely if you love something, you'd love more of it! So yeah, maybe I just wanted to maker America happy. I mean, if I could have written an episode featuring GIR doing nothing but making waffles, I would have-- Let's leave that for later.

PROPOSAL: Comedy! And just how the hell does that work, anyway?

Invader ZIM was a comedy. To most people, anyway. To others it was a wet slab of rotten ham thrown in the face of all things wholesome and decent. Still to others, it was a coded message sent from a race of higher-dimensional beings from another universe who want us to build a nest in the neighbor's recycling bins. This last group is definitely in the minority. In fact, that group may consist of only one member, and that person has fortunately found psychiatric help in a professionally-monitored medical facility. (Good luck, Maureen! Glad you got the treatment you so badly needed.)

Regardless, there's no question that I thought "GIR Goes Crazy and Stuff" would be a scenario fertile for harvesting laughs. Good old lovable GIR turning violent sounds like a giggle factory, doesn't it? What if he can actually carry out orders to a dangerous degree? What if the cute little guy starts shouting orders like a Cylon centurian? That's funny, right? It is... at first.

The odd thing about comedy, though, is that it relies a lot on the unexpected Comedy is great when it short-circuits our expectations, and we laugh at the surprise. Charlie Chaplin was once asked how he would do the old "man slips on a banana peel gag." He said he'd have the guy walk up, notice the banana peel, carefully move it out of the way, then walk on straight into an open manhole. Once we see the banana peel, we're pretty sure how it's going to end, and it's subverting that expectation that actually gives us the stinkin' laugh.

That's why I'm a big fan of absurdity. Absurdity jumps over our expectations completely and lands square in the ridiculous. The laugh comes from the sheer audacity of the reality bending used to make the joke. The trouble with "GIR Goes Crazy" is that our expectations are set up pretty early, and honestly, the demands of the plot don't lead us anywhere we couldn't have guessed if we didn't think of it. And where it leads is pretty horrific. The episode climaxes with GIR sticking brain probes into a score of library patrons, and then chasing down ZIM in a basement hell-bent on offing him for good. In the delicate irony of the horror in the ZIM universe, maybe this isn't too horrific. Everything in this world is on some level horrible, so if it's horrible and elicits a chuckle, then one could argue it's working. Right? Maybe?

I think, no. Or rather, it's not as funny as it could be.

To me, the funniest thing in this episode is Officer Squidman. He's a random addition to the story that takes on a life of its own, for no other reason than he's funny. His arc is about seizing on a plot detail I found hilarious -- the squid -- and running with it longer than anyone with any sense would have. This is exactly the sort of humor that I enjoy, and looking back on it, he turns up just about the point where I might find myself worried that the story is turning too predictable.

Squidman is a dramatic problem -- oh no, GIR's brought a cop into the secret base -- that ZIM has to solve using something effective but characteristically wrong-headed. "Now I have to wipe his brain," he says, with no real logic backing up *why* he ends up trading it with a squid's. Thus we are off with squid jokes for no reason. Honestly, this could have easily been a throwaway in the story. ZIM declares he's erasing the cop's memory, and that's the last we see of him, but no, we have bigger fish to fry with old Squidman.

The joke about his ink builds in a way that's not only suggestively gross, but keeps the story going. He then follows ZIM to the library, when by all logic ZIM should have left him in the lab, and his story arc culminates with him triumphantly using his "ink" to save the day, thus Squidman gets his mojo back and the audience cheers his triumph, while simultaneously worrying just where that ink came from.

The end with Squidman returning to the ocean -- along with his speech including a galactic space battle happening off-screen, which I have Jhonen to thank for -- firmly puts us in the realm of the ridiculous, when we maybe drifted away from it in the main story.

And thus, after this long analytical trip I'm not sure anyone needed to take -- but thank you anyway for taking it with me -- I can firmly state that Officer Squidman is the unsung spiritual heart of "GIR Goes Crazy and Stuff." He is the *raison d'etre* for this outing, and without him, we are poorer as a nation and as a species. Thank you, Squidman, for making this story all worth while.

And now I better wrap this up before I decide this is all bullshit.

Anyway, here's the script:

SCRIPT: GIR GOES CRAZY AND STUFF

illustration: Aaron Alexovich

Eric Trueheart

EXT. FIELD - NIGHT.

A field of cows placidly doing cow things. A SHADOW passes
over accompanied by a THROBBING HUM. A TRACTOR BEAM hits one
cow. She tries to maintain her dignity as she's pulled up.
A hatch opens in the bottom of the cruiser. An EERIE LIGHT
streams out and a robotic figure emerges on a tether. **GIR**   *
pops a hat on the cow and rubs his butt on its face.   *

                         GIR
               Hi cow!

                         ZIM   *
               GIR! Get in here!

                         GIR
               Bye cow!

He's yanked back inside.

INT. VOOT CRUISER - NIGHT.

ZIM stares angrily at GIR. Behind them is a large bubbling
tank sporting a long tube with a rubber nozzle.

                         ZIM (REPROACHFUL)
               No playing with the dirty cow monsters,   *
               GIR. This is serious work we do.

                         GIR
               Ooooh!

                         ZIM
               We'll switch. You man the tractor beam,
               I'll pump the cows full of human **waste**.   *

A deadly serious GIR moves his face eerily close to ZIM's.   *

                         GIR (ALMOST WHISPERING)
               Cows are my friends.

                         ZIM (AFTER A BEAT)
               The controls, GIR.

GIR is at the controls. WHEEEE!

2.

EXT. FIELD - NIGHT.

DOWNSHOT: ZIM descends from the hatch. The sewage tank is on
his back, nozzle ready.

                    ZIM (WICKEDLY)
          Once I've tainted the human's meat supply
          with filth, they will be ripe for
          conquest. Soon, the name of INVADER ZIM
          will be synonymous with DOOKY!! GIR,
          bring one of the cow beasts to me!

INT. VOOT CRUISER - NIGHT.

                    GIR
               (his eyes go to the red of his   *
                 obedient mode)   *
          Yes sir!   *
               (back to his goofy blue)   *
          I like dooky!

                    ZIM (O.S.)
          Sometimes I'm afraid to find out what's
          going on in that insane head of yours...

We push in on GIR's insane head to see... GIR'S POV: A
digital read-out, blue like his eyes, everything labeled with
digital type and icons. But the labels are bizarre and
constantly shifting. "Jelly", "Leprechaun." "Nose," etc.   *
The little cows on the screen look like dancing HOT DOGS.

                    HOT DOGS
          Dance with us GIR! Dance with usssss!   *

EXT. VOOT CRUISER

A tractor beam grabs a cow, swings it and tosses it.   *

                    ZIM
          GIR! What are you doing?

                    GIR (O.S.)
          WEENIES! WEENIES! DANCING WEENIES!   *

GIR zaps another cow and whips it across the landscape. It
smashes into a SILO. The lights in the farmhouse go on.

                    ZIM
          Stop! You'll blow our ingenious cover!   *

A beam grabs a third cow and yanks it straight up into ZIM.
It SMASHES him against the underside of the cruiser.

INT. VOOT CRUISER - NIGHT, LATER.

ZIM, now coated in filth, pilots the ship. He's obviously
giving a happy GIR the silent treatment. GIR whispers some
little song to himself and dances in his seat.

INT. HOLOGRAPHIC THINGS ROOM.

A large spherical room with projector lenses all over it and   *
a panel sprouting from the floor. A cleaned up ZIM holds a   *
BEHAVIORAL MODULATOR. **He turns the knob about halfway up.**   *

                    ZIM
          It's time we did something about your
          behavioral glitches, GIR.

                    GIR (SINGING)
          Boop Boop Bee Boooop... WAFFLES!!

                    ZIM (TRYING TO IGNORE)
          I'm going to attempt to lock you into
          duty mode with this behavioral modulator.

He presses a button. A street appears, and a HOLOGRAPHIC DIB
materializes, wielding a club and looking mean.

                    DIB (STUNTED)
          I will make you suffer large, alien!

                    ZIM
          GIR! Attack! Destroy the HUMAN!

                    GIR (RED EYED)
          YES SIR!

GIR goes red eyed while ZIM fiddles with his remote. GIR'S   *
POV: A TARGET over DIB's face. "TARGET: BIG HEAD BOY: *
DESTROY". GIR runs at DIB but the display changes to   *
"TARGET: POOP CAN." The target moves to a Poop Cola can.
GIR runs and snatches up the can, waving it around and
GIGGLING insanely. He smacks it against his face.   *
Irritated, ZIM presses buttons and the background **goes** white.   *

                    ZIM
          No more distractions, GIR! ATTACK the   *
          HUMAN!! **This time on a dangerously high**   *
          setting...   *

He turns the knob on the modulator a little higher.   *

                    GIR (RED EYED)
          YES SIR!

                                        (CONTINUED)

CONTINUED:

He runs at the holographic Dib. ZIM clicks the remote too
late. GIR's eyes go blue and he rolls on the white floor.   *
He makes SIREN SOUNDS while he rolls. **ZIM is getting really**   *
frustrated. He cranks the modulator to its maximum setting.   *

              ZIM   *
        ATTACK!

              GIR **(NOT REALLY OBEYING)**   *
     YES SIR! **DOODEEDOODEEDOO!!!**   *

              ZIM   *
        ATTACK!   *

This time he hits the button just as GIR's eyes go red. For   *
a brief second, they are a dark and sinister red color, but   *
then they fade back down to the lighter red. GIR'S POV: His   *
red-display analyzes Dib: "TARGET: HOLOGRAM. NO THREAT.
ABNORMALLY LARGE HEAD" **He talks in a serious tone.**   *

              GIR **(SERIOUS)**   *
        Sir, TARGET is a hologram and therefore
        not a threat to our mission.   *

              ZIM
        And what IS our mission, GIR?   *

              GIR **(DEADPAN)**   *
        Blend in with indigenous life. Analyze
        their weaknesses. Prepare the planet for
        the coming badness. Yay.

              ZIM (ELATED)
        Yes... Yes! YES!!! With you fully
        functional and by my side, we shall rule   *
        this world sooner than without you... by
        my side... not being fully...
             (getting tired of speech)
        Ah, let's get out of here.

PUSH IN on GIR'S EYES. One of them is TWITCHING and   *
fluttering into the darker red.   *

INT. ZIM'S LIVING ROOM - MORNING.

ZIM enters with GIR by his side.   *

              ZIM
        You are now the evil henchman I so
        rightly deserved all along, GIR. An
        assistant worthy of me. I AM ZIM!!   *
            (a SIREN sounds in the   *
            distance)   *
              (MORE)

(CONTINUED)

Eric Trueheart

CONTINUED:

                    ZIM (CONT'D)
          Now, with your amazing new programming,   *
          investigate that sound!   *

                    GIR   *
          Sir, it is merely a police siren-   *

                    ZIM   *
          Do as I say!   *

                    GIR **(SWITCHING TO DARKER RED)**   *
          Yes, sir! Opening door! Runnning!   *
          RUNNING!!

GIR runs out the door. Outside there's the sound of the
SIREN getting louder, then TIRES SQUEALING and a **police car**   *
CRASHES into the living room upside down. GIR **leaps through**   *
the windshield with a policeman (OFFICER SQUIDMAN) slung over   *
his back, bound with a seat belt.   *

                    ZIM
          GIR! What have you done!? **This isn't**   *
          information retrieval. Are you insane?   *

GIR throws the officer **on the floor**, and strikes POWER RANGER   *
style poses as he speaks. **Squidman starts to come to.**   *

                    GIR
          I have captured **the enemy** for meat   *
          testing. Praise me. PRAISE ME!!!   *

                    OFFICER SQUIDMAN (O.S.)
          AARGH!!!... all my bones... jammed up
          into my neck! **Huh? ALIENS!**   *

                    ZIM (DISGUSTED)
          Great. Now I have to wipe his brain to
          make him forget all he's seen.   *

GIR looks irritated by ZIM's comment as ZIM gags the cop.   *

INT. ZIM'S LAB

The policeman is strapped to a table. ZIM sticks probes in
his head.

                    ZIM (IRRITATED)
          This **memory transplant** will take hours!   *
          I'd planned to spend this afternoon   *
          experimenting on the happiness centers of
          that earth child's brain.

He points to a kid, NICK, in a tank with probes in his head.

                                        (CONTINUED)

6.

CONTINUED:

                    NICK (TEETH GRITTED)   *
        I'm so happy! All the time! It's great!   *

ZIM pulls off the cop's gag. He SCREAMS!

                    OFFICER SQUIDMAN
        Please! I have a house, and children,
        and pets, and a toilet!

                    ZIM   *
        Make silence now, human!   *

ZIM sticks probes into his mouth. **GIR goes to dark red eyes.**   *

                    GIR (SERIOUS)   *
        With all due respect, you must know the   *
        S.I.R unit code enables free will in the   *
        event that the mission is threatened.   *
        This police human was a threat.   *

                    ZIM
        You dare tell ME what I already know!?

                    GIR
        Did you know that?

                    ZIM (FRUSTRATED)
        Of COURSE I... YOUR LEGS ARE STUPID!!   *

ZIM looks down a row of tanks containing brains. The last
one contains a SQUID. He picks the squid tank. GIR's POV: *
on ZIM "ANALYZING: INTELLIGENCE." Results "QUESTIONABLE."   *

                    ZIM (CONT'D)
        Go upstairs and... **um**... monitor earth   *
        broadcasts until I think of something
        better for you to do. **That's a good GIR.**   *

GIR's POV: "ORDER: COUNTERPRODUCTIVE. ZIM = COMMANDER?" GIR
just stares at ZIM like HAL deciding whether to kill him.   *
His eye twitches, flickering from red to DARKER RED.   *

                    ZIM (CONT'D)
        GIR?

                    GIR (HESITANT, **LIGHT RED**)   *
        Right away, SIR.

ZIM hooks the squid to the brain transfer machine.

INT. ZIM'S LIVING ROOM - DAY.

GIR flicks a switch and a dozen TV monitors branch out from
the main TV. The monitors change from program to program.

                                        (CONTINUED)

Eric Trueheart

7.

CONTINUED:

                         GIR (ANGRILY)
              Observing. Observing. Observing.   *

                         TV VOICE **(OVERLAPPING)**   *
              Do you suffer from intestinal itching?

                         TV VOICE #2 **(OVERLAPPING)**   *
              THE **OINKIES** HAVE SCOOTER!!   *

                         TV VOICE #3 **(OVERLAPPING)**   *
              DOO DEE DOO DEE DOOOOO!

                         TV VOICE #4   *
              If people could eat sand we wouldn't have
              this problem!

                         GIR **(FED UP)**   *
              Television is stupid! The master is not   *
              utilizing me properly. I will show my   *
              "master" how information collecting is done.   *

He looks out the window at the surrounding town. In his POV:
Images of buildings appear, surrounded by target reticles,
but they are all quickly passed over. The final building we
see is a "Library". **His eyes are now permanently DARK RED.**   *

                         GIR **(SERIOUS) (CONT'D)**   *
              An information center. **Excellent.**   *

GIR marches off screen. There's a horrible sound of RENDING
METAL, then GIR walks back with a big DATA STORAGE CONTAINER
on his back. He marches through the front door and outside.

INT. PUBLIC LIBRARY - DAY.

Your ultra-modern public library. People look at DATA DISCS
on VIEWING STATIONS, but there are the usual LIBRARY DWEEBS.
A CUSTOMER is checking out some discs at the counter. A
RETINA SCANNER scans his eyeball. It BUZZES a reject.

                         SCANNER
              Retinal scan. REJECTED.

                         LIBRARIAN
              I'm sorry. You have two discs overdue.   *
              We'll have to confiscate your retinas.   *

Just then, the huge metal doors blow open, and GIR comes
floating in, the data cannister glowing ominously.

                         GIR
              I require access to all human knowledge.

                                        (CONTINUED)

134

8.

CONTINUED:

                    LIBRARIAN
          That would be under reference.   *

                    GIR
          Not acceptable, library drone!

Tentacles sprout from his data storage tank and attach to the   *
heads of library **patrons**.   *

INT. ZIM'S LAB.

ZIM wears his human disguise with a stethoscope. He turns   *
off the brain transfer machine. He pulls the probe out of
the policeman's mouth. The cop wakes up and SCREAMS.

                    OFFICER SQUIDMAN
          My tentacles! WHERE are my tentacles?!

                    ZIM
          Don't worry, officer, you are in a filthy   *
          earth brain hospital. Your feelings are   *
          normal. There's a squid brain in your head.   *

The cop's portable radio BUZZES.

                    POLICE DISPATCHER (O.S.)
          Calling unit 12, unit 12.

The Policeman YELPS and squinches up his face in response.   *

                    OFFICER SQUIDMAN
          SOMETHING'S WRONG. MY INK! Why can't I
          shoot ink anymore?! What kind of squid
          can't shoot ink!?? GAHH!! SQUID!!!!!

                    POLICE DISPATCHER (O.S.)
          Situation at the public library. Flying   *
          metal child draining the brains of
          citizens. Respond immediately.

                    ZIM
          GIR! I've gotta stop him before he ruins
          everything! That horrible robot!

ZIM runs out, the policeman squirms after him on the floor.

                    OFFICER SQUIDMAN
          Please! Just take me back to the sea!!

INT. LIBRARY - DAY.

ZIM enters wearing a policeman's cap, the cop is by his side.
When he sees the scene, the policeman YELLS and jumps onto
the glass door sticking there with his puckered up mouth.

                              (CONTINUED)

CONTINUED:

> ZIM
> Relax, humans, the police are -- ew.

REVEAL the library in shambles. People lying across tables like brain-dead zombies. Data discs scattered everywhere. GIR hovers in the middle of the chaos like a multi-armed god. Tentacles whip around the room, grabbing discs off the shelves and slotting them straight into the storage bin where they are scanned and discarded. He also has tentacles in viewing stations. Images flash by at rapid speed. GIR's eyes throb, emitting an electronic HUM. ZIM walks up to him.

> GIR (OMINOUSLY)   *
> The knowledge. It fills me. IT IS NEAT.

> ZIM
> GIR! You've drained enough humans today.   *

> GIR
> Data cannister is not yet full.

> ZIM
> I command you to get out of here before   *
> we're noticed... some more.

ZIM pulls out the behavioral remote, but before he can hit a   *
button, a tentacle snakes over and ZAPS his hand. ZIM drops   *
the remote. The tentacle picks it up and drops it into head.   *

> ZIM (CONT'D)
> HEY! QUIT IT!!   *

> GIR
> You are no commander, you are a threat to   *
> the mission. Your methods are stupid.
> Your progress has been stupid. Your
> intelligence is stupid. For the sake of
> the mission you must be terminated.   *

> ZIM (ANGRY)
> You DARE speak to your master in such--   *

He's cut off as two tentacles ZAP him. He jumps away. Tentacles sparking lightning swipe at him.

> ZIM (CONT'D)
> Squid Man! Assist me!

The policeman squnches up his body again.

> OFFICER SQUIDMAN
> Arg! INK... not working. All that comes   *
> out is... you don't wanna know what comes
> out!   *

> (CONTINUED)

10.

CONTINUED: (2)

GIR's eyes deliver a laser blast. ZIM jumps out of the way.
The lasers cut a hole in the floor. ZIM falls through it.

                         ZIM
             GIR!! LISTEN TO ME!! We HAVE to get out   *
             of here!! You're malfunctioning!!   *

                         GIR   *
             STUPIDITY IS THE ENEMY. ZIM IS ENEMY!!   *

GIR chases him down. The policeman follows,pleading.   *

                    OFFICER SQUIDMAN
             Wait! Don't leave me on land!

INT. LIBRARY CATACOMBS.

Dark and gloomy. ZIM runs through rows of data racks. He
climbs up a shelf and listens. GIR comes toward him.

                         GIR
             Target found. Eliminating moron.

ZIM flees further into the dark alley of data racks. GIR
pursues, glowing with some spooky power. ZIM turns down a
corridor. He runs past rows of viewing stations to find a
dead end wall of vending machines.

                         ZIM
             CURSE YOU SNACKS!!! CURSE YOUUUU!!!!

GIR appears at the end of the corridor, light streaming
behind him, in silhouette. He extends a tentacle into a
monitor. GIR's face appears on all of them.

                    GIR (REPEATED ON THE SCREENS)   *
             For the good of the mission.

                         ZIM
             GIR, you were my servant once, remember?

                         GIR   *
             Yes. I didn't like it.   *

A tentacle lunges at ZIM. He dodges, trips. The tentacles
reach in for the kill, when...

                    OFFICER SQUIDMAN (O.S.)
             HEY!! OVER HERE!!

GIR's face is sprayed by a jet of INK! He spins blindly.

                         GIR
             Vision impaired! CAN'T SEE!!

                                        (CONTINUED)

Eric Trueheart

11.

CONTINUED:

PAN OVER to find the policeman, looking triumphant.

                    OFFICER SQUIDMAN
          My ink! I DID IT!!

ZIM jumps on GIR's head. GIR flails around. ZIM opens GIR's
head up and pulls out the behavioral remote. He pushes a
button and GIR falls over, blue eyed face down on the floor.

                    GIR (HAPPILY)
          HI FLOOR!! Make me a sammich!!

                    ZIM
          That's better... I guess.   *

                    GIR (INSANELY)   *
          SAMMICH! HEE HEE!! SAMMICH!! HEEE!!!   *
                                                              *

EXT. OCEAN - SUNSET.

GIR, ZIM and Squidman **stand** on a beach **before** a **gorgeous**   *
sunset.

                    OFFICER SQUIDMAN
          I want to thank you. That was quite an
          adventure, the car wreck, the library
          fight, and then the galactic space battle
          that happened on the way to this beach.

                    ZIM
          Yes, very nice. Now into the ocean with
          you where you can tell no one of these
          things.

                    OFFICER SQUIDMAN
          I'm coming home!

The policeman walks off into the ocean triumphantly.

                    GIR (WAVING)
          G'bye! G'bye! G'bye! G'bye!

The cop turns and waves, then walks until his he's completely
under water. A few bubbles come up, then stop completely.

                    GIR (DREAMILY) (CONT'D)
          He **gettin'** eaten' by a shark.   *

STRAY OBSERVATIONS

- For some reason, iTunes calls this one "GIR's Gone Crazy and Stuff." I don't know why. And I will never know. I will go to my grave with this question unanswered, and my restless ghost will haunt the iTunes store for eternity.

- ZIM stealing cows was a reference to the rash of cattle mutilations that had been reported in the news. Back in those golden days when *The X-Files* was big and people still had to dig for conspiracy theories on the Internet rather than having them piped directly into their news feeds. It was still cool and spooky to look for evidence of aliens everywhere. These days, dead cows with mysterious gashes in them just seem quaint.

- The joke about Dib's big head was now firmly in place by this point. Enjoy it, people. Dib's head isn't getting any smaller.

- "Dance with us, GIR! Dance with us into oblivion!" was a line ad libbed in the booth. In context, it nearly implies that some part of GIR's subconscious is longing for suicide. I mean, if his brain is giving him hallucinations of dancing hotdogs beckoning him to oblivion, maybe he's not so happy after all.

- We couldn't get away with using the word "dooky" now. At least Nickelodeon says we can't use it in the comic books. Maybe the airwaves are still dooky-friendly.

- This episode marks the first appearance of Nick, the kid with a happiness probe stuck in his brain. "I'm so Happy! All the time! It's great!" Take a guess what this was a reference to. You get one. If you guessed our opinion that Nickelodeon was promoting an image of childhood that was pathologically happy all the time, you guessed right! Nickelodeon's brand constantly pushed this idea of kid-dom as non-stop fun. Even when getting a bucket of sticky green fluid dumped on their head, a Nick kid was grinning with glee, even though this would make most people red-eyed with rage. There was even an official Nickelodeon coffee table book filled with nothing but insulin-spikingly sweet pictures of kids being just plain *adorable!* After flipping through it, I immediately pronounced it "Photographic Heroin for Grandmas." I was that kind of person then.

- Ironic that a man named "Officer Squidman" would get a memory transplant from a squid's brain. It's almost like destiny knew of his tentacled fate, or the writer made a dumb joke on a revised draft when he realized he had to give the guy a name.

- A line from the script that never made it in: "The Oinkies have Scooter!" It's one of my favorite lines in the whole show. I want to use that for something big some day. Something big... and dangerous.

- I apologize to all library patrons for the use of the term "Library Dweeb" in the description. I don't know what I was thinking, and I am now ashamed. Anyone who hangs out in a library these days should be endowed with sainthood, not mocked. You are not dweebs, O denizens of this fortress of knowledge, you are like demigods in a bleak, soulless wasteland of illiteracy! Ironically, these days GIR's quest to find all human knowledge would be tackled more easily on Wikipedia. He could just download the entire thing and then go straight to killing ZIM. Good thing there was no Wikipedia when we wrote this, or the story would have been much shorter.

- The screenwriter critiques himself: I noticed my descriptions in script are actually kind of sloppy, and often compress more visual beats into a paragraph than they should. Maybe I was trying to make the page-length. Or maybe I was just not thinking as much as I thought I was. Either way, screenwriting children, do not do what I have done.

- Hard core *Doctor Who* fans may recognize "Vision impaired! Can't see!" as only half a notch a way from what every Dalek shouts when it gets its eyestalk blown off. This is no coincidence.

THINGS THE ZIM WIKI GETS WRONG

- "When Squidman joyously returns to the ocean accompanied by happy music, it probably references the 1970's *Godzilla* movies when Godzilla defeats a monster and goes back into the ocean."

Actually, it doesn't.

- The part where GIR refers to ZIM's method as "stupid" is a reference to the character Eros from the Ed Wood film *Plan 9 from Outer Space*, when he says to Jeff Trent: "Your stupid mind's stupid!"

No, I'm afraid not. But you got a lot of other things right, so good on ya, ZIM wiki! You're growing every day.

STORIES WHAT NEVER WAS: ZIM CHOABS FOO!

A Funny Idea Goes in Search of a Story, and ZIM Gets Cyber Bullied Before It's a Thing.

This time I had one idea. A single idea. And it wasn't even an idea, it was a funny phrase. The phrase was "ZIM Choabs Foo," and all I knew about it was that it wasn't a nice thing to say.

Here was the basic premise:

ZIM would arrive at school to discover words were being shined on the back of his head via some kind of laser beamed from somewhere he couldn't see. The words: ZIM CHOABS FOO.

He doesn't know what this means. Dib doesn't know what it means. Nobody at school knows what this means. Heck, nobody at all knows what this means.

However, because of this little act, ZIM is suddenly the focus of ridicule, derision and physical attacks from everyone at school, who now tease him mercilessly that he "Choabs Foo." No, they don't know what "choabing foo" could even entail, but that doesn't matter to anyone. ZIM sees his already tenuous status at school plummet as he's hit with an unending stream of foo-based abuse from his fellow students.

Why doesn't he blow up his tormentors? Well, something to do with not wanting to expose himself as an alien, which his death rays would most certainly do in whatever scenario I ultimately set up.

It was an obvious parable about bullying, shining a light on the fact that in the miserable crucible of pain we call "school," any difference -- any difference at all -- becomes a target for harassment and abuse. Kids will tease each other mercilessly over nearly anything. Just give them the reason and they'll go nuts. A strong idea, yes? Poignant! Topical! The sort of bare-knuckle sociological pugilism that wins the Humanitas Prize and the adulation of peers, superiors, and sycophants alike.

The problem is I didn't really have a story. Just the idea. I only sort of had an ending, with ZIM discovering the perpetrator was someone he'd been a jerk to arbitrarily many years ago and of course totally forgotten.

When I ran the idea by Jhonen, he was wrapping Rikki Simons in a layer of pizzas to make him look like an Egyptian mummy.

Jhonen suggested that the story climax with ZIM embarking on a galactic quest to track down the source of the offending letters. Tracking the beams as they bounced off several hyperspace satellites (or something), ZIM would eventually reach a small space bound station near the center of the galaxy, inside which was a small, snarky alien who had been beaming this insult at ZIM from this base.

ZIM would confront the little guy -- "Why are you tormenting me, alien thing person??" -- only for the little guy to say, "I dunno." Yes, it would turn out our man ZIM was just a random victim of pan-galactic arbitrary lolz. When asked what "Choabs Foo" even means, the little creature would be similarly unhelpful, "I dunno." Really, he just made it up because it sounded annoying.

That's as far as I got. Thinking about it now, I'd have it then end with the little creature agreeing to "cut it out," and turning off the beams, only for

ZIM to discover the words were still on the back of his head as he flew away. So he'd turn around and blow up the base, just because.

Maybe then we'd pan out farther and farther, to the level of whole galaxies, where we discover that the galaxies themselves have been aligned to spell the words "ZIM MOOPS BLOOGIES" by some higher-dimensional beings, just out to have a laugh.

Unsurprisingly, the network never went for it.

Figures.

DEELISHUS WEENIE!

"Deelishus Weenie! Deelishus Weenie!
Deelishus Weeenieeeeeee!"

"The restaurant is most likely a parody
of Oscar Mayer Foods Company"

- The *Invader ZIM* wiki

"The Invader ZIM wiki is wrong."

- Me

The famed "Deelishus Weenie" restaurant that featured prominently in "Tak the Hideous New Girl" and cameoed in a handful of other stories was actually an inside joke that wouldn't die. It started in a car ride on the way to lunch.

It was probably me, Jhonen, Rikki, maybe Rob Hummel and/or Aaron Alexovich piled into one of our reasonably-priced cars driving up the lackluster Burbank artery that is Olive Drive. Someone asked where we should go.

Someone else asked wasn't there a hot dog restaurant somewhere in Burbank? Either a third person or perhaps the original question-asker asked what it was called. Now either a fourth person, or perhaps the third person, or perhaps the second person if there was no third person engaged in this conversation (see scenario 2 of the previous sentence) said, "Delicious Weenie."

This sparked gales of juvenile laughter, which then sparked people saying "Delicious Weenie" over and over again in even more juvenile ways. This in turn sparked the usual compulsive kicking around of joke ideas building on the original joke, which culminated with an ad: A lone man standing against a black background, shouting louder and louder, "Delicious Weenie! *Delicious Weenie! DELICIOUS WEENIE!!!*" Then a logo swooshes in and slices him in half.

The ad never made it into the show. We hoped to have it playing on a TV somewhere in one scene or another, but for whatever reason, it was not to be. I even recorded the vocals of the man yelling, and I think the boarded sequence exists somewhere on an early animatic, a bit that was cut before the final animation. To this day, I still wish that ad had made it in.

But I suppose the Delicious Weenie ad lives on in the hearts and minds of weenie-lovers everywhere. Well, in my heart and mind, at least.

ZIM EATS WAFFLES

The Shot is Held. A Waffle Captivates a Nation.

"ZIM Eats Waffles" should never have happened. It was a car crash of ideas that, unlike the chocolate in the peanut butter or the velvet fist in the iron glove, was a stupid combination, conceived by a dangerously over-inflated sense of competence, that should have led only to disaster for all involved. "ZIM Eats Waffles" is exactly what it says. An 11-minute cartoon about an alien eating breakfast food while his chief antagonists sits on the other side of the camera watching.

Yet, somehow, through the intervention of cosmic puppeteers who somehow manipulate the psyches of all sentient beings through their invisible strings, "ZIM Eats Waffles" has ended up as a confirmed classic, loved by fans worldwide, and critics who bother writing reviews of something as largely inconsequential as waffle-based episodes of *Invader ZIM*.

Side note: I wish famed film critic Pauline Kael was still alive and I was also a billionaire with enough money to pay her to review every episode of *ZIM*, just to see her wrap her brilliant head around it. So that's my second wish if I ever find a magic lamp. The first wish will be to rewrite history and change the first US president to — *of all people!* — George Washington. If you're reading this and George is on the one dollar bill, then you know I found the genie, and Pauline's *The Semiotics of Doom* will be on the shelves soon.

I owe the genesis of this story to a few things.

1. My obsession with making dull things entertaining. (see also: my childhood)

2. My obsession with creating the longest single shot of animation in TV history. (I do believe I failed.)

3. A conversation with a bunch of artists one night when everyone was working too damn late.

For the sake of this volume, I will start with three and work backwards. Those who object to reverse numbering can, as they say, suck it.

As I've mentioned earlier, my office was about two or three doors down from an office shared by a couple of storyboard artists, Chris and Ian Graham. More than once, when inspiration was failing me or I was just two damn antsy to get any pages productively done, I would walk down to their office, a place that stunk of drawings and sweat, and make sure they didn't get any work done either.

It was on one such occasion, late one hazy Burbank night when everyone was staying too late to meet whatever inhuman deadline was on the table, that I found myself in that office with storyboard artists Chris Graham, Ian Graham, (if I recall correctly) Shawn Murray, and character artist John Fountain.

We had two character artists on the show. John was the first, the second was Aaron Alexovich, who went on to create some very impressive comics — including the incomparable *Serenity Rose* — and occasionally lending his talents to Oni Press' *ZIM* line. John started on *ZIM's* first season, and then went on to become a director on another Nick show. Despite John's success, he still came back to spend time with his board artist friends in the undesirable ZIM section of the building. He probably snuck in with a production assistant wheeling a cart full of coffee supplies so no one would see him.

The artists were lamenting the fact that our show was so damn complex, and they were routinely working late into the night to board the complicated sequences people like me were casually throwing down in the scripts. There's a reason board artists can grow to resent writers. We write "The flying pig leaps the meridian and zooms onto the highway against traffic," and then someone has to spend a metric f*ckton of time figuring that shit out panel by panel. To be fair here, *ZIM's* artists were famous for going above and beyond the call of the script. Many board artists in this business would visualize that sequence in the most straightforward way they could for the sake of the production, and the sake of their own sanity. *ZIM's* artists always tried to take everything to the next level of awesomeness. A pig chase wouldn't be a simple pig chase. It would be an epic pig chase featuring near-misses with traffic, a school bus full of screaming children, culminating in an epic crash with a bee. See the difference?

On this particular night, I had once again been going on about my desire to do a single shot of animation as long as we could possible pull off. Like an extended opening to *The Player* or *Goodfellas* but way, way simpler so as not to break the artists' brain. Maybe I'd just seen Hitchcock's *Rope* or something, and had this stuck in my head.

John Fountain turned to the topic of lightening the load of the board artists by making an episode simpler. He said something along the lines of, "We should do an episode where ZIM eats a bunch of pancakes or something." This set off ringing carnival bells in my brain. The elephants had broken loose from the big top and were trampling the clowns to get to the cotton candy truck. I would find a way to combine these concepts. Maybe it was my own ego that thought a stack of waffles would be *way* funnier than simply pancakes. I don't know. Or maybe it was a secure and granite-solid certainty that the laws of comedy dictated that "waffles" edged out "pancakes" in any sentence with "ZIM" in it. I don't know, but my wheels started turning.

This is one of the ideas I pitched at the Irish Mexican restaurant, and Jhonen was into it immediately. Jhonen, like me, I think was very much on board with turning something boring into something hilarious. I think the conversation went something like this:

ME: I want to make the most boring episode of *Invader ZIM* ever.

JV: (looking up from fighting off a pan-dimensional brain-beast trying to swallow his head through a hole in reality while he was trying to eat a burrito on a plate that was too hot) Sure!

Actually, I have little memory of whatever conversation he had. I'd ask him, but he'd probably make something up, too.

Steve Ressel was also on board. I was going to say "shockingly on board," but this sort of challenge was the sort of thing Steve liked. He even asked me about how the hell we would cut from Dib to ZIM without things getting boring. I suggested we do it with a series of whip-pans, usually as quickly as possible. A few survived. And that hilariously slow pan from the screen showing ZIM to Dib frustratedly waiting for ZIM to do something survived, too. Steve was probably right in thinking an entire episode full of those would get old real quick.

The network also gave little push back. Maybe by this point they trusted us to be able to pull off an idea as ridiculous and wrong-headed as this one. Maybe by this point they were too tired to argue. Or they'd been so exhausted by notes on (the ultimately unproduced two-parter) "The Trial" that this one just sailed under their radar. Regardless, they didn't try to stop us.

These people are all unsung heroes in the Waffles Saga.

The other mostly unsung hero is one of the board artists on this story, Bryan Konietzko. If his name sounds familiar to you, Nick fans of the early 2000s, it's because Bryan went on to co-create the show *Avatar: The Last Airbender*.

Bryan was an incredibly laid-back guy, and while I believe *Invader ZIM* was his first full art director job, he was the sort of artist who seemed unfazed by just about anything the show threw at him, even if that wasn't completely true. Jhonen assigned him and him alone to do the character-based static shots in the storyboard.

Because he could put all his attention into just this section, and because this was an episode largely free of the massive action sequences that characterized the show, Bryan was able to bring a level of character animation to the boards that we usually didn't have the bandwidth to accommodate. Artists are usually focused on how to best get the beats of the story across visually while making the damn deadline.

Rightfully so. (I mean about the story part, not the part where the deadline is damned.) Good visual storytelling is something that's invisible when done well, and something most people don't spend much time thinking about when they're watching TV. An argument scene staged with two characters standing side-by-side talking on a flat plane is pretty standard for the fast-faced production of animated television, but that confrontation is way more dramatic when the artist spends time composing the shots in such a way to make the viewer feel the conflict in their unconscious mind. One character could be looming in the foreground while another is smaller in the frame due to perspective. for example.

But before any of that visualization happened, I had to write the script, and even though I was still pretty much a newbie screenwriter, I at least had some deep inkling that writing a script where nothing happened was actually far more complicated that it looked.

As I mentioned earlier -- and since it was a boring section of the book, you've probably forgotten, so I'll mention it again -- drama has conventions that drive it forward. Sometimes this is called the "story engine," sometimes it's called... Oh, it's probably called other things, but we usually talk about the component parts. Conflict. Stakes. Tension. Squid jokes. No drama can function without these. There's an entire division of Shakespearean study devoted to the hidden squid jokes in "Othello."

Even though my screenwriting powers were still in their padawan stage, I knew just sitting and eating waffles wasn't enough to support 11 minutes without people getting bored and switching off. Sure, it's true that kids will watch anything -- both *Teletubbies* and *Hey Arnold* are testament to this -- but I knew that if we expected audience to sit and watch ZIM do nothing but eat waffles, there'd have to be some kind of story framing it, something -- however trivial -- that kept us interested. We had to on some level wonder just how this was going to turn out. Whether or not ZIM ate another waffle probably wasn't going to keep a nation raptly focused on their screens. Not THIS nation, anyway!

And so I turned my attention on Dib. A series-level antagonist is always a great tool when having to come up with stories, and Dib was the obvious choice as the force that kicks all of this off. I thought that giving him a plan to spy on ZIM would also give the audience a window to watch all that waffle-based comedy we were scheming up. (And at this point, by "We" I mean "Me." These are the moments as a writer where you really realize it's all on you. "You pitched a story about eating waffles, you better write it, assmonkey.") Great! Dib has a plan! He wants to spy on ZIM and find out his EVIL PLAN! Perfect!

Or was it?

This framing device was simple, but it put me in a tough place. By making Dib with the character most at stake, I had essentially made "ZIM Eats Waffles" his story. This is also an old shopworn tool in the screenwriters workshop -- a workshop not unlike Santa's Toy Workshop, except there are no elves and there's a lot more head-banging on tables.

"Whose story is it" is a question writers and directors ask themselves when trying to decide who to focus on in any piece of drama. It helps us decide who we follow, who the audience cares about most, and who to focus on when you're telling the tale. To pull a super obvious example from the Marvel Cinematic Universe, *Iron Man* is Tony Stark's story. We learn his history, are given reasons to empathize with him, spend time worrying about how his actions are going to turn out, etc. It is *not* Happy Hogan's story. We don't see Happy's long journey to become Tony Stark's body guard, we don't see flashbacks to him working nights washing dishes to put himself through bodyguard school, or see him begging his father to finally accept him after he left the family shoe-burning business to pursue his dream of protecting the world's most brilliant douchebag.

"ZIM Eats Waffles" is Dib's story. It's Dib's plan. Dib is the one most wanting things to turn out his way. Dib is the one with his fists clenched hanging on every word ZIM says between forking GIR's slabs of breakfast nightmares into his mouth. The problem is, by the nature of making him a simple witness to ZIM's evil, I'd made Dib one of the most dreaded things in drama: a passive main character.

Yes, a passive main character is death to a story. You may not realize it until you've read (and also written) too many screenplays where your lead has life just happen to them rather than taking the initiative. It the difference between a story of someone sitting in a room waiting to be evicted for not paying his rent, and a story of a broke old woman who goes on a bank robbing rampage because she's tired of being broke and ignored by society, and hell, rent's due in six days. No matter what happened in this little outing Dib could *not* be passive, and yet I'd given him the miserable task of just sitting and watching ZIM.

And so I set about raising the stakes for Dib, and hopefully giving him something to actually *do* while he sits on his black-clad butt. Enter the Swollen Eyeball Network, the mysterious organization of conspiracy theorists, crypto zoologists and weirdos who count Dib as a member, but never quite seem to respect him. Dib's eternal quest for validation was a running theme in the show. The cosmic mechanics of the laws of comedy somehow demanded that he never quite be believed, respected, or even taken seriously. The Swollen Eyeball Network would be our mirror for this. Dib had a reason for wanting to catch ZIM in the act of planning something evil for reasons beyond just staying ahead of his enemy, he wanted to *prove* something to the cooler-than-thou peers at the Swollen Eyeball who never give him the respect he thinks he so richly deserves. This gives the story what they call in the engineering business, "emotional stakes." His self esteem is now on the line, and everything he does will be to avoid looking like an idiot in front of his peers.

This also gives him a framework for something to do besides sit on his butt. He has to get his hard drives working. He frantically calls up the Eyeballs when it looks like ZIM's on the verge of spilling something big. He's out to make the Eyeballs proud of him. Though at a certain point, even this isn't enough. Dib later calls the FBI when he thinks a kid is in trouble, though this also serves the function of throwing monkey-wrenches in ZIM's plans, too, and really, Dib also does it in the hopes the Eyeballs will see it just in time.

MY EVIL PLAN!

Now that Dib had something to keep him occupied for 11 minutes, and to keep the audience worrying, I had to turn my attention to ZIM. Believe it or not, I couldn't let ZIM simply eat waffles in peace. The second problem of my framing device was that it did nothing to address ZIM's story. One person, no matter how alien, just sitting down to eat breakfast is not a story at all, and I had to do something to fix that. Since ZIM was going to be confined to the kitchen, I thought about trying to make his struggle more internal. And thus was born "MY EVIL PLAN!" Or ZIM's evil plan. Or his quest to find an evil plan while having a dozen distractions thrown at him from every direction. As I said earlier, drama is someone wanting something and being blocked from getting it. ZIM wanted to think up a plan, and the story was going to try to stop him at every turn. It was a story as old as the Bible itself.*

*Not really.

The choice of "My Evil Plan" was deliberately on the nose. I wanted it to be simple to the point of stupidity. By this point in the process, barely two seasons in, I was feeling like the strings that held the puppets up were getting more obvious, and I personally believe that pointing at the strings is always a good way to get a laugh. In evil cartoons, evil characters have evil plans, and ZIM was the sort of green little egotist who would openly call his plan "My Evil Plan" without a hint of irony. Most villains never look at themselves as evil. James Bond villains are just ruthless in getting what they want, and if a nuclear bomb goes off in London, so be it. Even through the dozen *Star Wars* movies piling up, not once does a black-clad agent of the dark side call themselves "evil." Sure, they've openly turned to The Dark Side, but the term "evil" is so judgmental.

(Side question: By the time the Empire was in its hey-day, did everyone openly know Palpatine was a Sith Lord? I mean, when you look at the politics of it, the Empire itself was just a giant totalitarian government out to take over planet after planet, but was the fact that their leader was a servant of space-evil out on the table? Or did he do it in private only? Was he a closeted Sith? Would it just not have played well in the outer rim if they knew the imperious leader was Space Satan on top of just Space Hitler? I mean, I figure it would be tough to get legislation passed if the prime minister of Canada was an open worshipper of Beelzebub. But I digress…)

ZIM's Evil Plan™ would be his goal, and throughout the story he takes steps toward completing it, while being taken off the path from finding it for reasons both trivial -- GIR made waffles! -- and not-so-trivial -- the evil demon squid has escaped! Watch the story with this idea in mind. ZIM wants a plan, he starts toward it, he gets yanked away. See how many times it happens.

See? I'm more than just a man who tells waffle jokes, I'm an elegant craftsman of drama, bitches!

FETCH ME NICK!

As I mentioned during the chapter on "GIR Goes Crazy and Stuff," Nick was my obvious stand-in character for certain aspects of Nickelodeon that were rightly or wrongly driving us more and more crazy with each passing week. For all of their good qualities — and there were many — we felt at the time like Nickelodeon's brand identity waved a massive sky-darkening flag of cheerfulness over the earth at every moment, and yeah, it was getting to us.

An executive at Cartoon Network once confided in me that the difference between how the two networks presented themselves came down to this: Cartoon Network (at least back then) was the class clown, the kid sitting in the back row who maybe wasn't getting the answers right, but was making everyone laugh, and was also wondering what the teacher did to deserve the power of telling everyone what to do in the first place. Nickelodeon, on the other hand, came down to one idea: "Isn't it great to be a kid?" Not "a child." Not, I dunno, "a little scamp" or "an adult in tiny pants," but "kid" and all that word implied.

That's not a bad thing, really. In some sense it really *can* be great to be a kid, right? But everything always had to be "GREAT!" all the time. No human being is that way. It's pathological to think so. But Nickelodeon's marketing department deemed kids were always happy, always excited for something that in the big picture wasn't that exciting at all, always going off on some non-threatening adventure.

They were also happy to get slime dumped on them, which always pissed me off. When I was a kid I would have been furious to get sickly green substance dumped on my head, even if I knew it was what I signed up for. Those the kids always smiled during it. Maybe the money really was that good. Or maybe my head is particularly slime-sensitive. Or maybe deep down I'm just a miserable buzzkill. This last explanation does hold some merit.

Anyway, poor Nick, the kid with the happiness probe stuck constantly in his brain, comes back again for more semi-abuse at the hands of ZIM. Actually, Nick gets off easy in this little tale, being completely ignored by the demon squid and his robot minions.

And thus having thought through every conceivable angle, I went off wrote the durn thing!

And when the script was done, the story boarding began in earnest. Or in Bryan's Konietzko's office. Or really, in both.

The simplicity of this story gave the a chance to really focus on character animation on a level we hadn't been able to before. Without the usual manic leaps from shot to shot, he had to come up with ways of keeping our attention through character moments. Yes, there were no shortage of over-the-top action moments -- the demon squid being the biggest vehicle for those -- but so much of this story's success or failure rested on the tiny, very human beats of ZIM sitting alone at a breakfast table, thinking.

Bryan had an office not far from mine, and I remember poking my head in more than once during the boarding process just to ask him how it was going. His devious, spectacled elf face would look up from the board and smile with his characteristic cheerfulness and he'd say something to reassure me that this was actually turning out great. Bryan liked finding those tiny character ticks, and he showed me just one single panel that made me realize he was going to do something genuinely cool: It was just ZIM at the table, idly moving a fork between his two hands, and blowing air out of his mouth in a big Irken sigh. It was the sort of moments we'd all had at one time or another while waiting with nothing to do, a very basic, boring relatable thing, and seeing it on an alien known primarily for screaming loudly at one thing or another made me happy just looking at it.

Walt Disney -- I mean the person, not the giant multimedia behemoth that threatens to blot out the sun and charge us to sit in the shadow — had talked about wanting to convey "the illusion of life" with just his hand-drawn two dimensional characters. Early in my time in L.A., I was lucky enough to work on a documentary called *Frank and Ollie* about two of Disney's original animators -- or "The Nine Old Men" as they were called -- Frank Thomas and Ollie Johnston. They worked at Disney's animation table from a period that started a few years before *Snow White*, and lasted roughly to the time of *The Black Cauldron*. They even wrote a book about the art of animation and titled it *The Illusion of Life*.

In this documentary, Ollie remembers the very first time he wandered into a theater and saw a Disney animated short. It was a piece that featured Pluto fighting a battle with a piece of flypaper that just wouldn't dislodge itself from his doggy self. Pluto would pull it off one foot, it would stick to another. He would yank it free with his teeth, toss it into the air, and it would settle to the ground just in time for Pluto to sit his butt square on it. Then a look of realization crossed his face that communicated a very powerful idea with no words at all, "I've sat it in again!" When describing it, Ollie said something like, "I couldn't believe they made a dog look like he was thinking." This was the illusion of life. A series of drawings made you think something was living, breathing, and most importantly, thinking. A creature with its own brain and own inner life.

As I've come to learn from talking to other animators, it doesn't take detailed drawings to create at least a basic illusion of life. Every episode of *South Park* convinces us that Eric Cartman is a real-life asshole, even if we never once think those simulated construction paper cut-outs are flesh and blood human beings. One stop-action animator friend told me it all comes down to three things: "timing, pose and expression." The timing of the movements, the poses they hold to communicate the emotion, and the expression on their faces. And I invite all the animators out there to tell me no, it takes a hell of a lot more than that, but there does seem to be a certain logic in this, so I'm sticking to it.

South Park is great in that the expressions always hit the emotions of the characters dead on. Meanwhile, we've all seen some under-budgeted under-scheduled kids shows where the character faces all seem a bit "off" from the voices, like the tone of the actor somehow doesn't match up with the look on the character's face. For a good example of this, go google up an old episode of a Hanna-Barbera show from the 1970s called *Wait Til Your Father Gets Home*. It was an attempt at a grown-up adult-targeted sit com, but animated in the vein of *The Flintsones*. The writing is really pretty funny, and the voice acting is good, but the expressions are so limited that you just feel like you're looking at something unreal. What's the opposite of the uncanny valley? The shitty mountain? The view from that mountain probably looks a lot like this.

ZIM's characters never suffered from this kind of emotional disconnect, maybe because the emotions were usually big, and madness of these characters was almost always worn on their sleeves. It would be hard to misdraw the expression on ZIM's face during most of his lines. Also, our storyboard artists were talented people accomplished in their craft, so they never whiffed this sort of thing like those overworked Hanna-Barbera guys. But "Zim Eats Waffles" gave everyone a chance to slow down and focus on the small moments between the huge outbursts. ZIM's bored sigh while toying with a fork is just as funny as his "YOU'RE LYING!" outburst.

Because I was curious about the details of just how this thing came together, I dropped Bryan "Avatar" Koniezko a line, and he gratefully allowed me to interview him. By e-mail. He wasn't letting me get anywhere near his personal space.

Q: How long had you been working on the show before you got "Waffles" assigned to you, and at that point did you think about quitting?

BRYAN: I think it was around a year and a half into my time on *ZIM* when I got the assignment. I was initially a storyboard artist on the show, but for season two I became the art director. But during that, Jhonen asked me to draw the storyboards for the static shot in "Waffles." I think it was in the early stages of writing when he pitched it to me as a single, intentionally flat shot — maybe with a few cutaways to Dib watching the video feed. I loved the idea and was excited for the challenge. In the end, there ended up being some more stuff in the episode, but we still got to have a lot of waffles.

As for thinking about quitting, frankly I thought about it frequently towards the end there. ZIM was an amazing experience for me on many levels, but it was also a big mess of stress and tension. One day I hit a real low point and wasn't sure how I could continue, and I heard some sort of muted gathering outside of my office. I opened the door and saw the crew gathered in the lounge. They were getting the news that the show was cancelled and they had to clear their desks by the following day. It was a shame, especially as we had to shelve a bunch of cool episodes in the works. But stress-wise, I was relieved. Due to my art directing duties, I ended up staying on the production for a few more months. But the day we got the news was when I decided for sure I wasn't going to look for another job. Instead, I decided to put all of my energies into trying to get my own show going once we wrapped. Luckily, that plan worked out and *Avatar* happened.

Q: You boarded the actual "eating waffles" segment? Was that to punish you for something you can't talk about?

BRYAN: I think we were all being punished in some way or another working on that show! And I probably deserved it. But in this case, I think Jhonen liked my character acting, and since that's pretty much all that shot was supposed to be about, I got the task — on top of my art directing duties. But that's what I loved about *ZIM* and working with Jhonen. It might have been a stressful mess, but it was also super creative and daring.

Q: What were the challenges of boarding what was essentially an extended lock-off shot? What were the up-sides and down-sides?

BRYAN: There weren't any downsides for me. As much as I loved trying to come up with a cool sequence of shots — especially on *ZIM*, where we were encouraged to really push the camera angles and make everything dynamic — I also loved the pure comedy inherent in Jhonen's character designs. So, I thought it was such a great idea at that stage in the series to do the total opposite of our camera style and just let the character comedy shine. It was an opportunity to showcase the brilliant simplicity found in a lot of Jhonen's comics work, like *Fillerbunny*. Also, I'd say ZIM typically had a really high shot count, which made the pacing rather frantic. So, I enjoyed the opportunity to do the complete opposite for a change.

Q: Can you talk more about the character comedy?

BRYAN: Jhonen's style is known for really extreme expressions, but he also does a lot of stuff where a character is just standing there with a blank expression and it's just as funny to me, so it was a treat to give that aspect a lot more screen time. Honestly, I wish we could have stretched out that single shot even longer, so we could really slow down the pacing and milk the mundanity, and then contrast it with all the madness that ensues. But that was often the case on *ZIM*, we were trying to pack a lot into eleven minutes. That would be my pitch for the next *ZIM* Netflix movie: ZIM eats waffles for 71 minutes. One shot.

Q: How different was it finding the comedy in this story as opposed to your other ZIM stories?

BRYAN: It was so streamlined that it was just pure character acting fun for me. I'm a really slow artist and would usually burn up most of my time toiling over shot ideas and trying to create interesting camera moves. So, on "Waffles," other than drawing a ton of poses, my job was easy. The writing and vocal performances were great. And again, those character designs look funny doing nothing, so the whole time ZIM is being attacked by the demon squid, GIR is just standing there, not reacting, looking hilarious. Also, I just like waffles. When I got to draw a cover for the ZIM comics, of course I put some waffles on there.

Q: Do you have a favorite moment from your boards, or anything you're most proud of?

BRYAN: Maybe pulling off ZIM's "lip-fart" raspberry noise acting? The storyboards from "Waffles" were probably my most on-model ZIM drawings, and I love getting deep into really specific, detailed acting poses, so they make me happy whenever I look through my box of old stuff and see them again.

Q: Lastly, how did "ZIM Eats Waffles" influence the epic story arc of Avatar: The Last Airbender?

BRYAN: Ha ha… Well, again, finding those moments to let the character comedy breathe with really specific, detailed acting poses was a good lesson. I think that made its way into Avatar. Being a part of *ZIM* was tough, but it was an incredibly creative and inspiring experience. I learned a ton from working with Jhonen and seeing his incredibly idiosyncratic vision and sense of humor in action. And from working in close proximity to writers like you and seeing a show go from a paragraph-long premise to a finished script. And from getting to spend three weeks working closely with the animators in Seoul, and from storyboarding alongside all the amazing artists on the crew, and designing, art directing… It all fed directly into figuring out how to make Avatar. Just working on and surviving ZIM was its own epic story arc, so I'm sure that influenced Aang's journey too.

A lot of people cite "Waffles" as their favorite episode. This is because they're crazy.

But I see the appeal. And there's always something about the odd-ball episode of any series that grabs people's attention. "The Trouble with Tribbles" in *Star Trek* is a level of comedy the show didn't usually indulge in. Likewise, my favorite episode of *Bojkack Horseman* may be "Free Churro," where (SPOILER ALERT!) he spends a full 22 minutes delivering a eulogy to his mother. None of the oddball episodes can exist outside of their context, though. If "Waffles" has a charm beyond the fact that everyone loves breakfast food, it only exists as a counterpoint to the other, more normal episodes of *Invader ZIM*.

That's right, I just used the words "normal episode of *Invader ZIM*" as though they were a real thing. Weird, right?

SCRIPT: ZIM EATS WAFFLES

illustration: Rikki Simons

INVADER ZIM   08/21/01   *

                        "ZIM EATS WAFFLES"
                              #4B
                           Draft 2   *

EXT. SPACE

Big majestic music as we fly through galaxies, nebulae and
other space stuff. TITLES fly at the camera, big and
Superman-like. "ZIM EATS WAFFLES!"

We fly through space to the EARTH, and spin down through the
atmosphere to:

EXT. ZIM'S HOUSE - DAY.

GIR walks up the sidewalk with a bag of groceries, sucking on
a SUCK MUNKEY, singing to himself. A STRANGE SHIMMERING
TRANSPARENT SHAPE sneaks along behind him.

GIR saunters up the sidewalk. The shape (might as well tell
you -- it's Dib in a "Predator"-style cloaking device) sneaks
from gnome to gnome behind the oblivious GIR.

GIR reaches the front door, Dib hovers behind. GIR then
unaccountably stops, does a jig, screams, then happily throws
his drink. On Dib. Dib's suit shorts out, leaving him all
too visible, holding a spy camera.

                         DIB
               Argh!

                         GIR
               INTRUDER!

Then GIR stops and just stares and eats cookies from his bag
of groceries. Dib starts to run, then stops.

                         DIB
               Hey, would you mind maybe putting this
               spy camera inside ZIM's house so I can
               spy on his evil and stuff? You know?

                         GIR
               Okeedokee!

GIR takes the camera and goes inside.

                         DIB
               I should have tried this a long time ago.

A gnome shoots him in the head.

Eric Trueheart

2.

INT. DIB'S BEDROOM - NIGHT.

Dib sits down at his desk, computer in front of him.

DIB
At last I've got a real video camera inside ZIM's house. This time I'm prepared.

Half a dozen video screens drop down from the ceiling. Recording decks sprout from the floor. The monitors read "SPY STATION DIB: RECORD."

DIB (CONT'D)
Check in **camera one. CHECK. Check in record decks** Alpha, Beta, Gamma, **Epsilon.**

Dib hears a whirring sound from the hard drives.

DIB
WHAT!? The drives aren't working! I can't record any of this video feed until those decks are fixed. Computer, run the disk repair. Tell me AS SOON as the drives are functional again.

A computer screen displays a little doctor icon repairing the four hard drives. Dib looks back at his main computer setup and stares at a blank screen.

DIB
Well, if ZIM does anything alien before the decks are fixed, I'll just have to CALL the Swollen Eyeball to see it while it's happening.

ZIM's kitchen pops up on the screen: ZIM sits at the kitchen table, reading a newspaper and eating Irken licking sticks. The audio is cheap, scratchy. It's decidedly anti-climactic.

GIR marches into frame, and very seriously, pours himself a bowl of cereal..

ZIM
(reading the paper)
Hey look. They're gonna start making artificial **beaver.**

DIB
He's after our **beaver** technology! Is THIS his newest plan!?

ZIM
Well, time to work on my next evil plan.

166

3.

                    DIB
         YES!! Talk about perfect timing! The
         Swollen Eyeball Network should see this!

Dib spins around and activates a rear monitor, which lifts up
and floats. The shadowy face of AGENT DARKBOOTIE appears..

                    AGENT DARKBOOTIE
         Agent Darkbootie here. What is it Agent
         Mothman?

                    DIB
         I have a video feed from the alien's
         house! Neat huh? You gotta see this!
         YOU CAN WITNESS HISTORY WITH ME!!!

Dib spins back around to face the ZIM screen. Darkbootie's
monitor floats up behind Dib to watch with him.

ZIM sits there, reading the paper, eating his snack. GIR has
his face dipped into a bowl of cereal. He blows bubbles.

                    AGENT DARKBOOTIE
         Um... Agent Mothman? The Swollen Eyeball
         isn't against having fun with jokes.
         Once, I tied Bigfoot's toe hairs
         together. It was very funny, until his
         insane fit of howling rage ended in
         tragedy for a family of campers. My
         point is, this is not funny. Call me back
         when you have a point, Mothman.

Darkbootie signs off. **Dib looks at the hard drive repair**   *
screen again.   *

                    DIB
         AARGH! HURRY UP AND FIX THE RECORDING   *
         DECKS ALREADY.   *

ZIM stretches and acts important.

                    ZIM
         Yes. Time to work on my EVIL PLAN!

                    DIB **(LOOKING BACK AT ZIM)**   *
         OOH!!!

                    ZIM
         My plan to cripple the humans by des--

GIR has walked up. He's holding a plate of waffles.

                    GIR
         GUESS WHO MADE WAFFLES??!

4.

                    ZIM
          GIR, you know human food has horrible
          effects on my amazing body of ZIM. I'm
          not going to--
                    (GIR WAILS HORRIBLY)
          ENOUGH!! I'll try some already!

He carefully takes a few bites.

                    ZIM (CONT'D)
          Well... they don't seem to be making me
          sick. You know, this actually might be a
          good way to build a tolerance to the
          human's filthy food. I'd look even MORE
          normal if I was always eating a pile of
          waffles. OK GIR, I will--

GIR screams with joy, clapping his nubby hands together. He
dances off and comes back with more waffles.

                    ZIM (SINISTER)
          And as soon as I'm done with these
          "waffles", I will reveal my EVIL PLAN!

                    DIB
          YES! This is IT!!

                    ZIM
          For this plan I will create a nasty
          computer virus that... Hey, these aren't
          bad. What's in them?

                    DIB
          Arg!

                    GIR
          There's waffle in 'em.

                    ZIM (IRRATIONALLY INSANE)   *
          YOU'RE LYING!! Anyhow...GIR, I need a
          break from the talking of my NEW plan.   *
          Let's have some silence for a bit, huh?

ZIM sits and chews, while GIR stands motionless. This goes
on for a bit. Dib looks irritated.

                    DIB
          Okay, already. C'mon, the plan already.

                    ZIM
          Hey, you know who came by today? That
          ugly neighbor lady. She was wearing this
          horrible-

5.

Something huge and horrible darts in from the side of the screen and tackles ZIM to the floor. ZIM's limbs can be seen flailing as he screams from below the table. GIR watches.

                    ZIM (IN SHEER HORROR)
          OH MIGHTY DUMP!! THE GIANT FLESH EATING
          DEMON SQUID HAS ESCAPED!!

ZIM appears again, lifted up by the revolting limbs of the many-armed mutant. It bangs ZIM against the table.

                    DIB (MOVING IN CLOSER TO SCREEN)
          OH MAN!!

                    ZIM (CONT'D)
          SECURITY!! PROTECT YOUR MASTER!!!!

The Robo-Parents roll up to the Squid which holds ZIM.

                    ROBO-MOM & DAD
          Welcome home, son!

The squid eats the heads of the parents, chokes, then spits the heads out.

                    ZIM
          AAAAAAGH!!!! COMPUTER, DO SOMETHING!!
          GIR!! DEFENSIVE MODE!!

GIR makes sno-cones from his head and offers them to the squid, which takes each one and eats them, while continuing to throttle ZIM. Laser beams criss-cross the room. Toast flies from the ceiling. A security robot lumbers by.

                    DIB
          Someone's gotta see this!

Dib spins around again and activates a different floating screen. AGENT NESSIE appears. At this moment everything in ZIM's house goes silent.

                    AGENT NESSIE
          Agent Nessie here. What is it Mothman?

                    DIB
          CHECK THIS OUT!! IT'S AMAZING!!

Again, Dib spins back to view ZIM's screen. Nessie's monitor floats up behind Dib to watch. On the screen, ZIM is back in his chair, eating more waffles. GIR is brooming something away, but we can't see what it is.

6.

                    ZIM
        That should take care of it. You be sure
        to sweep that thing away before it wakes
        up again. I'll be eating these waffles
        and growing ever more powerful. LOOK AT
        ME EAT WAFFLES!!

                    AGENT NESSIE
        Darkbootie told me about YOU, Mothman.
        You must think the Eyeball Net has
        nothing better to do than watch a weird
        looking kid eat waffles, huh?

                    ZIM
        I'm eating waffles like never before!

Nessie Leaves. Just then chaos erupts again in ZIM's house
as the squid roars from offscreen.

                    ZIM
        Arrgh!! IT WOKE UP!!

He's knocked offscreen by the mutant. GIR watches as there's
a THUNK from off screen. Then ZIM comes back.

                    GIR
        What happened?

                    ZIM
        Eh, he escaped. Oh well, he wasn't part
        of my NEW plan anyhow.

Dib perks up, but deflates again when GIR shoots to ZIM's
side with more waffles.

                    ZIM (CONT'D)
        Ah, yes. More waffles. I can feel my
        tolerance for earth food growing
        stronger. Or at least my tolerance for
        waffles. HERE I GO AGAIN!!

ZIM dramatically raises his fork, then undramatically just
eats again.

                    DIB
        This is the most boring thing I've ever
        seen.

                    ZIM
        GIR, for my plan I'll need a test
        subject. Bring me NICK!

GIR returns with a plate of waffles.

                        GIR
            These got peanuts and soap in 'em.

Then runs off again and wheels in NICK, a kid with a brain
probe stuck in his head so he's always happy.

                        DIB
            He's got a human test subject!

                        ZIM
            Ah, yes... um... Nick. Neural Experiment
            #231. And how is the happiness probe in
            your brain doing today, filthy human?

                        NICK
            It's great! I never want to leave this
            magical place! I'M SO HAPPY!! AAARGH!!

                        ZIM
            Excellent! Want some waffles?

                        DIB
            That poor kid!! ZIM's making him eat his
            WAFFLES! I gotta get help!

Dib spins around, but hesitates before activating another
monitor. He looks back at the ZIM screen, nervously.

                        DIB
            PLEASE, PLEASE don't stop being a freak
            ZIM. I need SOMEBODY from the EYEBALL
            NET to believe me. Here goes.

AGENT DISEMBODIED HEAD appears on a window.

                        DIB (CONT'D)
            Agent Disembodied Head! I need a Mobile
            Eyeball Unit to --

                        AGENT DISEMBODIED HEAD
            Agent Mothman? STOP CALLING US!!!!

He signs off.

                        DIB
            Then I'll try the F.B.I.!

One of the floating screens reveals an FBI agent.

                        FBI OPERATOR
            Hello, thank you for calling the F.B.I,
            my name is Greg, how may I help you?

                        DIB
            I have an emergency! There's a kid--

8.

                    FBI OPERATOR (LAUGHING)
            Hey, you're Dib, right? Did you ever get
            that ninja ghost out of your toilet?

                    DIB
            Yes, no thanks to you! There's a kid in
            trouble!

They look at the screen. It's just ZIM and Nick eating
waffles. NICK is almost gagging he's so happy.

                    FBI OPERATOR
            MAN, that kid sure loves his waffles.
            Stay right there. We're sending someone
            over to beat you up for playing jokes on
            the FBI.

                    DIB
            But look at the brain probe.

                    FBI OPERATOR
            Oh, all right. We'll send someone over
            there to investigate when **we** get around   *
            to it.

The FBI hangs up. On the screen, GIR brings more waffles.
NICK is stuffed, clutches his belly between smiles. ZIM's
looking a bit stuffed, and sick, too.

                    GIR
            You look like you need waffles!

                    NICK (THOUGH STUFFED)
            YAY!

                    DIB
            Gotta stall him for time.

Dib opens a window on the same screen as ZIM's.

                    PIZZA MAN
            Bloaty's Pizza Hog. We deliver in 5
            minutes or its free. Usually.

Dib types an address into the computer.

                    DIB
            I need you to send a dozen large cheese
            things to this address right now!

                    PIZZA MAN
            We guarantee we'll see what we can do.

He signs off. NICK is getting delirious from all the
waffles.

9.

                    DIB
        ZIM won't get that pizza for another 5
        minutes! I gotta make sure he doesn't
        hide NICK! Where's the phone!! I have a
        plan!!

Dib runs offscreen. On screen, ZIM's phone RINGS. ZIM walks
off screen to get it. NICK sits eating the waffles that are
forcefed to him by GIR.

                    ZIM
        Hello? Who is this? I can hear you
        breathing. Is this Dib?? If this is the
        best prank call your planet can muster,
        you've got a lot to learn!

He hangs up and walks back. Dib runs back to the computer.

                    DIB
        Maybe I bought some time. But the
        suspense is unbearable. HURRY UP FBI!!

ZIM moves closer and closer in to the hapless NICK, LAUGHING
EVILLY. GIR runs offscreen.

                    ZIM
        And now GIR, to test my EVIL PLAN on this
        child here!

                    DIB
        Noooooo!

GIR appears with more waffles.

                    ZIM
        No more waffles, GIR.
            (GIR wails)
        No, really. No more. I'm starting to
        feel sick.
            (GIR wails even louder)
        All right! I'll eat just one more piece.

ZIM eats a little waffle. He gags. He GAGS more. As his
gag crescendos he hears the sound of a ROAR off screen! ZIM
points at something offscreen.

                    ZIM (**FRANTICALLY EATING WAFFLES**)   *
        THE HIDEOUS MUTANT SQUID HAS ESCAPED
        AGAIN AND HAS CREATED AN ARMY OF CYBORG
        ZOMBIE SOLDIERS TO DO ITS EVIL BIDDING!

Suddenly ZIM is over-run by an ARMY OF CYBORGS followed by
the SQUID.

                        ZIM
            NO! Stay back! Stay back! Nooooo!

Dib is in awe at the sight, then almost falls out of his
chair as he whips around to call Darkbootie!.

                    DARKBOOTIE
            What IS IT, Mothman?

                        DIB
            AGENT DARKBOOTIE! I KNOW YOU THINK I'M
            PLAYING JOKES, BUT THIS IS SERIOUS!!
            THIS IS JUST TOO AMAZING!! LOOK!!

Just as he says this, the CAMERA falls over in ZIM's house.
Now all we see is NICK's face. DARKBOOTIE's screen floats
over just in time to see-

                    NICK (REALLY VERY HAPPY LOOKING **AND**   *
                    EATING WAFFLES)   *
            It's horrible! The horrible army of
            cyborgs rending ZIM's very flesh! The
            carnage makes me so happy!!

THE DOORBELL RINGS

                    PIZZA MAN
            Hello! Pizzas! ARG!

The SOUND OF THE DOOR BURSTING OPEN.

                    FBI GUYS
            FBI! Don't move! Argh!

More sounds of a scuffle.

                    NICK (ECSTATIC)
            Now the cyborgs are eating pizza, and
            the FBI is being cocooned to feed the
            squid babies that just flew in from the
            window -- OH! What's that thing ZIM has?

                        ZIM
            Don't make me use this! I'll do it!

There's the sound of a HORRIBLE ELECTRONIC VORTEX. Objects
fly by the camera. Then nothing.

                    AGENT DARKBOOTIE (TO DIB)
            You make me sick.

He signs off.

11.

                              DIB
                    No! Wait! There was a mutant and
                    cyborgs and   *

          Out of frustration, Dib hits the recording device. We hear   *
          the sound of the recording device coming to life.   *

                              DIB   *
                    Yes! THEY'RE FIXED! I can show it to   *
                    the Eyeballs later. You're waffle-eating   *
                    days are over, ZIM!   *

          Dib slams his finger down on a record icon, and the decks   *
          begin recording. ZIM crawls on camera amidst a sea of   *
          waffles on the floor.

                              ZIM
                    Well, thankfully I was able to reprogram
                    those cyborgs at the last minute and send
                    them out into the world to do horrible
                    things to the humans. But my EVIL
                    PLAN... hey, I forgot what my evil plan
                    was. Oh well. GIR, your waffles have
                    sickened me. Fetch me a bucket.

                              DIB
                    AAAGH!! THE PLAN!! WHAT WAS THE PLAN!!?

          Dib watches, repelled as ZIM, offscreen, gets sick into a
          bucket.

                              DIB
                    Oh well, at least I have everything
                    recorded on disc. It wasn't a total loss.

          An army of pizza-covered cyborgs crash through the window and
          smash up all of Dib's equipment, then leap back out the
          window. Dib raises his arms in a moment of dramatic loss.

                              DIB
                    NOOOOOOOOOOOOOOOOOOOOOOOOOoooch whatever.

          He kicks a hunk of computer then slumps over to his bed to go
          to sleep.

STRAY WAFFLES:

- Much has changed from script to screen. What's presented here is known as "the record draft," or sometimes called simply "Gary" or "Mr. Draftpants." The animatic cut bits from the original script, and the final cartoon was produced from that. One of the bits missing is Dib calling in a fake prank call to ZIM to stall for time. I hope they actually recorded it. I would love to use ZIM's response to Dib's silent phone prancing as the outgoing message on my voice mail.

- The opening credits are a play on *Superman: The Movie*, who's notoriously long opening credits featured nothing but flying words for nearly ten minutes. The push-in from space to ZIM's house was inspired by a short film called *Powers of Ten*, which was a journey from a galactic scale down to the subatomic level as a way of demonstrating the scale of those titular powers of… What? Ten!

- Naming one of Dib's hard drive's "Stevie" was a tribute to the Nickelodeon "office guy" who serviced the utterly essential coffee stations every morning.

- Dib's last line "Nooooooowhatever," was a reflection of my own emerging fatigue with Dib's constant loss. Both Dib and ZIM ended up on the "fail" side of their endeavors more often than not, so by this point it's understandable if the poor guy had trouble caring any more. But while ZIM's built-in narcissism always insulated him from the pain of blowing it time and time again, Dib clearly felt all of his failures. Yeah, Dib's ego was bloated, but not bloated enough to be an airbag in the perpetual car crash that was his life.

- I noticed Dib yells an awful lot in this one. Clearly, showcasing Andy's larger emotional bandwidth was not my priority here.

- Credit where it's due: The sound design team did a great job on this one, what with all the insane stuff that goes on off-screen. Remind me to mail them all an Emmy.

- I also have to credit so many great details. Richard's delivery on the word "Waffles!" The timing during the squid attack. The action sequence communicated almost entirely by the shadows on the walls. etc.

- John Delancie -- a.k.a. *Star Trek's* "Q" -- provided the voice of Agent Darkbootie. He's one of the many celebrities I was sad to miss during their recording sessions. Why? Honestly, I was just too nervous to ask if I could stop in and meet them. Same goes for the *Kids' in the Hall's* Kevin MacDonald, who provided the voice of Tallest Purple. The whole f——ing series and I never once stopped in. *What is wrong with me?!*

- Nickelodeon gave us all crew jackets with the studio's logo on the back and our name's embroidered on the front. I requested that mine say "DARKBOOTIE." I still have it, but I keep it hidden in a secret location somewhere outside of my home, so don't even think about breaking into my house to steal it. You won't succeed! You won't!

- Longest single shot of animation if you include the zip-pans: approximately one minute and fifteen seconds. Though there are a few shots lasting from 45 seconds to a minute. And since Google won't tell me what holds the world record for the longest uncut shot of animation, I'm going to claim it for "Waffles."

WHERE THE ZIM WIKI IS WRONG:

- "According to the commentary,Rikki Simons said that the idea for this episode came about when the writers were in a Mexican Restaurant down the street from Nickelodeon. Rob Hummel was talking to Eric

Trueheart about coming up with ideas for future episodes and by the end of the dinner, Eric put down his napkin and said 'Zim Eats Waffles' to the surprise of Rob."

WRONG! It was lunch. And I threw my napkin over my own face.

THE GERMAN CALYPSO SONG

I Have No Idea Why I Have This.

In searching through my old *ZIM* files, I came across a document called "The German Calypso Song." Why do I have this? Did I write it? Was it for something in a story? Was it to appease a Lovecraftian Caribbean god who could only be placated by the sound of steel drums?

I have only a vague, shaky memory that I might have written this, or perhaps I wrote an English version that someone translated in to German. Or perhaps I passed out drunk behind the studio and woke up with it written in felt tip on my arm. *Or perhaps I never wrote it at all!*

I don't know!

Still, I present it here for the good of humanity. Maybe we can learn from our mistakes. Maybe we can grow.

THE GERMAN CALYPSO SONG

Calypso, Calypso,

der yanwing Ozean schluckt meine Seele,

die ich meine Augen mit den Delphinzähnen

Calypso durchbohre, Sie ein whore zu mir

Calypso sind, ich wünsche meine fünfzig deutchmarks zurück

GOOGLE TRANSLATION:

Calypso, Calypso,

The yawning ocean swallows my soul,

I blindfold my eyes with the dolphin teeth

Calypso pierce you a whore to me

Calypso are, I wish my fifty deutchmarks back

If any of you out there ever set it to music, please send me the band-camp link. I'll happily pay the 99-cents for the download

.

STORIES WHAT NEVER WAS: PLASTIMART RISING

ZIM Meets his Deliverance

Here's another one that never quite came together. Hooray!

For a long time we'd kicked around the idea of ZIM running out of fuel somewhere in the middle of nowhere, and having to find help at a scary 24-hour convenience store run by scary 24-hour rural redneck stereotypes.

Somewhere along the line, I tried to pack in a half-dozen only semi-related ideas, none of them strong enough to really support the story. Is it about ZIM eating junk food? The scary rural desert types? ZIM being confused about Earth's "convenience" store? The struggle of a failing coal town in a changing world? A man turned against himself by a fracture in time that puts him at war with his own infant form, now given deadly power by cybernetic enhancements given to him from a secret government lab?

Or is it really about the angry hippo that lives behind your eyes and tells you to steal the gun out of that policeman's holster? Go on. That cop is fat from donuts, and will never be able to stop you in time.

The big takeaway: Never listen to the hippo.

NOTE: Ending up on the fail pile freed up the word "Rising" for the Dibship episode title. Rejoice, history.

INVADER ZIM
Premise
PLASTIMART RISING
06/02/2000

The deep desert in the dark of night. ZIM and GIR are finishing up tormenting some trailer park residents, ZIM practicing his "abduction" techniques. (He just sucks them up with a gravity ray, but then drops them back on the ground from a great height, not bothering to actually take them on board.) On his way home, the saucer runs out of fuel (blame GIR) outside a lonely convenience store — The Plastimart. ZIM is now stuck in the middle of nowhere without his human disguise. The only hope for finding fuel is in this strange and mysterious establishment: The Plastimart. He's never seen anything like it, and his scanner indicated that there's substances inside that he could use to power his saucer. Unfortunately, the burly guy behind the counter doesn't like green-skinned "minorities" in his store. Of course, he calls the police.

Surrounded by so much junk food, GIR begins sampling everything in site. ZIM is amazed: So much food, and NONE of it has organic content! (He might actually be able to eat some of it.) He begins analyzing the contents of the store with his Subtansolyzer and discovers that the contents of the Slushbuckets (the slurpee like frozen drink) might actually work as fuel. ZIM has GIR hook up a hose (improvised from a long string of "candy hose") to the Slushbucket machine, and prepares to fuel the saucer. But while trying to start the siphon flow, ZIM accidentally gets a huge gulp of Carbonberry slush. Not only does he like it — it's the first Earth food that hasn't made him literally sick — but he likes it a little TOO much, and starts to get a little drunk on the stuff. ZIM starts bingeing on the Plastimart's junk food just as two redneck cops arrive. They grab ZIM and GIR and tie them up in the back room, accusing them of stealing from the store. ZIM is too "drunk" to put up a good argument for his defense. In some really clever way, GIR escapes. He's about to just wander off, but has a Pulp Fiction moment, and decides he has to help ZIM.

The cops torment ZIM by offering him more junk food, but ZIM turns the tables on them. He's realizing that the synthetic chemical additives are altering his metabolism, and he eats so much that his bidubblee glands burst, emitting a noxious gas which knocks everyone unconscious. GIR returns with "help," in the form of the trailer park abductees. They now beg ZIM to take them away to another planet, and he must fight his way out to his saucer, and finally escape.

MORTOS DER SOULSTEALER

An Inside Joke Sees the Light of the Outside World and Blinks in Hapless Wonder.

I don't think I'm making a huge revelation when I tell you I love it when inside jokes make it into TV shows. Even if I don't get it, even if I don't completely understand the context, the in-joke always makes me laugh. I always feel like there's some strange energy built behind it, like the joke is a rotten cabbage put on the end of a string and swung around and around in circles before being launched straight at the side of a public building, where it splats hilariously against the window of the most annoying bureaucrat there. Perhaps it's because the cabbage has survived re-telling many, many times in the conference rooms and hallways of the production, and is funnier for it. This gives the cabbage its power.

On the other hand, sometimes this cabbage can be thrown too far, or just slightly off its intended course. It slams against the windshield of an ambulance, blocking the view of the intrepid driver who's trying to rush a dying heart attack victim to the hospital. The ambulance veers off course, careening dangerously toward a school bus full of nuns, puppies, and orphans. Perhaps none will survive the crash. Perhaps the person who hurled that cabbage will run screaming into the woods; the weight of what they've done too much to bear. They'll find a small cave to live in, unable to stomach the thought of showing their face in civilization ever again.

Usually this doesn't happen, though.

"Mortos Der Soulstealer" is a cabbage of an in-joke that went too far, and ended up splatting on the side of a cartoon that aired in front of millions of children, and I owe it all to one man…

This guy:

Meet Mortiis: musician, composer, and performer of Norwegian black metal for what I assume is an adoring audience of appreciative fans.

I've never heard his music. Not once. And at this point, it would be a shame to ruin that record. It's like how the Chicago Cubs finally winning the world series ushered in an age of unparalleled misery and despair. If I ever hear the tiniest piece music Mortiis has recorded, something very special will be destroyed. So I will forever know him from his picture, and his picture alone. So say we all.

We stumbled across Mortiis one day while hanging out in the office of the colorists, affectionately known as "The Color Room," despite being mostly black. I don't remember how. It was probably a Google search gone wrong. This was the early days of Google, when the Internet was an interesting frontier, and a search could accidentally turn up genuinely strange and wonderful results because two dozen companies hadn't already colonized your search term as part of their business plan.

Regardless of how we found him, there on our screen was Mortiis, a "dark metal" artist so committed he performed in full goblin make-up.

But in our minds, something greater was going on.

Mortiis wasn't a guy who dressed up just for a gig. Heavens, no! Mortiis was so committed, he would go out in public in full Mortiis regalia. He would hang out at the bar after the show, trying to pick up girls, and would say in a voice not unlike the final voice we used for the show, "Mortiis thinks you're pretty. Can Mortiis call you sometime?"

In our far-more-interesting and glorious version of Mortiis, he went about his daily life, a Lebowski-like gothic goblin who never quite had his act together, and of course, always referred to himself in the third-person.

"Mortiis left his wallet at home. Can you can you cover Mortiis for the sandwich?"

"Excuse me, could you tell Mortiis what aisle the toilet paper is in?"

"Could Mortiis sleep on your couch while Mortiis gets his life back on track?"

"Mortiis donated a kidney for the money, then lost it all at the dog tracks."

And yes, the aforementioned "Mortiis thinks you're pretty" line that made it into the final show.

It went on. And on. Until somehow I was pitching Mortiis as a story called "Mortos der Soulstealer." The original pitch is in that multi-pitch document earlier in the book, but here's the final premise I submitted to the network. Notice my positively *expert* focus of detail!

```
INVADER ZIM
"Mortos der Soulstealer"
Revised Premise
06/01/01
```

In order to stop ZIM once and for all, Dib decides to summon Mortos Der Soulstealer, a supernatural being capable of stealing the life force of one's enemies. Mortos, it turns out, has many amazing powers, but he must "recharge" them. Recharging has something to do with the consumption of junk food and it doesn't take us too long to figure out that Mortos, in addition to being a superpowerful, otherworldly creature, is also an easily distracted mooch. Dib must keep Mortos focused and moving ZIMward as Mortos continuously discovers new foods and entertainments for his recharge. Dib corners ZIM and keeps him busy while Mortos finishes up his final recharge soda. Once recharged, a distracted Mortos grants the wish of a random passerby, draining Mortos' powers. Tired from the strain, Mortos retreats back to the underworld. Dib curses Mortos as Mortos fades back to the spirit world.

Of course, we needed a story if we were going to actually make a cartoon, so I came up with the idea of Mortos as a powerful creature of the underworld who by legend, had the power to grant a wish. But true to our fictional Mortiis, he was basically a mooch who would find any excuse in the book to avoid making good on his promise if it meant procrastinating just a little longer.

Something I noticed looking the script again: It was becoming obvious at this point that the conceptual tent poles of the series were firmly planted, and we could shorthand them to get to the story at hand. Yes, ZIM had some kind of evil scheme, because he always had an evil scheme. Yes, Dib was trying to find new ways of stopping him, because Dib was always trying to find some way of stopping him. The fact that ZIM's plan turned out to be stupid was just the topper for the joke.

The script went over surprisingly well, and everything was on track. Until we hit one small hitch from the might castle of Standards and Practices: Mortos couldn't be from "the underworld" because it sounded a little too much like being from hell, and we couldn't have anything from hell on our show because... um... reasons?

To this day I'm not totally sure why. Was this just an intensely cautious approach to offending radically fundamentalist Christians? Were they worried that if we so much as suggested Mortos was from the place that TV preachers threatened people with if they didn't donate to their international church organization *right now,* that our poor evangelical audience would yank their children from the TV and run screaming into the street, finally in possession of the evidence they needed that yes, everyone in Hollywood is secretly on Satan's payroll?

Fortunately, this is one of those treasured situations where addressing a note from Standards and Practices makes you change the show into something even weirder. And in this case, dumber. We couldn't say "underworld," but for some reason "from above the overworld" was A-OK! And while horrible hell-like cracks appeared in the earth, Mortos appeared by dropping from the sky for no good reason at all. In making no sense, it became more funny. Unlike, say, real life.

SCRIPT: MORTOS DER SOULSTEALER

illustration: Rikki Simons

Eric Trueheart

"MORTOS der SOULSTEALER"
#22B
Draft **2.1**   *

EXT. GRAVEYARD - NIGHT.

A shadowy figure observes a strange scene. As the MOON
rises, the shadows from ancient grave stones slowly align and
form a MAGIC SYMBOL that looks like a not-smiling face.

An UNEARTHLY CRACK opens in the ground. Bats fly out, stormy   *
winds blow from another dimension, turning the graveyard into   *
a cyclone of nightmares.   Lifted up by the winds, bathed in
lightning and swirling energies, is MORTOS DER SOULSTEALER.
The crack closes below him and he lands on the ground.   *

The shadowy figure reveals itself to be Dib, who taps Mortos
on the shoulder.

                    DIB (RECITING)
            Umm...ANCIENT TRAVELLER...uh.. are you
            Mortos der Soulstealer?

                    MORTOS (LOOKING DOWN AT DIB)
            Ehh? Yes, I am Mortos der Soulstealer.
            Every thousand years when Th'tuul aligns
            with Chu'kunga, I escape from the
            underworld to walk among mortals. Men   *
            hide behind furniture. Women spit
            loogies of terror. Animals void their
            bowels at the sight of Mortos der
            Soulstealer. Bwaaaaaaahggaga!

Mortos's roar of evil turns into a nasty wet coughing fit.
Mortos recovers then stands, scoping out the place with his
hands in his pockets. Dib is nonplussed.   *

                    DIB
            OK, GREAT! **I have a job for you.** CAN   *
            YOU STEAL AN ALIEN'S SOUL?!

Mortos turns to Dib. He looks very serious. He listens.

EXT. GRAVEYARD - LATER.

On a grave stone, Dib spreads out photos of ZIM dragging a
MYSTERIOUS BOX. Mortos looks confused.

                    DIB
            ...and so that's pretty much what ZIM is,
            understand?
                    (MORE)

                                            (CONTINUED)

CONTINUED:

                   DIB (CONT'D)
And I've seen him walking around the city
dragging a spooky looking box. I just
KNOW he's up to something. Something...
EVIL!

                   MORTOS
Mortos like evil.

                   DIB
No, this is bad evil.

                   MORTOS
Oh.

                   DIB
That's where you come in, Mortos.

                 MORTOS (AGREEING)
I AM Mortos!

                   DIB
Uh, yeah you are. I've been going at ZIM   *
using technology all this time, but that
hasn't been working out too well. It's
time to use more supernatural tactics!
And that's YOU Mortos! Mortos?

Mortos is behind the grave now, rubbing his face on it.

                   MORTOS
Stone feel good. Look, Mortos been away
a thousand years. Don't want to waste
time stealing lifejuice of bug man from
outer space. Mortos go now.

                   DIB
HOLD IT! According to the ancient
pamphlet, **you must grant at least ONE**   *
mortal a wish before you can return to   *
the spooky realm. I figured I'd catch   *
you before anyone else did. SO, I'd like   *
a wish, please.   *

Dib holds an Ancient Pamphlet open under Mortos's eyes.

                 MORTOS (RELUCTANTLY AGREEING)
Pamphlet stupid. OK. But powers very   *
weak from thousand years in underworld.

                   DIB (EAGER)
Well, how do we fix that?   *

Eric Trueheart

3.

INT. MAC MEATY'S - NIGHT.

Mortos orders at the counter. Dib's behind him.

                    MORTOS
          Two quarter porkies with cheese. One
          MacGrease, no cheese. Meaty MacMeat   *
          shake, cheese. And appley pie with Meat.   *

The drone plops a tray of greasy meat-stuffs on the counter.
Mortos begins eating foods. In the light, Mortos doesn't
look nearly as impressive as he did in the graveyard. He
looks like a doughy bum, stained and ratty, actually.

                    DIB (WATCHING MORTOS EAT)
          Mortos, is this really how you recharge
          your unearthly powers?

                    MORTOS
          YES! SINCE BEFORE TIME BEGAN!
               (stuffing more food in)
          Mortos not carry cash.

                    DIB (CONFUSED)
          Oh...okay.

Dib digs in his pocket.

EXT. CITY STREETS - NIGHT.

Dib drags Mortos, wearing a MacMeaty's hat, through the city
streets. Mortos chews on the last of a Burger.

                    MORTOS (LAZY WITH FOOD)
          Mmm. Mortos' Power returning.   *

                    DIB
          We lost some time, but that's okay. **ZIM's**   *
          last location was somewhere in this city,
          and WE'RE in this city so... Mortos?

Dib looks back half a block to see Mortos at a TOY MONKEY
CHURROS STAND. A vendor demonstrates the dancing monkey.

                    MORTOS
          Monkeys AND Churros? Together AT LAST??   *

                    DIB
          MORTOS! **You're not recharged yet??**   *

                    MORTOS
          Mortos been away a thousand years. Take
          long time to get back to full. Delishus
          Dancing Monkey contain much power.

                                        (CONTINUED)

192

CONTINUED: 4.

Mortos takes a bite out of a monkey churro, and then dances
what's left around on a string. Dib spies ZIM and GIR
dragging a cardboard box way down the block. ZIM pulls a
"thing" from the box and lobs it through a window.

                         DIB
          There's ZIM! **And his box is full of**   *
          THINGS! Let's go... Mortos?? MORTOS!!   *

But Mortos is gone. Dib starts to chase him.   *

                    CHURRO VENDOR
          HEY, **that monkey costs money!**   *

Dib looks irritated and reaches into his pockets.

INT. CLOTHING STORE - NIGHT.

Mortos looks in a mirror, modelling a pair of RUBBER PANTS.
The sales clerk (let's call him LORS) scopes out the fit.

                       MORTOS
          Do Mortis butt look big in these?

Lors gives Mortos's butt an odd glance. Dib bursts in.   *

                         DIB
          Mortos! Come on!   *

                       MORTOS
          Mortos is trying on... rubber pants!!
          Look, they squeak when I bend knees.   *

                         DIB
          That's a stupid way to recharge.   *

                       MORTOS
          YOU DARE INSULT THE PANTS OF MORTOS?
          Mortos recharge faster when he look good.
          When Mortos look good, Mortos FEEL good.

                        LORS
          A rubber jacket would make you feel
          fabulous.

Dib grabs the jacket from LORS.

                         DIB
          No! Mortos has work to do!

Off-screen we here a SQUEAK SQUEAK SQUEAK and a door closing
as Mortos runs off.

                              (CONTINUED)

5.

CONTINUED:

           DIB (CONT'D)
  Mortos?

           LORS
  The pants aren't free.   *

EXT. STREETS - NIGHT.

Dib runs through empty streets, then another, and another.

           DIB
  Mortos! Where are you? Mortos! Mortos!

He runs down the street and sees ZIM, waaaaaay at the end of the block. He yells to him. ZIM looks up, but he can't make out what Dib's saying.

           DIB (CONT'D)
  ZIM!   *

           ZIM (NOT HEARING)
  WHAT?   *

           DIB
  You won't get away with it!

           ZIM
  That's very nice of you!!

           DIB
  No! **Your plan!** I'm going to stop you! *
  I've got a secret weapon!   *

           ZIM
  Where is it?

           DIB (AFTER A LONG BEAT)
  Around.

           ZIM
  Can it protect you from this?

           GIR   *
  SAMMICH!!   *

A wet sandwich launches from GIR's head and hit's Dib in the face. ZIM LAUGHS and walks off.

           DIB
  Laugh now, spacemonster! But my weapon is
  so powerful, it... it buys rubber pants. *

He hears a SQUEAKING NOISE far off in the distance.

                (CONTINUED)

6.

CONTINUED:

                         DIB (SUDDENLY HOPEFUL) (CONT'D)
            Mortos??   *

Dib runs around the corner to find...

EXT. STREET CARNIVAL - DAY.

A street carnival, complete with rides and everything. Dib
runs onto the grounds, looking everywhere.

                         MORTOS (O.S.)
            WHEEEEEEEEEE!!!

Dib looks up to see Mortos on the kiddie bumblebee ride,
sitting in a happy bee that spins around. Seeing his great
hope acting like such an idiot, Dib's heart sinks.

                         DIB
            What is WRONG with him?

EXT. CARNIVAL - BUMBLEBEE RIDE - LATER.

Mortos is talking to a girl in a booth (DARLENE O'BOOBOO).

                         MORTOS
            Mortos think you pretty. Mortos, maybe
            call you sometime?

                         DARLENE O'BOOBOO (DISTRACTEDLY)
            Allright.

As he talks, he uses **unearthly** powers to lift snacks from   *
carnival goers. One child, having lost her cotton candy,
screams like a gutted piggy.

                         DIB
            Mortos! You ditched me!

                         MORTOS (ALL SERIOUS)
            Yes. Mortos ditch you. And Mortos
            sorry. But many years ago, Mortos trust   *
            little boy like you. Little boy named
            Floochie who sang songs **to Mortos**. That   *
            little boy break Mortos heart. Now, dark   *
            energy **of** universe Mortos' only friend.   *

                         DIB
            I'm sorry.

                         MORTOS
            And Darlene here.

                         DARLENE O'BOOBOO
            Hi.

                                        (CONTINUED)

Eric Trueheart

7

CONTINUED:

                    DIB
          GAAH!! I can't believe I almost bought
          that sob story! Mortos, you're no mighty   *
          master of spooky powers like the pamphlet
          said! YOU'RE just a big MOOCH!   *

                    MORTOS (IN SHOCK)
          YOU CALL MORTOS MOOCH??

                    DIB
          Yes, a MOOCH!

                    MORTOS (ANGER AND DISBELIEF)
          MOOCH??

                    DIB
          That's right.

                    MORTOS
          MOOCH MOOCH MOOCH MOOCH MOOCH?!! YOU   *
          WANT SEE POWER!?? I SHOW YOU POWER!!

Mortos summons power from deep within him, makes strange
motions with his arms, and lets out a mighty ROAR! CRACKS
open in the earth and EVIL FIRE SPIRITS scream forth. They
wreak havoc over the carnival, setting things on fire, making
lights explode, etc. People flee in terror. Dib stops and
stares, wide-eyed. The spirits fly into the carnival rides,
which transform into GIANTS BEASTS and attack each other.
The Clown-O-Wheel battles the Vomi-tron. There is chaos in   *
the background as Dib turns to Mortos.

                    DIB
          WOW!! MORTOS, I BELIEVE YOU NOW!! I   *
          always believed you, but you just seemed   *
          so... oh, anyhow, LET'S GO GET ZIM!!!

                    MORTOS (GESTURING AT CARNIVAL)
          Mortos use up all power with that. Must   *
          return to spooky home... Mortos weak...   *

Mortos begins to fade. Dib panics.

                    DIB
          NO!! MORTOS! DON'T LEAVE!! I NEED YOU
          TO HELP ME STOP ZIM!

                    MORTOS
          Well... MAYBE I stay if SOMEBODY help me
          recharge some more.

Dib gives Mortos a suspicious eye, then holds his hand out.
Mortos grabs Dib's hand dramatically, and solidifies.

8.

INT./EXT. HAPPY FUN MONTAGE - NIGHT.

SKEE-BALL. Mortos wins a stuffed ape.

DANCECLUB - Mortos dances. Dib looks at the clock.

MOVIES - Mortos cries. Dib looks at someone's watch.

INT. 24-HOUR PUPPY STORE - NIGHT.

Mortos sits by a pen of puppies, playing. They crawl on his
head. He holds one up in his arms.

                    MORTOS
          Who likes the soulstealer?

Dib, heavy with bags of collected trinkets from various
purchases for Mortos, hangs his head down in frustration.
He's disgusted by Mortos. The PUPPY SHOPKEEPER (MAURICE THE
PUPPY MAN) slams down the phone.

                    MAURICE THE PUPPY MAN
          HEY!! I SAID NO LOITERING! I've called
          the police already! YOU HEAR ME?!

                    DIB (ANNOYED AS HELL)
          Come on, Mortos.

                    MORTOS
          You scaring the puppies! Mortos
          apologize for mean boy, puppies.

Dib sighs and looks to the front window. Suddenly GIR hits
his face against the glass.

                    GIR
          PUPPIES!

                    ZIM (IRRITATED)
          No GIR! You can eat later!

He yanks GIR away.

                    DIB
          ZIM's out there! Mortos, LET'S GO!

                    MORTOS
          Mortos alllllllmost recharged.

                    DIB
          What? What do you need! What could you
          possibly need now?

Mortos points to a soda fountain. It's a holy moment.

                                        (CONTINUED)

Eric Trueheart

CONTINUED:

> MORTOS
> Sooooodaaaaaa.

> DIB
> Why do they have sodas at a pet store?

EXT. YET ANOTHER CITY STREET - NIGHT.

ZIM walks down the street while GIR drags a cardboard box on a rope. The box has "MUTANT VERMIN" stenciled on it.

> ZIM
> GIR, another mutant biting thing!

> GIR
> Yes Vermin Lord!

GIR pulls a SNARLING CHUBBY RAT-THING from the box and hands it to ZIM. ZIM throws it through the window of a building.

> ZIM
> Onward to victory!

Dib comes running up the street.

> DIB
> ZIM! I don't know what your plan is, but
> I'm going to stop it!

> ZIM
> I am infecting this city with genetically-
> enhanced vermin, but YOU'LL NEVER KNOW!!

> DIB
> You just told me.

> ZIM
> YOU'RE LYING!!

> DIB
> Mortos! Now! Steal **ZIM's** LIFEFORCE!!   *

Cut to MORTOS, in the street, still sucking on his soda.

> MORTOS
> Almost there. Almossssst therrrrre.

> ZIM (UNIMPRESSED)
> That's your secret weapon?

ZIM shrugs and walks on. Dib tackles him.

(CONTINUED)

10.

CONTINUED:

                    DIB
          I'LL HOLD HIM HERE WHILE YOU FINISH UP,
          MORTOS!! JUST HURRY!! HURRRYYY!!!

                    ZIM
          GET OFFA ME, YOU SMELL LIKE HUMAN!! **Ah!**   *
          The vermin!   *

ZIM and Dib knock over the box of vermin. VERMIN scatter, a   *
few jump on ZIM's head. Mortos keeps drinking. GIR just sits   *
on the sidewalk and claps his hands.

                    GIR
          YAAAAY!!

                    DIB
          MORTOS! WHERE ARE YOU?

Mortos is still drinking agonizingly slowly. ZIM gets Dib in   *
a headlock and sits on his head. FINALLY, intensely, Mortos
takes his last suck on the straw..

                    MORTOS
          Ah! Refreshing. Mortos grant wish now!
          What did you want again? **HEL-LOO!?**   *

Dib breaks free of the headlock, and slams the vermin box
down on ZIM. Dib strains so hard to keep ZIM down that he   *
doesn't notice the GUY who walks by **and comments:**   *

                    GUY
          WOO! I sure could go for an ice cream.   *

                    MORTOS (MIGHTY AND BOISTEROUS)
          YOUR WISH IS GRANTED!   *

The city RUMBLES. CRACKS open in the fabric of reality.   *
Spirits swarm. Lights shine from beneath the earth. ZIM,
DIB, GIR, and all the VERMIN stop fighting to look in awe at
the display. A SPECTRAL ICE CREAM MAN **descends,** scoops out a   *
cone, hands it to the guy and vanishes. The vapors clear.   *

                    GUY
          Hey! Whatdyaknow! Ew, Raisins.

He walks off, sullenly licking his cone.

                    DIB
          NOOOOOO!!!!!

                    MORTOS
          Mortos so weeeak. Must go return now.

                                   (CONTINUED)

Eric Trueheart

CONTINUED: (2)   11.

A crack opens in the earth. Mortos begins to descend. Dib
squirms away from ZIM and tries to pull Mortos back.

                    DIB
          Nooooooo! Mortos, **you still owe me**!   *

                    MORTOS
          Maybe next time you not be so cheap with   *
          Mortos.   *

The rift closes. Dib is alone in the street.

                    DIB
          Nooooo!   Nooooooooo!

He keeps crying. ZIM pokes at him.

                    ZIM
          Hey. Uh. OK. Well, guess I'll get on
          with my evil scheme then. Come on, GIR.

He collects his box and walks on. As soon as ZIM leaves, Dib
is surrounded by police cars and a police harrier. Dib is
snatched up and thrown into the harrier.

                    DIB
          WHAT? WHY!!!?? WHAT'S HAPPENING??!!

A newspaper spins into the screen, showing Dib being
arrested. A headline reads "INSANE BOY TERRORIZES PUPPIES IN
LOCAL PET STORE".

                    END.

STRAY OBSERVATIONS

- The collection of tombstones in the opening is a garden weird references. "Chris H" and "Lisa" are inside tributes to various crew members. One grave simply says "1905-2002," which implies that the show takes place some time in the year 2002 or later. Unless, of course, it takes place earlier, and someone in planned to die in 2002 and carved their tombstone early.

- Mortos' "Important plot point this is" was added after the script. I'm guessing somewhere in the animatic phase to satisfy a note that the ticking clock wasn't clear enough. And because it was funny.

- Listen for the fart when Dib says "OK, great!" The whole series is filled with tiny, nearly-inaudible farts, and some day someone should compile a complete list of them. Someone other than me.

- Dib's line about trying supernatural tactics was added to address whether or not the show took place in a sci-fi universe, or a universe where hell and demons existed. I get the point, but as the sort of person who read a lot of H.P. Lovecraft, Mortos didn't feel too out of place in a show driven by sci-fi logic, especially since *ZIM* was a show barely driven by logic at all.

- There was a scene involving a churro vendor that was cut for time. Or because someone was racist against churros. I don't know which.

- In the script, you can tell I was keeping myself amused with the names of character that would never appear on the screen. "Lors," "Darlene O'Booboo," and "Maurice the Puppy Man" were all put in for no other reason that I thought they were funny, and I figured the people down the line in the production would get a chuckle out of them. Character designer Aaron Alexovich particularly liked Maurice the Puppy Man. Actually, I think Maurice the Puppy Man might be my favorite name of any character in the whole series, for reasons I can never explain.

- The repeated shouting of "WHAT?" by ZIM and Dib across the intersection is something that was added in the animatic stage, and I adore it. Funny detail: The original storyboard featured traffic roaring by between them as they shouted, but for some reason it was left out of the animation. However, the sound of traffic is still there, invisible cars roaring by them as they shout threats at each other.

- GIR's shooting sandwich gag is perhaps one of my favorite visual gags of the season. It's the sort of overwrought milking of what should be a small, dumb moment that the show did so well. Good on ya, sandwich!

- There are so many horror moments done so well — like the carnival rides coming to life, and the demonic ice cream man, etc. — that I wish we could have done an entire horror-based animated series. You know, the sort of thing you find so often on kids' TV. Non-stop demons and murder, that children's television. Uh-huh.

- I heard Jhonen Vasquez say this is his least favorite story. Yeah? Well, Mortos told me Jhonen Vasquez is *his* least favorite story!

NOTE: I asked Jhonen if he'd agree to an interview about why he hates "Mortos," but at the time of writing he's only responded with the text message equivalent of dark stares.

THINGS THE ZIM WIKI GETS WRONG

- "Mortos der Soulstealer's voice is based off of Lothar from a recurring Saturday Night Live sketch."

No, it was based on our in-office Mortiis impersonations, which sounded way nerdier than Lothar ever did. Wally Wingert (a.k.a. Tallest Red) provided the final, deeper voice, and did a Mortastic job, in my humble opinion.

STORIES WHAT NEVER WAS: SQUISHY: HUGGER OF WORLDS

A Destructive Space Behemoth Just Wants Love.

Can we talk about Rikki Simons?

I know most people can't, not without tearing-up or shaking uncontrollably. He's a man whose path through this earth is as ethereal as it is squidgy. He's both enigma and un-igma. He is the olpha and the almega of Rikki Simonsness. A tall man with small round glasses, hair he clearly stole from The Cure's Robert Smith while Bob was too depressed to stop him, and a face that looks alternately cherubic or full of madness, Rikki was the voice of GIR on the show, a color artist behind the scenes, and a recurring presence in my time there.

Rikki had been friends with Jhonen since his comic book days. An artist and writer himself, Rikki and his wife Tavi had published several manga-style comics under the moniker "Tavicat," and had carved a sterling niche for themselves among fans of Japanese style comics. Their book *Reality Check* featured an anthropomorphized cat lady long before either of them knew what a "furry" was. In fact, based on this comic, the pair got themselves invited to a furry convention to hawk their comic wares, only to have the reality of what a furry was driven home like a baseball bat into a palooka's forehead when they discovered the artist at the table next to them was selling sketches of foxes with erections or something.

(For the record, no disrespect meant to furries. They've got enough problems in this word with everyone leaning on them for sexualizing anthropomorphized animals. I mean, yeah, it's not a recreational fetish that's anywhere close to "for everybody." But in the year 2019 when I'm typing this, it seems like a painfully adorable lifestyle compared with the sheer madness running wildfire through our society. But anyway...)

When he wasn't recording -- which was the majority of the time just by the pure math of it all -- Rikki spent his time doing color in a dark room with two other color artists. "Color," for the uninitiated, is the department on an animation production who -- wait for it -- puts the color into various object, characters and backgrounds the show will then use in its animation. The backgrounds are sometimes used directly off the page. (More or less. I think. I'm not sure. And the only background artist I know won't talk to me after what I did to his Ford Taurus.) But the characters and props are put on reference sheets and then used when creating the storyboards and animation.

So Rikki spent most of his day in a dark room turning a lot of things purple on his monitor. Also in this office was a tall, lanky color artist named Jay who was also a dance DJ at certain times of the night, and a sometimes-surly Swedish woman named Keshdie who, despite being sometimes-surly, was quite a nice person at heart, and at Christmas time brought in "Glug," which is a spiced wine drink the Swedes use to get drunk at Christmas, and Ikea sells because that's the sort of thing Ikea does. (We heart you, Ikea.)

Side note: There was an Ikea in Burbank then. There still is. I can't imagine Burbank without an Ikea. I think the Ikea may anchor Burbank to our dimension. If the Ikea ever goes away, Burbank will drift off into hyperspace at an eight-dimensional trajectory leaving only a crackling hole in the ground between Glendale and Toluca Lake. Or maybe Burbank's blandness would reach some kind of critical mass and it would collapse in on itself in what scientists call a "beige hole," an astrological phenomenon so boring that not even light can escape it.

Many a time I would wander into the color room to try to uncompress my brain, and end up lying on the dark couch listening to Jay talk about DJ sets, or watching Keshdie quietly disapprove of things, or making jokes with Rikki about... Jesus, I don't remember all of them, but they often were something about Japanese pop culture, though rarely about tentacle porn.

Anyway, Rikki was a comic book writer, and Rikki wanted to write an episode of ZIM with me. In actuality, he probably wanted to write it on his own, but there's no way the network was going to let him go solo on a script when there was a very real chance it could turn into something that furries would like without him even realizing it. (That's a joke.)

Rikki had an idea about a giant creature that roamed through space hugging planets to death. This creature just wanted love, but didn't realize every time he reached out to embrace a world full of tiny souls, he ended up crushing it to bits. Rikki had named this creature "Squishy," and thus we titled it "Squishy: Hugger of Worlds."

While communicating only through hand signals so the other color artists wouldn't see us and disapprove, we decided that Squishy has probably cut a path through the galaxy, and trailing him was an armada of space ships composed of races whose planets he'd hugged to death. This brave armada was trying to catch Squishy hoping there was some way they could stop him before he hugged again, but really having no strong ideas, because, well, if they had the power to stop him now, they probably would have stopped him before he hugged their world in the first place.

As the story developed, we determined that good old Earth was right in the path Squishy was wandering through the galaxy, and yes, Squishy posed a very real threat. The Earth was in danger of being hugged to death.

This was also to be the episode where Dib finally got Tak's ship running, and took his first solo trip into space. Of course, this honor now goes to the

Enter the Florpus movie, which used it to much greater effect, in my humble opinion. It also had a bigger budget. Life ain't fair.

So we had elements, but we didn't have a story. How was ZIM involved? What would Dib actually *do?* Ultimately, where was the conflict? Because if you've learned anything by now, you've learned that there is no story without conflict. Pressured by the fact that we'd have to pitch this story to Mary, and we didn't want to walk in without an actual story, I came up with the idea maybe ZIM and Dib would be in competition over who would save the Earth. Dib would want to save it because that's what he does, and ZIM would want to save it because he wants to be the one to destroy it, not some massive space-hugger, and neither one's ego would be able to stand the idea of the other succeeding.

Their competition would see them being taken on board the armada, where they spend more time bickering than getting the help they could use in stopping Squishy. Then both ZIM and Dib would fly into Squishy's brain in their space ships and try to communicate with him, hoping to drive him away.

I had the idea that Dib's impassioned plea would be something along the lines of, "Squishy! Stop hugging planets! *Nobody likes you!*" This cause Squishy to pause and shed a tear, before sadly turning around and trudging back into space again, now carrying the burden of the knowledge that he's horrible and nobody likes him.

Yes, I know it's kind of awful, but awful is sometimes very funny.

The response we got from the network was "Does the ending have to be so mean?" Mean? Hugging planets to death is mean, is how my logic went, and telling a giant space creature no one likes him when he does it seems only sensible. Why were they suddenly worried about "mean?"

Apparently at this point Nickelodeon was trying to figure out why the show wasn't getting better ratings, and one theory up in the higher echelons of cartoon power was that the show was somehow too mean spirited to attract an audience. The idea that they weren't promoting it very well, sometimes even changing the air time without any notice, didn't seemed to enter their minds. Yes, ZIM was at one point yanked unceremoniously from its time slot and replaced with a bad CGI show called "Butt Ugly Martians." (Google it. If you dare!) Of course the ratings weren't building. People tuned in for ZIM and saw bad CGI martians, and got mad, vowing never to darken the orange network's door again.

So the ratings monster was now scratching at the door of our stories.

One thing Nickelodeon *had* considered was that the show was getting ratings, but it was getting it among college students, who the Nielsen ratings system wasn't tracking at the time. It seems all Nielsen ratings were conducted via "Nielsen Boxes," that were placed in a randomly selected sampling of representative households. These boxes then recorded every last viewing habit the family had, translating it into numbers that the networks could then show to their advertisers when the time came to demand money in exchange for showing ads for fruit roll-ups or whatever. Nielsen boxes simply weren't distributed to college dorms because either they felt student's lives were too itinerant, or they figured the boxes would be summarily turned into bongs.

But Nickelodeon had considered that more people were watching the show than they were tracking, beyond just the college students. They knew the show was catching a good audience with older viewers. The problem was their advertisers didn't want older viewers, it wanted the highly-coveted "Kids 6-to-11" demographic, the biggest target of their toys, breakfast cereals, fruit roll-ups and whatever else they thought kids could talk their parents into buying for them. They just couldn't run an ad for the new Buick LaSabre next to an add for Cookie Crisp cereal. Why? I don't know.

Surprisingly, though, they green-lit the story to go to script.

I found the revised, less mean premise in my archives, such as it was, and I present it here for no other reason than you've all probably come to expect it now.

INVADER ZIM
SQUISHY: Hugger of Worlds
Premise Stuff
11/14/01

ZIM discovers that Dib is conducting outer atmosphere
tests using TAK's spaceship. Dib pushes his ship all
the way to the outer reaches of Earth's solar system,
beyond Pluto, and beyond the more recently discovered planet Wally. When ZIM catches up to Dib, he
is about to destroy him, until they both notice an
adorable little chubby man somehow floating in space
near Wally. The two stop fighting and both fly towards
the little man, curious, but they soon realize the
figure is actually thousands of miles away and the
size of a planet. The orb-shaped, smiley creature
approaches Wally and hugs the planet, which buckles
like a watermelon. Having hugged Wally, the happy
creature then moves on towards Earth! A ragged Space
Armada chases the giant. ZIM and Dib dock with the
armada and are told that the giant is SQUISHY, the
last of an indestructible race of really friendly
creatures who hug planets into destruction. Squishy
has destroyed all of their planets and now they plot
revenge by destroying any planet SQUISHY tries to
hug before SQUISHY can hug it, just to show him. ZIM
doesn't want Earth destroyed by anyone but HIM, and
Dib just doesn't want his planet destroyed. The two
get very competitive in who will save the Earth.
Since Squishy is indestructible, the only choice is
to persuade him into changing course. ZIM and Dib fly
into each of Squishy's enormous ears, both intent
on being the one who will convince Squishy into not
destroying Earth. Squishy gets overwhelmingly irritated and confused by all these thoughts in his head.
He pounds himself on the head, then grabs a ship from
the armada and uses it as a Q-tip, squooshing Dib.
ZIM, now the only voice in Squishy's head, manages to
sweet talk him into going to hug something else. When
Dib finally escapes from the rubble in Squishy's ears,
he is furious that the Earth has been saved by ZIM!

This was the story we were writing when we were all called into the
main space for the announcement that *ZIM* was cancelled. Rikki and I had

started work on page one, passing the laptop back and forth, trying to figure out just what Dib would be saying as he finally fired up Tak's ship for his first big trip off planet earth, and then we heard Mary Harrington's voice from outside our door, calling everyone for a full staff meeting.

When we came back into my office — which now seemed even darker when lit by not just the one green novelty lightbulb I'd bought at that hipster store in Burbank — but by the news that this ride we'd been on was now over, we simply looked silently at each other, and quietly, almost ceremoniously, closed the laptop.

RIKKI SIMONS: THE SQUISHY INTERVIEW

The View From the Wrong Side of the Submarine Window

Thinking about "Squishy: Hugger of Worlds" made me want to talk to co-writer Rikki Simons about his memories of it. I stood outside his window with a bullhorn and a giant helmet until he agreed to text with me. The text message transcription follows.

ERIC:

Thanks for agreeing to this interview thing. I know Squishy is a sore subject and often sends you into blind rages.

RIKKI:

Sometimes it makes me happy though. Today could be one of those days. Let me think. Nope. Still angry. Wait. I'm okay now.

ERIC:

You didn't punch someone in the neck again, did you?

RIKKI:

No. I just got stared down by my cat, Pippi until I realized what true rage was. I will never be that angry.

ERIC:

I understand.
So let's talk about "Squishy: Hugger of Worlds."

RIKKI:

Okee dokee.

ERIC:

You were both a voice actor and a color artist on ZIM. What made you want to write a script as well? Was it to make the rest of us feel bad?

RIKKI:

No. I would never do that. I never think about what anyone thinks thanks to my youthful solipsism. Writing is the one thing I enjoy more than anything else in the world. The only reason why I'm not known for being a writer is because I was known for being a voice actor more. I wrote all of the comics that I did with Tavisha in the 90s and those comics had fans, but nothing on the scale of what being GIR brings. When I go way back to my beginnings I thought I was going to write children's books or novels. I never meant to get into comics at all. Just like I never meant to get into voice acting at all. Just like I never meant to get into coloring at all. Everything has been one huge mistake And there is an alternate universe Rikki who is known only for writing. So I always wanted to write ZIM story.

I mean, I only draw because I want to know what my stories look like.

ERIC:

Did Alternate Universe Rikki actually get to finish "Squishy?"

RIKKI:

Oh, he did. I still remember the day we found out ZIM was being canceled and we had to close that laptop and walk away. It literally felt like the universe was torn in half, like one of those movies where two people are stuck on the other side of the door closing on a submarine and one guy is drowning on the other side while the other one looks on through the little window. Except the other Rikki is having a really good time and doesn't even know that this one got stuck in the collapsing universe. So he finished that script, and he went on to be President of Space. That asshole.

ERIC:

Wow. What do you suppose his biggest achievement was as President of Space?

RIKKI:

Making the universe's biggest sandwich.

ERIC:

We missed out on a lot on our side of the submarine door.

So...

About "Squishy."

Was that your favorite idea you pitched the ZIM execs? Or were there others?

RIKKI:

That one was my favorites. It was originally called Hugulon 5000. It was Jhonen who suggested Squishy be the title. I had another story that Jhonen liked about Dib being infused with nanites that made him totally indestructible, but also filled him with a complete monomania for watching television. So the story was about him trying to get home and then a single jaywalking offense ends up with the entire Membrane house eventually being surrounded by police and the army because here's this person that can't be arrested and is completely indestructible, and although they only want to watch TV, they have broken the law and they must be stopped at all cost. Nickelodeon didn't like the idea of an all Dib episode though, so it got panned.

ERIC:

Well, America hates Dib.*

*NOTE: America does not hate Dib. "America Hates Dib" was a slogan the voice actors used to throw around in record sessions to give Andy Berman a hard time for no reason. At least that's what I heard. I suppose it's possible Andy himself came up with it to give himself a hard time. Or maybe — whoah! — America really does hate Dib!**

The truth is… a mystery!

** America does not hate Dib.

RIKKI:

It's true. I'm getting angry just thinking about him.

ERIC:

What was it about a giant creature that hugs planets to death that you think appealed to you? Is it autobiographical?

RIKKI:

Well, you know what they say, write what you know!
But really I just have always love the idea of Galacticus. This big guy and a giant helmet who just wants to eat planets.

ERIC:

Did you envision Squishy in a big helmet?

RIKKI:

Oh sure! I thought he would be a big round potato shaped guy who is mostly helmet.

ERIC:

I hadn't realized the helmet played so much into it when I started writing. If I had, I may have devoted more time in the script to just the helmet.

RIKKI:

I think I have a picture of what I was thinking of around here somewhere.
You've got to have a helmet!
How do any of us get by without helmets?

ERIC:

Yeah, but we could have spent easily seven of the eleven minutes on the helmet alone. Like, slow pans over the helmet. Then, you know, Dib falling into a long haunted soliloquy about how the helmet is vaster than the human soul. That sort of thing. Then the helmet would fart for no reason.
But you know, "shoulda woulda coulda" as my Aunt Shirley used to say.

RIKKI:

Oh man. What I would give for a farting helmet.

How is Aunt Shirley?

ERIC:

Sad.

RIKKI:

Yeah.

ERIC:

So back to Squishy. We never got to the point of writing any lines for GIR, but if we had, would you have handled his dialogue differently, given that you were his voice and all?

RIKKI:

This may sound strange, but I can't recall if I ever thought of GIR in the episode. I guess he'd have to fly out into space with ZIM and screw things up for him. I think he probably empathize with Squishy on some level and then completely forget about him.

ERIC:

I would have assumed you'd take the opportunity to give GIR the biggest speech of his entire television career.

RIKKI:

That's the problem with GIR. I want more dialogue for him but he's not really verbose guy. He mostly makes statements. It doesn't really work if he sounds suddenly aware of what he's doing except maybe in short bursts, but he also can't sound like he meant to act on anything, or that he's aware that he's cute.

One of my favorite things in the comics is GIR making a virtual donut as a friend and then deleting him after waving goodbye to him, completely unaware of this thing's terror at sudden nonexistence.

ERIC:

GIR always seems completely unaware of the implications of anything he's doing. I suppose that mirrors your life.

RIKKI:

Sometimes I think that would be a great life. But the truth is I have obsessive compulsive disorder and can't stop thinking about anything ever. Sometimes I think it would be amazing to be something like GIR. But then I think he must have these lucid moments where he's absolutely terrified. That seems like it would be worse than OCD.

Although I think he must be completely trapped in whatever moment he is currently existing in. Like a dog is upset when it's done something wrong and then its whole world is that wrongness . Or when its owner has left for the day and that owner will never come back. But then the owner is back and it's the best day ever forever!

ERIC:

I remember our original ending for "Squishy" had Dib defeating Squishy by telling the giant space monster that nobody liked him, and Squishy just trudging sadly into space. Nickelodeon thought

that was too "mean spirited." Do you remember how we planned to
end it instead? Because I have totally repressed all of that.

RIKKI:

I remember that the alien armada was also going to destroy the Earth
just to make Squishy feel bad. I really liked the mean-spirited ending.
I can't remember if we actually nailed down an actual ending though.
I checked my notes recently and I don't see anything about it. It's possible we may not have gotten there because of being canceled that day.

ERIC:

Yeah, I remember both of us just going back into the office and closing the laptop without a word.

RIKKI:

And then the sound of the submarine door closing and the rush-
ing water.

ERIC:

And Aunt Shirley pounding on the glass.

RIKKI:

Weird how they built the office like that.

ERIC:

Weird that Shirley kept showing up there, too.

RIKKI:

Must've had a thing for Orange.

ERIC:

One last question: Do you think you'll ever try to do "Squishy" as a comic?

RIKKI:

I would love to. I should try pitching it to Oni maybe. You'd have to write it with me though. That's what God told me. You don't wanna go to hell do you?

ERIC:

I don't think so. What's in hell these days?

RIKKI:

The usual. Ewoks and accountants and preachers.

ERIC:

Then no.

RIKKI:

24 hour Jub Jub music

ERIC:

Please stop.
This is making me shake involuntarily.

RIKKI:

No one would ever volunteer to shake.

ERIC:

Thanks for your time, Rikki. I have to go check on Shirley's medication now. May you never rot in a hell of your own devising.

RIKKI:

Thanks for having me! I hope we can build a giant helmet together someday.

ERIC:

Look out your window.

RIKKI:

Whoooooaaaa!!!

THE CANCELLING

"Everything dies, asshole."

— *Buddha**

*Not Buddha

Why was *ZIM* cancelled?

It's a question that often comes up at conventions, or in boxcars, asked between hobos as they ride the rails up and down the Pacific Northwest. Oh, the romance of the rails. Oh, those incorrigible hobos.

This is what I was told later.

A recession had hit the country hard after 9/11. The entire economy was in a slump, and Viacom -- the parent company that owned, among other jewels, MTV Networks, which was the parent company that owned Nickelodeon -- was seeing losses. It's stock had (I was told) fallen. Profits were down. Sumner Redstone -- the raven-clawed withered billionaire who owned it -- was alternately shaking in his sealskin slippers and wandering dazed in the corridors of power bellowing a powerful war cry that "heads will roll!" with anyone asking him to elaborate being kicked in the shins.

Thus the word came down from on high: company-wide Viacom had to make cuts.

We'd felt these cuts already. The studio had stopped giving all its employees a catered lunch every day, reserving that only for Fridays, on the idea that nothing launches the weekend like a steam tray full of foil-wrapped burritos from the burrito joint down the street. The MTV Network Christmas party — which the previous year had been held in the House of Blues, and had featured hand-rolled cigars, tarot card readers, several professional Santas for confessional lap-sitting, and an entire acrobat group performing on the main stage -- had been cancelled and replaced with free Christmas coffee and tiny round chocolate-covered pastries that I could only describe as "Cream Pods."

Never mind that MTV Networks was the cash-cow of Viacom, and Nickelodeon was the cash-cow of MTV networks, every last tentacle of the Viacom octopus was told to trim a few inches off the end or face the wrath of Business Affairs. Inside the halls of Nickelodeon Animation Studios, this trimming could be accomplished by cutting the production of one show.

You can guess how easy a decision cutting *ZIM* was for them.

Look, at the time the shows in production were, if I recall correctly, *Fairly Oddparents, Hey Arnold,* and *Invader ZIM*, so I can only imagine that meeting went pretty quickly.

"So, which show should we cut?" said fictional suit number one.

"How about *ZIM?* We hate *ZIM!*" said fictional suit number two, never realizing he was paraphrasing the Almighty Tallest.

Okay, that's unfair. But I can't fault their logic for choosing us. *ZIM* was the problem show, the show they had no idea how to market, the show that constantly pushed back in the creative meetings, the show that just wasn't Hoovering in the viewers like the other shows were. Any Business Affairs executive worth the price of their MBA and Brooks Brothers suit would have been an idiot not to pick *ZIM* for the chopping block.

This is why Business Affairs ruins everything good. Even at the best networks. (I could go on a long conversation about that, but I won't. If you happen to be the head of a network or massive media company, please fire half of your Business Affairs people right now and use the money you save to produce more TV shows, which is your actual business in the first place.)

The news hit us all very hard. We had recently been renewed for a second season, and given the logic of most television production at the time, that meant we were almost a proverbial shoo-in for a third. Most networks tried to rack up 65 episodes of any given show, as that was the minimum number for a "syndication package." That's the fancy word for "reruns on your local station." When you grew up watching *Seinfeld* or *The Cosby Show* or even *M*A*S*H* shown weekdays at 4:30 or 7:00 or whenever, that's a show in syndication. The minimum required episodes is generally 65, because that way a local station can run a different episode every weekday and get through about three months of shows before repeating anything. Of course, *ZIM* may not have been the "weekdays at 4:30" type of show, but nevertheless, the logic still stands. Get 65 episodes and the studio is home-free on its investment. All those millions they put into the show will finally come back in spades.

Since *ZIM* had been picked up for a second season, I was sure a third season was practically guaranteed. Under most circumstances, that would probably have been true. But Nickelodeon pulled the plug on us just six episodes into season two, thus yanking the rug out from under a show we felt was finally finding its feet, if not it's audience. OK, definitely not its audience.

What I see now looking back at the magic-hour light on the yellow brick road of history (I have no idea what any of that twisted metaphor means) is that in some ways, cancellation may have ensured *ZIM's* place in the hall of television immortality.

Some of the biggest genre hits in history were cut down in their prime. *Star Trek* being the most famous. A show that had its plug pulled just before the invention of demographic analysis would show that actually, it was incredibly popular among the sort of people advertisers wanted. Televisius Interruptus.

It's what sealed the fandom of *Firefly*, too. Televisius Interruptus. Shows pulled off the air before the audience had a chance to get sick of them -- cf.

The X-Files -- or get so annoyed by the ending they questioned why they ever fell in love with the how in the first place -- cf. *Lost*.

There's nothing like being cut down in your prime to leave a hole in the audience's heart that they can only fill with fandom of their own making. And to their credit -- and to my occasional horror -- they have. Since cancellation, *ZIM* fandom has grown in the dark corners of popular culture like fungus grows in the back of your refrigerator.

Invader ZIM became one of those shows, like *Star Trek* and *Doctor Who* before it, that could entirely support its own fan convention. A series of three "InvaderCons" were held over the intervening years, and there's something special about a whole con devoted to a single fictional entity. Imagine hotel hallways filled with people all cosplaying from the same show. Of people quoting lines they all know-- OK, this now sounds a little terrible. But really, it's kind of cool. Look, the best thing I ever saw at one of these conventions was a girl dressed as the bee that struck down ZIM's Voot cruiser in "Attack of the Saucer Morons." Yes, a kid was dressed as a bee, and everyone knew exactly what it was.

ZIM also seems to be one of these shows that somehow manages to snag a new audience every year. It's a dark little secret that teenage babysitters share with kids while their parents are out. It's the mutant stepchild Nickelodeon keeps locked up in the basement, but never quite hiding the key well enough for nobody to find it. It seems to attract misfits from every era, and with any luck it may go on attracting them for another decade or so.

But back on that day when we were all called into the main space, none of us knew the future. The whole crew had gathered from the not-all-that far corners of our open office workpit. Both Mary Harrington and Jhonen were there, standing in front of the TV where the board artists routinely played *Star Wars Super Bombad Racing* on a PS2. (It was a different time.)

Of course, I thought this was the moment we'd get our third season pick up. They'd green-lit us for season two, there's no way they'd let us slide into obscurity without reaching the magic 65 episode syndication package, ratings problem or no. It was just common sense.

One look at the expression on Mary's eyes and I knew I was wrong. Oh, the poor innocent farm boy that I was. The network axe will swing down on even the most prized heifer at any time, and it doesn't care who the blood splatters on. Is that figure of speech gross enough? I'll work on a grosser one later.

Mary was emotional, and her voice cracked as they told us the news. She was almost apologetic. She knew that this show had been just as unique and weird as we all did. It was the sort of thing that didn't come along every day, and probably wouldn't come along again for a long time. The sadness slowly fell over us, as though it had drifted down from the rafters, where the skylights hadn't been pink for a long, long time.

Jhonen was also upset, though I honestly don't remember what he said. The whole moment -- the gathering of a crew to be told their show is cancelled -- is a moment as old as the TV business itself. Nobody ever knows what to say. Sometimes people are silently relieved, but that relief usually pales against the feeling that everyone worked very hard on something that's now being tossed in the trash. (Unless, of course, the show is terrible, the star is a huge pain in the ass, or the producer is a raging asshole, then that feeling of relief towers over the skyline like King Kong on a meth binge, pounding its chest loud enough to drown out the anxiety of coming unemployment.)

It wouldn't be until later that I'd learn an old adage among TV writers: Never decorate your office with more than you can carry out in one cardboard file box. It's true. The life of the TV writer borders on itinerant. Not only can your show be cancelled at any moment, you can be unceremoniously tossed from a writing staff if the showrunner doesn't feel like you're fitting in. Never make your home in one place for too long.

My office was jam-packed with stuff. Posters. Photos. Weird Japanese toys. Plush hamsters. I knew the job would some day end, but the thought that the ride could end so soon and so abruptly had never even crossed my mind. I wasn't officially kicked out of the building that day. They gave me about two more weeks to do whatever revisions were necessary on the current scripts, followed by many more weeks after my exit to fight with the network over paying me the rest of my pay-or-play contract. (cf. Business Affairs ruins everything.) The artists stayed on longer than I did, and we managed to scrape the Christmas special out of it, but there's something strange about working on a show you know is a dead man walking.

That day I saw our network executive in the hall. He hadn't been in on the announcement, but someone had probably told him he should stop by to lend his condolences. I'm afraid I was a complete dick that day and passed him right by without saying a word. That wasn't fair, and I regret it, but damn I was angry, and I felt like he had a hand in our demise.

I mean, he hadn't, really, but like I said, I was angry. And a dick. And in retrospect, I'm very not proud of that exchange, or utter lack of one.

I always wonder if we somehow set ourselves up for failure by all of us subconsciously thinking this couldn't last. That the network would hate us no matter what we did. That "The Man™" would do us in for being too out there, too edgy, too... you know, the usual hipster crap that young people pride themselves on. If we'd all imagined we could somehow get along, would things have turned out differently?

Eh, probably not.

However, that early demise ensured us a shrine in fandom history by being a show that was yanked before it wore out its welcome. People still talk about Firefly, but few people resent "Buffy the Vampire Slayer" not being resurrected. Seven seasons was enough to get your teenage vampire fix. It's long enough for a fan to start watching in high school and be out of college looking for a job when the show wraps up, ready to move on to more mature endeavors like paying bills and not-starving. We gave the audience no such closure. We left people wanting more mutant ridiculousness, and that kept the fires of fandom burning.

Until...

THE COMICS!

Oni Press Raises the Dead, a Star Donkey Kicks the Earth, Lost Episodes are Finally Found.

After *ZIM* was cancelled, I got on with my life. Years passed. I rode the rails, taking jobs wherever I could find them from kindly farmers and rural housewives who needed help with fence painting and cleaning up the yard before pa got home.

No wait, that's hobos again. What is it with this show and hobos, anyway?

For myself, I took more jobs in the animation business, at some point managing to work for just about every major toon-slinging network in town -- Disney, Cartoon Network, Dreamworks, Netflix, PBS, the Hub (remember them? yeah, nobody else does, either). Fans of another Nick show called *Fairly Oddparents* might want to check out Disney XD's *Yin Yang Yo*, a show I wrote for about two Kung-Fu rabbits, run by Steve Marmel, head writer for "Oddparents" and *Danny Phantom* before he fled Nick for less-orange pastures. Realistically speaking, you will probably go your whole life without getting the chance to work with Steve, but if you do, jump on it. It's a good time.

I also was part of a comedy group that landed a couple of pilots on various networks, and learned first hand how it feels when your pilot doesn't get picked up -- twice. (If you're at all interested, you can YouTube-up "The Ministry of Unknown Science." The stuff has dated, but well, haven't we all?)

But I largely put *ZIM* behind me, and walked forward into a sunrise completely free of flying pigs and robot bees, only occasionally hearing whispers that the series might get "revived," either on Nicktoons as a low-budget shadow of its former self, or as a series of GIR-based shorts, or as a comic book published by Oni Press. None of these panned out.

Oh wait, the comic book *did* pan out.

In 2015, I got a call from Jhonen asking if I'd be interesting in writing some issues of a comic book version of *Invader ZIM* that Oni Press was planning. It seems Oni had sought out the rights to *ZIM* about the same time they bagged the rights to do a Rick and Morty comic, and of course they wanted Jhonen involved. He started life as a comic-book person, after all. Gestated from a comic-book womb and born in a comic-book hospital. I have no idea what I'm saying here.

The conversation went something like this.

ME: Hello?

JV: [STRANGE GURGLING NOISES}

ME: Is this Jhonen?

JV: Yeah, sorry. Just strangling this infernal death beast from beyond the dark void.

ME: Why didn't you strangle him before you called?

JV: Come on, man, you know how death beasts are.

ME: I'm just saying, at least close the void first.

JV: I *did* close the void, but one beast got out and was hiding in my cereal cupboard, *okay*? Jeeze, I don't come to your house and knock the death beast out of your hand.

ME: Fine. Is it dead?

JV: It's a wisp of black smoke now. It stained my couch.

ME: That sucks, dude.

JV: Hey, Oni Press wants to publish some comics based on *Invader ZIM*. Would you want to write some of them?

ME: I don't know. Does it come with fortune and glory?

JV: No.

ME: Hmmm... Does it at least pay a wage commensurate with a union-covered television job?

JV: Absolutely not.

ME: Can I write something about a Star Donkey?

JV: Hells yes!

ME: I AM SO IN!

(NOTE: The actual conversation did not go anything like this at all.)

Jhonen had a lot of ideas for this new book, but he also only wanted to be so hands-on. He didn't want to write every word himself, and he wanted other artists to take a swing at drawing it In his mind, it would be way more interesting to see *Invader ZIM* interpreted through the talents of other people than simply do a version that was "just like the TV show, but not moving."

So off we went, writing stories as though the show had never been off the air.

It was surprisingly easy to pick up where we left off. Technology had marched on only a little -- imagining Dib doing all of his usual Dib stuff with a smart phone isn't a stretch at all -- and the characters were surprisingly easy to fall back into. Jhonen's one directive was that Gaz should be just slightly less horrible. Sure, she's still angry and annoyed by every last thing Dib does, but she should have at least have a shard of a conscience behind it all. She still has some feelings for her brother, even if they're buried behind a red-hot volcanic irritation at him.

We started with a story that saw ZIM hiding from Dib for an indeterminate number of years, only to lure Dib out of hiding for the sole purposes of humiliating him on a galactic scale by broadcasting footage of our morbidly obese paranormal investigator getting back into shape. The first part of this story would later be echoed in the "Enter the Florpus" movie, with an almost identical set of circumstances launching events in a completely different direction and giving us a story that was much, much different. I almost think Jhonen did it precisely to mess with people who wanted to fit the comics into the canon of the TV series. Almost. Really, I think he did it because he thought it was funny.

For myself, I just saw an opportunity to tell more uniquely strange stories with these characters again. A pile of years in the animation business had made me realize that shows with the inbred strangeness of ZIM didn't come along that often. Seriously, when I left ZIM in 2000-whatever, I figured I'd find plenty of odd science-fiction comedies out there who'd be dying to hire me. I was -- surprise! -- very wrong. The opportunity to go hog wild with weird ideas and surreal comedy was a rare thing in a business dominated by shows like... Damn, I've blocked most of them from my memory. I just remember a lot of *Hannah Montana* from that era, and it wasn't even animated. Then there was *Phineas and Pherb*, which was a great show, but there were no Star Donkeys. *Gravity Falls* was a show my manager didn't even put me up for. Such is the nature of this business.,

But I am rambling. Where was I?

Yes! Comics!

The comics gave me a chance to spin more strange tales from the world of ZIM, some of which rank in my favorites. The aforementioned "Star Donkey," where ZIM attempts to summon a cosmic burro from beyond the stars to do his bidding is one. Other favorites are "Zimmer World" where ZIM goes to a future where he has taken over the earth, and discovers he can't stand himself. "Interner Derb," where Dib sneaks into ZIM's base disguised as an alien wanting to intern for ZIM. "Li'l Meat Man," a road trip featuring ZIM and his newborn baby made of ground beef. And "Burrito King," a lost episode that I'd pitched to Nick near the end of the run where ZIM takes over a restaurant called "Burrito King" because he wants to become… wait for it… The Burrito King!*

*The ZIM Wiki says, the restaurant name Burrito King is an obvious parody of Burger King. Actually it is the actual name of more than one burrito shack in the Los Angeles area. Once again, the ZIM wiki is wrong. *Wrong!*

Speaking of lost episodes… The Oni comic gave me the chance to finally harpoon that white whale of a story that had been plaguing my nightmares since it was shot down all those years ago by Jimmy Neutron. I am speaking, of course, of "Pants!"

Pants!

The Pants Live! They Live!

Now free of any buzzkilling executive nay-sayers, I was able to bring "Pants" to semi-life on the page where it had once been denied life on the screen. In fact, our editor at Oni, the perpetually-awesome Robin Herrera, was excited to be bringing an actual lost episode to the page. Or at least she pretended to be excited. One of the qualities that makes a successful editor is knowing how to humor the writers.

If you're asking yourself why after all this time I still cared about this one, trivial script that the network denied, the answer is a very blunt, "I have no idea!" It's one of those uniquely human moments of completion that you wait years for without realizing it. Or maybe it's like a petty act of revenge you didn't know you wanted, like accidentally denting the the high school bully's car at the twentieth reunion, or letting your abusive alcoholic stepfather die alone in a squalid old folk's home after he hit you with a belt for eighteen straight years-- wow, that got unnecessarily dark. And now there's probably nothing I can say to convince you that that I don't have an alcoholic stepfather, and my real father is, in fact, a really nice guy.

Anyway, attached is the script for the comic book adaptation of "Pants!" Listed in the ZIM wiki as originally being titled "When Pants Ruled." That was, in fact, one of the titles that got kicked around back in the day, so in this case the ZIM wiki is not totally wrong and full of shameful lies.

A brief note here, unlike the comic scripts that most normal comic writers would churn out, this one is written in screenplay format. This was a decision on Jhonen's part early on, for the rather esoteric reason that it was easier to write screenplays than comic scripts. I agreed. And one of the early comic artists Aaron Alexovich said "Look, artists are capable of doing their own panel breakdowns. In fact, most of them would rather make the decisions themselves." So suck on *that,* Eisner Award Committee!

The script turned out largely as I would have done it if I'd gotten the chance to actually tackle the thing back in the day, and I had forgotten just how much fun it was to see Dib acting as a Fox Mulder-style paranormal investigator. I really enjoy stories where Dib is not just a doomed foil for ZIM's mad schemes, but when he actually takes the initiative and goes after that "uncovering evil" thing he actually craves doing. In that same vein, "Chickenfoot" was one of my favorite stories to write in the original series, and to this day I think the world actually could support an "Investigator Dib" spin-off series. (Though, now that I think about, I don't suggest anyone actually do it. Look, just because you *can* do a thing, doesn't mean you *should* do a thing.)

A very thinly-veiled commentary on the idiocy of fashion trends is at the front and center of this story, as is every last riff on *Invasion of the Bodysnatchers* and even *Aliens.* I even got the Donald Sutherland reference in there, which was an homage to something we used to do around the office as a joke. You'd walk into another coworker's office, point straight at them with an open mouth and give that classic Sutherland wail from the end of the 1970's *Bodysnatchers* remake. Then you'd casually walk out without a word.

The climactic dance-off between ZIM and the Ubertrouser was suggested by Jhonen for the original episode, and as much as I would have loved to see it animated, the artist Dave Crosland did a stunning job of making "Pants Pants Revolution!" light up the page. So to speak. (Dave has drawn some amazing comics in his own right, and you should absolutely check them out. Right now!)

One of my most favorite additions was being able to give a little more time to the new character named "Groyna," the jock-ish girl from a grade ahead of Dib who also somehow managed to avoid the alien pants invasion due to her strong sense that fashion is stupid. In the final as well as the original outline for the TV script, she teams up with him to break out of the Skool and find the pants queen. I was glad to be able to give Groyna just the tiniest bit more story by having her lose her best friend to the pants invasion, and suffering a breakdown when she sees the girl she once loved working at a bland Gap-like store selling the pants to the public, the brainwashing having drained away all of her individuality.

Everyone loves tragedy.

Had it actually been produced, Groyna, with her crew cut hair and gym clothes, would probably have been the first coded LGBT character on the show. And yes, I know that portraying the lesbian character as "a jock" is kind of a stereotype -- and putting "groin" in the name probably comes with its own objections -- but from a story perspective I felt like an athletic type would be a great counterpart to Dib's scrawny, brain-centric character, gay or not-gay. Of course, I never breathed a word of this to the executives. We had enough problems as it was .

It wouldn't be until years later that I noticed just how many women liked to cosplay as Dib, and how many of those women marked themselves somewhere on the Kinsey scale. (Google it.) What I'm saying is, it seems Dib has a lot more fans among LGBT women than I'd realized, and it would have been great if history had given Dib a lesbian sidekick for them to cosplay partner with at conventions. Sadly, history did not. Because history often sucks.

The comic, however, did not suck in the least. In fact, it turned out beautifully. With layouts by original series artist Aaron Alexovich and illustrations by the aforementioned Dave Crosland, it's a fantastic and fantasmagoric translation to the page, the images carrying enough motion to make me almost forget this was an animated show.

The script is attached below. It's a little longer than your average *ZIM* script of the era, but it still feels like it could have been pulled from the ranks of the TV show itself. Though you may notice a few references to "panels" here and there. (And there are more typos than normal because, well, I'm terribly at catching my own typographical errors.)

And in case you feel like actually seeing it in all its glory, it was officially "Issue 8." The individual comic issue may be hard to find, but it's still available as part of a couple of collections that I'll list when I remember to look up exactly which ones they are.* Oni press, we love you.

*I've remembered! It's in the soft cover trade collection vol 2., and the "deluxe" hard cover collection vol. 1. We can all sleep better tonight.

SCRIPT: PANTS!

Illustration: Rikki Simons

<u>**INVADER ZIM: THE COMIC**</u>
Issue #8: "PANTS!"
a.k.a. "WHEN PANTS RULED!"
a.k.a. "THE WALKING PANTS!"
a.k.a. "PANTS PANTS REVOLUTION!"
a.k.a. "BATMAN: ARKHAM PANTS!"
a.k.a. "PANTS: THE TAKEN KING!"
By Eric Trueheart
Draft of 11/25/2015

EXT. DARK AND STORMY HILLSIDE - NIGHT

It is a dark and stormy hillside, like the slug-line says.
And also night, like the slug-line says.

ZIM and GIR silhouetted against the storm clouds. ZIM
holds an IRKEN COMMUNICATOR as he looks to the sky.

                    ZIM
          It is nearly time, GIR! This
          alliance will secure my plan to
          dominate the humans utterly!

Closer on ZIM as he looks to the heavens.

                    ZIM (CONT'D)
          Until now, I have only dominated
          them semi-utterly! But tonight
          ZIM EMBRACES THE COMPLETE UTTER!
          No partially utter will--

                    ZIM (CONT'D)
          GIR! Stop building a tiny hobo
          camp on my feet!

WIDE TO SHOW - GIR sitting at a small campfire he's built
on ZIM shoes. GIR has a bindle slung over his shoulder,
and a classic hobo-hat on, while he roasts a weenie over
the fire. He also has a small HOBO made of straw sitting
on a tiny log.

                    GIR
          MmmmMMMmm! Hobo weenie!

Above him, the clouds part, a light shining through.

                    ZIM
          Silence! They have arrived!

An H.R. Gieger-inspired craft descends through the clouds,
roughly pod-shaped, but covered in the usual veins and
creepy nodules that make us love that crazy, sweaty German.
Two "appendages" act as thrusters as the craft descends.

ZIM COMIC ISSUE 8: PANTS   2.

PANEL: The craft touches down.

PANEL: A door cracks open.

                    ZIM (CONT'D)
              It's about time. Can't take much
              more weenie smell.

PANEL: Wider to see the light streaming from the open hatch,
and the shadow of what looks like an alien's legs.

                    ZIM (CONT'D)
              Yes!

A LARGE PANEL TAKING UP MOST OF THE PAGE. (OR A WHOLE PAGE
IF SPACE ALLOWS.) We see the whole scene now. The hatch on
the alien ship has opened and standing before ZIM is not a
whole alien... but just a pair of ALIEN PANTS! (Alien pants,
looking all H.R. Giegerish, veiny, dripping slime, but
unmistakably pants, you know, with a fly and pockets.)

                    ZIM (CONT'D)
              Yesssssssssssssssssbwahahahaha!

                    GIR
              Heylook! Pants!

EXT. CITY STREET - DAY

Wide "Long shot" of the streets of the town. Dib rides "The
Dibmobile" through the sidewalks. (For the record, the
"Dibmobile" is a really dopey-looking Segway-type device.)

                    DIB'S TEXT BOX
              Paranormal Investigator's Log:
              Agent Mothman reporting.

                    DIB'S TEXT BOX (CONT'D)
              After leaving a family vacation
              early, I am piloting the Dibmobile
              back to town.

                    DIB'S TEXT BOX (CONT'D)
              This is entirely because I need to
              file an urgent report on an amazing
              new discovery: Vampires are the
              mortal enemies of Cowboys!

CLOSER: We now see Dib in his full glory on the Dibmobile,
riding on a sidewalk through a town street. The street is a
bit odd, though. A bit menacing. The citizens all wear
strange, veiny, black alien pants, much like the alien ZIM
encountered earlier, and they have blank expressions on their
faces. Also, every billboard somehow advertises these pants.

ZIM COMIC ISSUE 8: PANTS   2.

PANEL: The craft touches down.

PANEL: A door cracks open.

                    ZIM (CONT'D)
          It's about time. Can't take much
          more weenie smell.

PANEL: Wider to see the light streaming from the open hatch,
and the shadow of what looks like an alien's legs.

                    ZIM (CONT'D)
          Yes!

A LARGE PANEL TAKING UP MOST OF THE PAGE. (OR A WHOLE PAGE
IF SPACE ALLOWS.) We see the whole scene now. The hatch on
the alien ship has opened and standing before ZIM is not a
whole alien... but just a pair of ALIEN PANTS! (Alien pants,
looking all H.R. Giegerish, veiny, dripping slime, but
unmistakably pants, you know, with a fly and pockets.)

                    ZIM (CONT'D)
          Yesssssssssssssssssbwahahahaha!

                    GIR
          Heylook! Pants!

EXT. CITY STREET - DAY

Wide "Long shot" of the streets of the town. Dib rides "The
Dibmobile" through the sidewalks. (For the record, the
"Dibmobile" is a really dopey-looking Segway-type device.)

                    DIB'S TEXT BOX
          Paranormal Investigator's Log:
          Agent Mothman reporting.

                    DIB'S TEXT BOX (CONT'D)
          After leaving a family vacation
          early, I am piloting the Dibmobile
          back to town.

                    DIB'S TEXT BOX (CONT'D)
          This is entirely because I need to
          file an urgent report on an amazing
          new discovery: Vampires are the
          mortal enemies of Cowboys!

CLOSER: We now see Dib in his full glory on the Dibmobile,
riding on a sidewalk through a town street. The street is a
bit odd, though. A bit menacing. The citizens all wear
strange, veiny, black alien pants, much like the alien ZIM
encountered earlier, and they have blank expressions on their
faces. Also, every billboard somehow advertises these pants.

Eric Trueheart

ZIM COMIC ISSUE 8: PANTS   4.

                    DIB'S TEXT BOX (CONT'D)
          They could be surrounded by a mob
          of zombies weasels and not notice.

He looks up to see a threatening crowd has gathered.

                    DIB
          Huh? What do you people want?

                    ZOMBIE STUDENT 1
          Paaaants!

                    DIB
          "Plants?"

                    ZOMBIE STUDENT 2
          PANTS!

                    DIB
          "Bants?" Do you mean the
          cryptozoological South American
          Badger-Ants who eat whole villages
          with their badgmadibles?

                    ALL ZOMBIE STUDENTS
          PAAAAAAAAANTS!

Now we see the whole hallway is filled with glass-eyed
students, all staring at Dib. All wearing the alien pants.

                    ZOMBIE STUDENT 1
          You're not wearing the pants, Dib!

                    ZOMBIE STUDENT 2
          Your legs look stupid, Dib!

                    ZOMBIE STUDENT 3
          Stupid, stupid Legs!

                    ZOMBIE STUDENT 4
          You aren't cool without the pants,
          DIB!

                    ALL ZOMBIE STUDENTS
          WEAR THE PANTS!!

Dib gets nervous. He's slowly backing up.

                    DIB
          Um... Sure! I'll wear the pants.
          I have a pair at home. I'll go get
          them! Right now!

ZIM COMIC ISSUE 8: PANTS   5.

He backs into a student coming at him from the other
direction, holing up a pair of pants. (If this were
animation, the pants would be twitching and making gurgling
noises. But it's not. So... There you go.)

                    ZOMBIE STUDENT 5
          YOUR LEGS LOOK STUPID, DIB!

                    DIB
          SHUTUPMYLEGSARECOOLAAAAIIIIIEGH!

NEXT PANEL, Dib is running down the hall, the student has the
pants wrapped around his face. The other pants zombies chase
him, their pants all making "SQUISH! SQUISH! SQUISH!" noises.

                    ZOMBIE STUDENT 1
          Wear the pants!

                    ZOMBIE STUDENT 2
          You are nothing and nobody without
          them!

Dib turns a corner. More Pants kids follow him.

                    ZOMBIE STUDENT 3
          YOUR LEGS LOOK STUPID!!

Dib opens a door to a classroom to find a teacher who looks
an awful lot like Donald Sutherland from Invasion of the Body
Snatchers, but in alien pants. The teacher points at him
with his pants-leg. (That is, foot.)

                    PANTS ZOMBIE TEACHER
          PAAAAAAAAAAAAAAANTS!!

INT. BROOM CLOSET - DAY

SLAM! Dib slams the door on a closet filled with brooms.

                    DIB'S TEXT BOX
          Agent Mothman's Log: It seems the
          entire population has been taken
          over by some kind of mind-altering
          bio-pants. It's made them crazy.
          And fashion-conscious. Which is
          kind of the same thing.

                    DIBS TEXT BOX
          So I've hidden in the broom closet
          while I formulate a plan.

Behind him: KLIK! The little vent at the base of the door
opens, and someone tosses in a PANTS EGG. (Yes, a Pants Egg.

ZIM COMIC ISSUE 8: PANTS   6.

Appropriately Giegerish. Maybe closed with a zipper, if
that's not too damn goofy.)

                    DIB'S TEXT BOX
          Who knows how far the pants have
          spread. Maybe just the town.
          Maybe--

                    DIB
          Man, this Skool has a lot of
          brooms.

Dib looks around the closet, somehow failing to notice the
PANTS EGG opening behind him.

                    DIB (CONT'D)
          But I never see anyone sweeping
          anything.

A pair of alien pants extracts itself.

                    DIB (CONT'D)
          Just what are they hiding?

The pants jump him.

                    DIB (CONT'D)
          GARRGH!

SMALL PANEL (or however you wanna to portray this fight): The
pants attack Dib.

SMALL PANEL: Dib kicks them off him.

SMALL PANEL: Dib swings at the pants with a broom.

SMALL PANEL: The pants swing at Dib with a broom.

SMALL PANEL: A random Dib-fights-pants scene, perhaps
inspired by old-school wrestling.

SMALL PANEL: The pants wrap themselves around Dib's head.

                    DIB (CONT'D)
          Mffff! Mffff!

PANEL: THUNK! Dib's head hits the floor as the pants now
crawl on his legs.

EXT. FIELD - DIB'S HALLUCINATION - DAY

Dib's hallucination: Dib frolics in a field where pants grow
on the tops of flower stems like daisies. He's wearing the
alien pants. In the sky, pairs of pants fly like birds.

ZIM COMIC ISSUE 8: PANTS   7.

                    DIB
          Beautiful! My legs are beautiful!

He comes face-to-face with a JOCK GIRL WITH A MULLET. (This
is GROYNA, whom we will get to in a moment.) She SHOCKS HIM
with a home-made cattle prod.

                    DIB (CONT'D)
          IEEEEGH!

INT. SKOOL AIR DUCTS - DAY

Dib comes to inside a classic metal air duct. He's being
dragged by GROYNA, a butch-looking girl wearing gym pants and
sporting a side-shaved-style haircut. She has a Ghostbusters-
like backpack on with a cattle prod on it. A shock-pack.

                    DIB
          Where am I?

                    GROYNA
          Shh! We don't want to attract the
          pants! And I have to fit your
          giant head through grate.

INT. SKOOL LAUNDRY ROOM - DAY

Skool laundry room. A big room full of angry washing
machines and driers. The kind that children only dream of in
their laundry-soaked dreams. Dib's head SQUEEZES through the
air duct grating at the top of the wall. He's being pushed
from the other side by Groyna.

                    GROYNA
          How do you do stuff with a head so
          big? It's like a turkey!

                    DIB
          NRRRGH!! NRRRGH!!

POP! They land on the ground.

                    DIB (CONT'D)
          Who are you? Where are we? And
          why does everyone say my head is
          big? It's barely above average!

                    GROYNA
          First, my name is Groyna. I'm a
          year ahead of you and captain of
          the girls Vooleyball team.

                    DIB
          "Vooleyball?"

ZIM COMIC ISSUE 8: PANTS   8.

                    GROYNA
          Second, we're in the skool laundry
          room. The pants avoid it. Laundry
          scares them like it scares all
          aliens.

                    DIB
          Laundry doesn't really scare--

                    GROYNA
          SHHHH! Third, your head is
          enormous. Stop lying to yourself.
          IT'S THE ONLY WAY WE'LL SURVIVE!

                    DIB
          OK, OK! The last thing I remember
          I was attacked by pants. I can't
          believe I'd ever say those words.
          But here I am saying them.

Dib starts to freak out.

                    DIB (CONT'D)
          "MY NAME IS DIB AND I WAS ATTACKED
          BY PANTS!"

                    GROYNA
          Calm down. It's a lot to take in.
          I killed the pants you were wearing
          with this SHOCKPACK I made.

She points to the cattle-prod backpack she has.

                    GROYNA (CONT'D)
          You're free now. Free to wear
          whatever you want on your legs.

She hangs Dib's dead pants on a rack with a few other dead
pants.

                    DIB
          What happened around here?

                    GROYNA
          I'll tell you...

EXT. TOWN STREET - FLAHSBACK

TEXT BOX: "FLASHBACK!"

People on the streets with glassy-eyes wearing alien pants.

```
               ZIM COMIC ISSUE 8: PANTS                9.


                         GROYNA TEXT BOX
                Everything was fine until a few
                days ago everyone started wearing
                alien pants!

                                            RETURN TO:

        INT. SKOOL LAUNDRY ROOM - CONTINUOUS

        TEXT BOX: "END FLASHBACK!"

        Dib stares at Groyna for a panel.

                         DIB
                I kind of figured that part out.

                         GROYNA
                Oh.  Then here's more!

        EXT. TOWN STREET - FLASHBACK

        Again, people on the streets in alien pants.

                         GROYNA TEXT BOX
                Nobody knows who Pants-Victim Zero
                was, but soon the streets were
                packed with PANTS ZOMBIES!

        A panel with a lone man NOT wearing the pants being chased by
        pants-wearers.

                         PANTS ZOMBIES
                YOUR LEGS LOOK STUPID!

                         GROYNA TEXT BOX
                They said the pants were cool.  If
                you didn't wear them, you were "not
                cool."

                         DIB'S TEXT BOX
                So?  Lots of people aren't "cool."
                Most "cool" people are horrible.

                         GROYNA
                Then they held you down and forced
                you to be cool!  With the pants!

        The mob holds down a non-pantser.  He SCREAMS.

                                            RETURN TO:

        INT. SKOOL LAUNDRY ROOM - CONTINUOUS

        Groyna weeps.
```

Eric Trueheart

                    GROYNA
          IT WAS HORRIBLE! They even took my
          bestest friend SHEATHER. She would
          never have worn pants! But now...
          I can't even think about what she
          must be wearing now!

THOUGHT BUBBLE of another jock girl like Groyna. Happy.
Smiling.

Dib starts to exit.

                    DIB
          Um... Hey, thanks for saving me,
          but crying makes me uncomfortable.
          So I'm just gonna get out of here
          and figure out a way to stop the
          alien pants menace.

Groyna steps up.

                    GROYNA
          Let's go together! You and me are
          the only ones left in town
          unaffected by the pants! We could
          be pants hunters together!

NEW PAGE: A big splash page that looks like a comic book
cover. The title reads "PANTSHUNTERS: DIB & GROYNA!" A
badass action pose of Dib and Groyna with their shock-packs
taking down alien pants on the flaming streets.

And I'm deliberately putting a little extra space in the
script here just to impress on us that this gag will take a
whole page.

Yep. A whole page.

Kind of a lot for one gag, but it's worth it.

Wait a bit...

And...

Okay!

NEXT PAGE: We're abruptly back in the laundry room.

                    DIB
          Um... No thanks.

ZIM COMIC ISSUE 8: PANTS   11.

                    DIB (CONT'D)
          Also, there are thousands of pants
          out there and just two of us. We'd
          be overpantsed in minutes!

He notices the dead pants hanging on the rack.

                    GROYNA
          Unless... We wear the dead pants as
          a disguise!

He holds a pair of dead pants under his nose.

                    GROYNA (CONT'D)
          That is <u>real</u> disgusting.

EXT. TOWN STREETS - DAY

Dib and Groyna walk through the streets, wearing dead alien
pants. "SQISH! SQISH! SQISH!" (Only Groyna has a shock
pack.) Everyone on the streets walk around with alien pants
and vacant expressions. And there's a LOT of them.

                    GROYNA
          Actually, even with this disguise,
          we could never take them all down.
          There's so many of them!

                    DIB
          Yeah, it's kind of obvious how
          stupid that plan was. This isn't
          the movies, Groyna, one or two
          people can't take down an alien
          invasion on their own. PSHH.

Dib looks across the street where a PANTS! STORE looms. (It's
a store that simply emblazons the word "PANTS!" on a sign
over the door.)

                    DIB (CONT'D)
          WAIT!

                    GROYNA
          What?

                    DIB
          That must be the source of the
          pants! WE CAN TAKE THEM DOWN ON
          OUR OWN!

Eric Trueheart

ZIM COMIC ISSUE 8: PANTS   12.

INT. PANTS STORE - DAY

The interior of the pants store looks like any other mall
clothing store, except with racks of the veiny, throbbing
pants as the only product.

                    DIB
          The pants must originate from here.
          You distract the woman behind the
          counter and I'll look for some kind
          of pants-hive.

A voice comes from the front counter.

                    PANTS CASHIER
          May I help you?

                    GROYNA
               (to the counter girl)
          Yes, I'm looking for some pants
          or... SHEATHER?

Show Groyna's friend SHEATHER behind the counter.

                    PANTS CASHIER (SHEATHER)
          I'm sorry, my name is "Pants".

                    GROYNA
          Sheather! It's me, Groyna! You
          must remember!

                    DIB
          Um... Groyna? Probably a bad idea!

                    PANTS CASHIER (SHEATHER)
          My name is Pants. Your name is
          Pants. We are all Pants.

                    GROYNA
          No! Your name is Sheather! Let's
          get those pants off of you!

Groyna pulls out her pants-shocker. SHEATHER SCREAMS!

                    PANTS CASHIER (SHEATHER)
               <IEEEEEEEEE>

A group of pants-zombies rush in.

                    DIB
          Groyna! No!

Groyna mobbed by pants zombies.

248

ZIM COMIC ISSUE 8: PANTS   13.

                    GROYNA
          Come with me, Sheather! I won't
          leave you! Mfff!

Dib steps back as she's mobbed.

                    DIB
          I'm... um... going to go downstairs
          now and look for the pants hive.
          I'd help but...

He opens a basement door.

                    DIB (CONT'D)
          Basement door right here. So...
          Yeah.

                    GROYNA (OFF-PANEL)
          Nrrghh! Arrgh! I will never give
          in!

INT. PANTS BASEMENT - DAY

Dib steps down the basement stairs with a flashlight. CLIK!

                    DIB'S TEXT BOX
          MOTHMAN'S LOG: Deprived of my
          sidekick, I stepped into the
          basement I knew not what I would
          find. But I expected to find...
          PANTS!

Dib looks around at a basement filled with PANTS EGGS. Much
like the egg chamber scene from ALIENS. (Obviously.)

                    DIB TEXT BOX
          Pants eggs! Thousands of them!
          Ready to hatch their trouseryoung
          and expand all over the globe! I
          assume.

Dib steps in closer inside the chamber.

                    DIB'S TEXT BOX
          But who laid them?

We see behind him where a large PANTS QUEEN descends its legs
from the ceiling. A pair of pants about ten feet tall.

Dib sees it and his eyes go wide.

                    DIB
          The pants queen...

It lays eggs with one of its legs.

                    DIB (CONT'D)
          ...is really gross! I should
          gotten that shock-pack from Groyna
          before--

The queen attaches the other leg to Dib's head.

                    DIB (CONT'D)
          GRK!

Suddenly there's a voice in his head -- probably portrayed by
an ethereal text box. (Though for consistent dialogue
purposes, I won't put the "TEXT BOX" in the descriptions
unless it's a "voice over.") It's the PANTS QUEEN talking,
whom we shall henceforth refer to as THE UBERTROUSER.

                    UBERTROUSER
          You are a brave human, big-headed
          one.

                    DIB
          You're communicating with me
          telepathically?

                    UBERTROUSER
          Indeed. It is the talent of the
          Ubertrouser. That is what your
          primitive brain would call me.

                    DIB
          Why aren't you trying to take me
          over?

                    UBERTROUSER
          I have never seen a human with such
          a big head. I assume you are the
          leader of Earth?

                    DIB
          Seriously, what is UP with people
          saying--! I mean... Yes, I'm
          leader of Earth.

                    UBERTROUSER
          Then as leader, it is a courtesy to
          show you who has taken over your
          planet. Open your giant head to my
          psychic visions!

Dib's eyes go wide.

PSYCHIC VISIONS!

```
                    ZIM COMIC ISSUE 8: PANTS              15.


      - The vast panoply of space.  A single planet hovers in the
      void.

                              UBERTROUSER TEXT BOX
                         The name of my kind is
                         inconceivable by your language.

                              DIB TEXT BOX
                         How about "Space Pants?"

                              UBERTROUSER TEXT BOX
                         Oh wait, no, you got it. We are
                         "THE SPACE PANTS!"

      - A strange alien jungle landscape marked by pairs of legs
      running wild.  A few run with ALIEN CAVEMEN inside them.

                              UBERTROUSER TEXT BOX (CONT'D)
                         We evolved on the planet SLKSSKZ,
                         where we lived in symbiosis with
                         the local creatures.

      - Now a modern, burned-out landscape where the pants are on
      evolved alien hominids, shooting each other with weapons.

                              UBERTROUSER TEXT BOX (CONT'D)
                         But we burdened our land to
                         extinction, and wars decimated the
                         planet.

      - A space scene: The trouser ship launches into space.

                              UBERTROUSER TEXT BOX (CONT'D)
                         Now we are a space-faring race.
                         Landing on planets.  Sharing our
                         pants-selves with local creatures.

                              DIB
                         You mean taking them over!

                              UBERTROUSER TEXT BOX
                         Their legs look stupid.

      - Earth hillside at night: The ship lands by ZIM on the
      hillside.

                              UBERTROUSER TEXT BOX (CONT'D)
                         And then we received a transmission
                         from the Irken ZIM.  He promised he
                         would share this world with us if
                         we worked with him.

                              DIB TEXT BOX
                         Wait-- ZIM?  THE ZIM?!
```

BACK IN THE BASEMENT:

                         DIB
             ZIM is a liar! He'll betray you!
             Let me show you! Bond with my head
             again.

PSYCHIC ZIM-IS-A-JERK MONTAGE: IMAGES OF ZIM coming out of
DIB'S HEAD. ZIM laughing at a burning earth. ZIM riding a
moose. ZIM with a rollerskate sideways in his mouth. Stupid
stuff.

                         DIB (CONT'D)
             Whatever ZIM promised you, he lied!
             And he's also an idiot!

BACK TO THE BASEMENT:

                         DIB (CONT'D)
             Ubertrouser, join forces with me!
             We can stop ZIM from taking over
             this planet!

"Shot" of the Ubertrouser looking majestic.

                         UBERTROUSER
             One with a head so big must be just
             as wise! HUMAN, GET IN ME!

                         DIB
             It's weird you think that
             considering your people have no
             heads.

                         UBERTROUSER
             -snif-

                         DIB
             Aw, geez. Are you crying?

EXT. HILLSIDE - DAY

On a hillside, ZIM works attaching an Irken device to the
giant array with some kind of Irken tool. GIR is at his
side, arm around his straw hobo.

                         ZIM
             I must hurry, GIR! My secret Pants-
             Jammer must be complete by the time
             the pants take over every human on
             Earth! Then I can use it to
             destroy the nervous system of every
             Pants on Earth!

```
              ZIM COMIC ISSUE 8: PANTS                17.


                         GIR
               Hobo says believe in yourself!

                         ZIM
               Actually, they won't do that for a
               while.  So I'm TOTALLY ahead!  I AM
               AMAZING!

     Dib's voice comes from off-panel.

                         DIB
               ZIM!

                         ZIM
               Heh?

     REVEAL: Dib rides in the Ubertrouser as they confront ZIM.

                         DIB
               Your lies have been exposed, ZIM!
               And the Ubertrouser and I have
               joined forces to DEFEAT YOU!

     ZIM LAUGHS!

                         ZIM
               Ha ha ha, human!  This is me
               laughing!  HA HA HA!  Did you not
               think I planned for every
               possibility?

     ZIM falls on the ground, his legs in the air.

                         ZIM (CONT'D)
               Anti-Pants Battle-Legs: DEPLOY!

     INSERT PANEL: A hatch in ZIM base opens and a pod is launched
     from inside.

     The flying pod rockets in over the horizon, and a pair of
     LARGE CYBERNETIC COMBAT LEGS unfold from it.

     They land on ZIM's legs.  PAP!

     ZIM vaults up into the air and lands on his battle legs.
     Weird weapon-energy pods protrude from them.

                         ZIM (CONT'D)
               The britches-battle begins!

                         DIB
               I have no idea what's going on.
```

Eric Trueheart

ZIM COMIC ISSUE 8: PANTS   18.

                    UBERTROUSER
          We battle using the ancient method
          of my people. I generate bursts of
          psychic energy made real via
          ancient pants-based martial-arts.

                    DIB
          Really?

                    UBERTROUSER
          ZIM, ONLY ONE WILL SURVIVE THE...

TEXT: "**PANTS PANTS REVOLUTION!**"

The two foes square off: ZIM in his battle-pants, Dib in his
Ubertrouser. (I haven't dropped SFX into this battle, but
feel free to put them in as the spirit moves you.)

SMALL PANEL - ZIM does an elaborate Dance move. Energy
builds up around him.

SMALL PANEL - An energy ball is released from his pants as he
finishes the move.

SMALL PANEL - Dib/Ubertrouser are struck by the bolt.
NRRRGH! But they're not down.

SMALL PANEL - The Ubertrouser does an elaborate dance move.

SMALL PANEL - The Ubertrouers releases an energy bolt at ZIM.

SMALL PANEL - ZIM is hit! OOOF!

LARGER PANEL - The two engage in pants dance moves, bolts
unleashing from their legs.

                    ZIM
          Take THIS!

                    DIB
          Oh yeah? Take THIS!

PANELS CONTINUE.

ZIM is hit by a bolt!

                    ZIM
          My battlepants! Overheating!

Dib/Ubertrouser gear up for the finishing move.

                    DIB
          And now, our finishing move!
          HOIYAA!

ZIM COMIC ISSUE 8: PANTS   19.

They release a massive outburst of energy bolts at ZIM.

ZIM lies on the ground, his PANTS IN RUINS. Dib stands triumphant.

                    DIB (CONT'D)
          We win, ZIM!

                    UBERTROUSER
          Thank you, Earth leader! Now I can
          envelop the legs of all of your
          citizens in my children!

                    DIB
          Wait. What?

                    UBERTROUSER
          Without ZIM, we are free to take
          over all the humans on your planet,
          as is our destiny!

                    DIB
          Um... You never said that part.

                    UBERTROUSER
          And after a year, we eat the legs!

                    DIB
          Hey! Not cool!

                    UBERTROUSER
          This planet is ours! KNEEL BEFORE
          THE UBERTROUSER!

                    DIB
          Never! For a start, I'm inside
          you!

SFX: FZZZZP!

ZIM's giant antenna sends out an ENERGY BURST.

We see ZIM down at the base of it, pressing the ACTIVATE BUTTON. The Ubertrouser writhes in agony.

                    UBERTROUSER
          Noooooo! My trouserkin!

PANELS OF THE PANTS DYING ALL OVER THE CITY.

- STREET - Pants fizzle. People come back to their senses.

- SKOOL - The pants die, while kids look around, confused.

```
                    ZIM COMIC ISSUE 8: PANTS              20.


    - PANTS STORE - Groyna and Sheather hug each other, happy!
                         GROYNA
             WHEEEEP!

    EXT. HILLSIDE - CONTINUOUS

    The Ubertrouser is a dead mess on the ground.  Dib still
    wears it.
                         DIB
             Gross.

    ZIM and Dib look at each other, awkwardly.
                         ZIM
             Oh.  Guess I accidentally saved
             every human on earth.

                         DIB
             Huh.  I guess you did.

                         ZIM
             I was kinda gonna wait until they'd
             eaten everyone's legs, but... Yeah.

    Dib's out of the pants now.  They exit, still awkward.
                         DIB
             So, uh... See you tomorrow?

                         ZIM
             Probably. Death to the humans,
             though.

    EXT. TOWN STREET - DAY

    Dib walks back through town, passing confused and shell-
    shocked people in dead pants.  Dib stops and points at one.
                         DIB
             YOUR legs look stupid!  HA!

                         BYSTANDER (SMALL)
             What?

    Dib walks into the sunset, but the guy just looks confused.
                         DIB TEXT BOX
             That's telling him.  Agent
             Mothman's log... Out.

    END.
```

STRAY TROUSERVATIONS

- Observant fans will spot that "Your Legs Look Stupid!" is a line from "Bad, Bad Rubber Piggy." I am now cannibalizing myself. It's a sign I should change careers, maybe to something like applied data analysis or toilet cleaning.

- The script definitely has more dialogue than would have been in the cartoon. The comic format lets you expand the dialogue, and sometimes you need it because you can't rely on moving action to convey the story. Other times you just don't have to cut it down to 11 pages, so you let yourself go a little. You can decide which time this is.

- The alien pants ship in the opening sequence looks either "H.R. Gigeresque" or "vaguely gynecological," depending on your point of view. If your point of view is the latter, please keep it to yourself.

- Dib's Investigator Diary is a device that I could only use in the comics, at least with that much verbiage. But I think it really works for setting a tone. Maybe the *Investigator Dib* series isn't that crazy after all.*

*No, it really is crazy.

- Aaron Alexovich did an amazing job with the layout of this issue, and I realize now there was just a massive volume of stuff to get across. Showing the entire evolutionary history of the alien pants in just one page is a feat in itself. Maybe I should have spread this one over two issues.

- Can I count the number of references to the movie *Aliens*? No, I can't.

- "Sheather" is supposed to sound like "Heather," but I realize now it could read like someone who sheathes a lot of things. Just so there's no confusion, for the record, Heather does not sheath things more than the average amount most people sheath things.

- I love the design of Groyna, though I have no idea if the "8" on her shirt is significant. I like to think it's infinity turned on its side, symbolizing the eternal made material, but on a shirt. Or something.

- The "Space Pants" gag was all Jhonen's, and it makes me laugh every time.

- I liked having Dib psychically show the Ubertrouser an image of ZIM with a roller skate sideways in his mouth, though I have no idea if it reads on paper. At least it's funny tho me, and that's all that matters. All. That. Matters.

- The ending "See you tomorrow" moment between ZIM and Dib speaks to just how long they've been at this rivalry. They can both recognize when a plan has exploded, and that they're both just going to walk away and sleep it off. It makes me wonder if they'd ever reach the "Morning, Sam"/"Morning, Ralph" level of the old Looney Toons shorts about the wolf and the sheep dog. (Google it.)

FAVORITE OBSERVATION
FROM THE ZIM WIKI

- "It's revealed that crying makes Dib uncomfortable."

WILL He eVeR ZIM aGaIN?

Look to the Future, Worm-Babies!

At the time of writing, the world is now post-*Florpus*.

The *Invader ZIM* TV movie *Invader ZIM: Enter the Florpus* dropped on Netflix on August 16th, 2019. It was dropped from a great height, and caused a lot of damage to the facilities, smashing through several offices on its way from the roof to the ground floor, killing one very nice lady in human resources, and a couple of business affairs executives that nobody will miss.

All of this is not true except the fact that yes, *Enter the Florpus* was released on August 16th, 2019, and received great critical response. As of writing, it's Rotten Tomatoes rating is still 100%. Suck on *that* tomato, *Avengers: Endgame!*

The long and tortuous road the movie took from conception to production is a topic for another book entirely. Let's just say there was a lot of gnashing of teeth getting that movie across the finish line after some considerable headaches involving the Korean animation studio. More than a few unsung heroes put in long, long hours to turn it into the glorious demented triumph you saw on your screen. (Including — but not limited to — Art Director Jenny Goldberg, compositing wizard Ami Goff, and some poor bastard named Jhonen Vasquez.)

For myself, I was only the tiniest bit involved in the script. Jhonen asked my advice on how to cut a few pages in a later draft, and I helped on some story consulting during the edit phase, but the screenplay for the wonderfully demented beast you saw on the screen is all Jhonen's doing.

The movie's positive reception begs the question of whether or not either Nickelodeon or Netflix will some day revive the show. Now that 90s nostalgia is fading away in favor of 2000's nostalgia, you'd think the idea has been whispered in the hallways more than once. Over the years, the potential of a new series has come up more than once. Somewhere in the early 2010s, Nicktoons proposed making a new series, but their budgets were so low, it would have had to be a far more claustrophobic version of the original. I don't know if the series could have thrived on nothing but "ZIM Eats Waffles" style bottle episodes. America just can't take that much wafflage.

But in a world where *Florpus* won the hearts and minds of children everywhere, is there a chance? Fans to this day keep a light burning in their squeedlyspooch.

Well, after the special aired, apparently neither Netflix nor Nickelodeon reached out to call Jhonen and congratulate him on a job well done. At least that's what he told me. The silence wasn't deafening, but it was powerful enough to deaden your sense of smell. That's another of my goddamn metaphors.

The point is, it doesn't seem like the halls of either establishment is now buzzing with *ZIM*. The way this business works, projects get championed by individual executives, and apparently the regime who was keen on the idea of a new *ZIM* series was swept away in one of the periodic purges that television networks are so famous for. So there's nothing to make us think think there's a new series in the works at this little moment in history.

Lucile Bliss sadly passed away many years ago, leaving the world without a Miss Bitters. Meanwhile, Andy Berman is working full-time as a big-league TV writer and producer on shows like *Psych* and *Rosewood*, so getting him to come in for regular recording sessions would be a challenge in itself.

Where does this leave fans?

Enter the Florpus left the world of *ZIM* in an ambiguous place. On the one hand, it could be the launching point of a new series with a new status quo. After the madness that swept planet Earth, Dib may have finally convinced his father -- and possibly the world -- the aliens exist. Likewise, for the first time in his career, ZIM is without the Almighty Tallest. This could be the starting point for something pretty interesting. How does Dib still get perpetually frustrated in a world where everyone now believes in aliens? How does ZIM see his mission now that he's alone? Would he start an empire all to himself? These shifts could either be tectonic, or they could be brushed off with one of television's reset buttons.

Or, like *Star Trek* before it, *Florpus* could be the first of a series of *Invader ZIM* movies, though probably not ones that would be shown in theaters or directed by J.J. Abrams.

On the other hand, *Florpus* could also stand as a capstone for the entire series, wrapping up questions that had been hanging over our characters since the beginning. The Membrane family is finally one notch less dysfunctional, and ZIM has finally learned the truth about just how not-important Earth was in Operation Impending Doom. Like *Firefly* gave its fans a final bow with *Serenity*, the Florpus could on some level fill that *ZIM*-shaped hole that was left in fandom's soul when it was ripped off the air.

In this way, *ZIM's* Television Interruptus becomes Television Completus, and can finally roll over and smoke a cigarette. *Invader ZIM* stops being the show that never got a break, and becomes a strange chapter in the history of animation, a show now easier to digest and then move on from since it has an obvious endpoint. Will this change the fandom forever?

Who knows what the future will bring?

Actually, I know way to answer that.

There's a homeless guy named Gerald who hangs out by the Greyhound station in Vernon, CA. He wears a dirty cardigan sweater over a second-hand clown suit. On his head he sports a fur winter ear-flap hat covered in tin foil and the peeled labels from plastic bottles of Japanese energy drinks. He's often heard muttering lyrics to old Snoop Dogg songs under his breath. Apparently he knows exactly what the future will bring. He predicted the rise of bitcoin. He predicted that Kanye West would go crazy, and that Donald Trump would develop incontinence and tell no one, but the Oval Office would smell of wee for decades to come.

But Gerald isn't telling anyone about the future of *Invader ZIM*.

For myself, I just consider myself lucky that in a business that has an unfortunate habit of suppressing originality, I was part of something genuinely strange. I was one of a group of humans who worked stupidly long hours to make a cartoon whose mere existence is baffling to this day. I got to write some of the weirdest bits ever to make it into a cartoon: a chase on a flying pig, a guy in a chicken restaurant locked in an endless argument about whether or not he has his slaw, a character named "Maurice the Puppy Man" for almost no reason, an anti-Santa battle-mech, a giant slow explosion getting loose because of a dog with meat, time traveling rubber piggies, a kid named Nick with a happy probe in his brain, candy made entirely of sawdust, "Chickenfoot, you're not a freak, you're just stupid!"

It's not bad, is it?

I could die in peace.

I could.

If not for that bargain I made with that strange blue-skinned traveler who was walking backwards in time. Now I can never die. I will outlive the earth itself. I will outlive you all!

And when the sun has gone out, and I'm floating in the cold vacuum of space, I'll look back at the darkness — with eyes that can see a thousand light years — and wonder whether that guy really had his slaw or not.

Fans Q&a

The Best Things in Life Are Tweets.

I thought it might be fun to do a little "Q&A" at the end of this book. Looking back, that was a foolish idea and I should have known better.

Still, I put the call for questions out on Twitter, and true to my word, I'm answering a small selection of them. Many others I am ignoring because they were too stupid, too vague, too pointless, or just obvious cries for attention.

I'm also hiding their twitter handles to protect the innocent. Never let it be said I have no compassion.

@1*****: Was there a planned ending? If so what was it?**

ME: There was no planned ending. Except getting rich and retiring on the residuals*.

*This is a joke. There are no writer residuals in animation. Which is in itself a joke.

But there is a persistent rumor about a series finale called "Invader Dib," which would feature Dib going to the Irken home world to try to stop Operation Impending Doom forever.

Sorry, kids, this rumor is not true. There were never any plans for "Invader Dib."

I'm going to say it again, because I'm sure it won't sink in it unless it's said many many times, and only way to stomp this irritating rumor into the ground is with persistence.

So let me reiterate: *There were never any plans for "Invader Dib." Ever! Stop talking about it before you embarrass yourself even more. Your friends are rolling their eyes behind your back. There was no "Invader Dib" finale!*

The truth is, "Invader Dib" was just a dumb in-joke about colons. The punctuation mark, that is, not the disgusting bodily organ.

Some background: The title for *Invader ZIM* was originally meant to have a colon in it, thus making it *Invader: ZIM*. Somewhere along the line, Nickelodeon wisely decided to cut it, but we never forgot. When someone suggested that if the series was popular, there would inevitably be a *ZIM* movie released in theaters, we threw out the idea of Dib going to Irk only — I repeat, *only* — so we could see just how many colons we could cram into a movie title. The resulting non-existent film would be called Invader: *ZIM: The Movie: Invader: Dib.*

It's way funnier when you read it out loud say the word "colon" at every colon. Try it now.

But that was as far as "Invader Dib" ever got: a throwaway colon joke we made up to keep ourselves amused. Now when you lie in bed at night and dream of the ending that never was, dream only of colons.

@S*****: Do you develop your stories differently based on whether they are animated or in the comics?**

ME: On the one hand, they're shockingly similar. The amount of story contained in al 11-minute episode is *about* the same as the length of a single issue of a comic book.

On the other hand, I clearly put more dialogue into the comic scripts than I would into a short for TV. The written word has to carry a bit more information on the page than it does when you've got animated characters communicating the narrative.

Also, I get to be more experimental with the comics, since every issue doesn't have to fit into the mold of what a network expects from a cartoon. I probably never would have gotten away with a two-episode cartoon about Poop wizards.

The downside is I don't get to make Richard Horvitz scream in a comic book.

That's right, "In a comic, nobody can hear Richard Horvitz scream."

@A**********: How much of your writing had to be scrapped due to censorship?

ME: All of it. Nothing any of us wrote ever made it to the screen. Weird, right? The so-called "show" was improvised in the booth and put together randomly by cutting out old Jack Kirby comics and drawing ZIM's face over them.

Um…. The real answer is not all that much, really. Just bits and pieces here and there. Usually if someone was going to be nixed, it was nixed early before anyone put too much work into it.

But when it did happen, it usually seemed really arbitrary to us at the time. For example, they hated people dying, even though they were cartoon characters, and kids knew no actual person was getting hurt. This is why, there's a disclaimer at the end of "Hamstergeddon" that no cartoon characters were hurt, and why Iggins bursts from the wrecked elevator at the end of "Game Slave," alive and kicking.

Is this attitude over-protective? Well, that's a matter for child psychologists, and everyone on the internet who has a keyboard and an opinion. However, I once had a chat with an animation executive who once asked her seven-year old son if he got upset at the way Elmer Fudd shot at Bugs Bunny. "Um… No," he replied. When asked why not, he simply said, "Uhhh… Because they're not real?"

@B*******i: How much ended up getting cut from an average episode? Not as far as censor stuff goes, though I'd be interested in that too, but stuff that just got cut for time. The two examples that come to mind from commentary are from Saucer Morons and Abducted.**

ME: All of the poop jokes. Which was always, like, half of it.

Seriously, lots of stuff gets cut just by virtue of the process. My first drafts always started too long, so I'd cut lines and jokes to streamline it. The storyboards usually had bits cut before they reached animatic. The animatics always came in long, so the director and Jhonen would cut some things once everyone saw the show "on its feet." It was rarely whole scenes, though. My biggest "cut" regret was the fantasy parade sequence to the United Nations ZIM was going to have in "Door to Door." I'll go into that if I write a second volume of this little script book. Unless it gets cut.

@I***: If there were any episode you could go back in time and rewrite, given the chance, what would you change and why?**

ME: How much am I being paid? Is it union wages?

Though for free I'd go back and fix "Dibship Rising" so the final chase/fight/action-sequence takes place with the ship in Dib form. To this day I'm kicking myself for not noticing that the first time around. I'm kicking myself now. Through the chair. It a trick that comes naturally to me.

@N****: What is the origin of the irken race? What happened to dib's mom? How is an inside of an irken? The hair strand of dib and membrane is a extremity? Chemically, what damages an irken? Were they going to make a ship canon? Will one day zim win?**

ME: I will answer your questions with another question: Have you sought treatment for your meth problem?

@I*********: Out of all of the rumors spread about the show, be it unfinished episodes or whatever else occurred behind the scenes, which of them are true, and which of them are false info?

ME: All of them are false except one.

@I*********: For example, was Dib really going to be revealed as a clone of his father, and were Zim and Gaz going to replace Tallest Red and Purple?

ME: No. See? False. And you'll never guess the true one, so don't try.

@G******: What happened to Dib and Gaz's mother? Are they really just clones of Professor Membrane?

ME: Okay, real answer this time. The truth on this one is it was never formally decided. However Jhonen did at one point say he might some day have Dib discover an empty jar labeled "Mom" in one of Professor Membrane's cupboards. Whether he was serious about this, who knows? A lot of things Jhonen was never serious about get quoted as fact, and I fully expect this to fall into that category.

@M******: There were rumors about a potential movie 15 years ago. Was there a script? Concept art?

ME: No. I'm afraid there was nothing. Nobody proposed a movie. There wasn't even an idea for one. There was no script. No art. No gleam in a child's eye. No tear shed for the fallen. Just a cold, gray world spinning around an angry, squinting sun in the vacuum of space.

@X*****: Are there any practices or warmups that you do prior to writing to have your scripts be more "in character" or does it all come naturally?

ME: I usually start with two gallons of ginseng coffee, a glucose danish, five hundred ab-crunches, six dozen push-ups, and an hour-long plank. Then I write the words "Death Before David Hasselhoff" over and over again until

I've filled eight pages. These pages are burned on an altar to T'hanzshanz, the dark elder of cartoons, and the ashes are collected to make toner for my laser printer. After that I'm good to go.

@F*******: Was there really a concept of Zim, accepting the life on Earth eventually and becoming sort of a guardian even for it?

ME: Nope. Someone made that up. Probably hoping it was true. Let us all take a moment to feel bad for that person.

@P********: What character was your LEAST favorite to write for?

ME: Aquaman.

@A******: Did they really have Richard Horvitz in the recording booth making Zim noises while everyone was on lunch? Not actually recording anything, just trolling him.

ME: If they did, it's Richard's fault. There's a window that looks out of the booth straight into the studio, so if Richard didn't see that everyone had left, he needed to pay better attention to his surroundings. I mean we know Richard has problems with object persistence and hallucinating talking dogs, but that's another level entirely.

@S*******: Were there plans to have more of the other irkens be more prominently featured in the story? Would we have seen more Tak, Skoodge, or Tenn?

ME: Tak - She was going to come back eventually if the series had kept going. In fact, she was slated to turn up in the scrapped dog show episode "Top of the Line."

Skoodge - Actually — and this is for real — Jhonen wanted to work Skoodge in as having been secretly living in ZIM's house for a while. He may have gone on to be a constant presence in his base, kind of an annoying roommate who never got much done.

Tenn — I have no idea. America hates Tenn.

@R******: There's a rumor that there was going to be a bloody gir in one of the scenes but nick refused to have it,if this rumor is true,how would bloody gir be used?

ME: For the record, Bloody GIR was never anything even the least bit "real." It was never intended to be part of any story. Chris Graham drew him on a whim, and everyone knew it would never properly get into the show, so the crew snuck him in for one-frame flashes here and there. But Bloody GIR was never, ever put up for approval, therefore Nickelodeon never said no. Also, the rumored Bloody GIR crossover episode with *Hey Arnold* was never once considered. Sorry, Arnold.

@c******: What was the best episode to write? What was one joke or reference you had wanted to add to an episode but had to be cut or removed?

ME: - Best episode: Anything I wrote with someone else. (Seriously, it was more fun. "Megadoomer," "Door to Door," "Chickenfoot," "Dib's Wonderful Life of Doom," all of those rank up there.) Best joke that got cut: As I referenced earlier, the big parade at the end of "Door to Door." It was cut for production purposes, but it was recorded and storyboarded and everything. It would have been glorious. *Glorious!!*

@Z*******: a big super question I have is why does skoodge have no pack?

ME: There are three answers in one here. The first is "The crew forgot it." The second is is "Skoodge was the experimental test subject of an advanced pak system that condensed the complete pak functionality into his boots. Hobo 13 was a field test of this system, which came through with flying colors. The

Tallest, however, never approved the boots for wide distribution because they couldn't be bothered. The third is, "Really, the crew forgot it."

@B*******: One more - can you tell us more about Lobster Claws(Claus?)?

ME: I did tell you, but then the Lobster Cops wiped your mind. I'll say nothing more. I've put you in too much danger already.

@rikkisimons: Where did I leave my keys?

ME: Rikki! Listen! Because I'm not going to repeat this *again*. They're Jammed in the skull of a drifter behind an AM/PM on a lonely highway through the lost soul of the Mojave desert. Ask for Jessica at the register. She'll show you to the body. Just don't tell the authorities. And please, lose my number.

ABOUT THE AUTHOR

ERIC TRUEHEART has been writing in the zone called "Kidspace" for nearly 20 years, despite his best intentions., and he's made animated creatures talk for every major — and minor — kids' network in town. He started on Nickelodeon's original cult hit, *Invader ZIM*, wrote for Disney XD's BAFTA-nominated *Yin Yang Yo*, helped Dreamworks develop the feature film *Turbo* into the first animated series for Netflix — garnering it a Daytime Emmy nomination in the process. He also spent time in sketch comedy, but took a shower afterwards. Along the way he sold pilots to Cartoon Network, Disney, SyFy, and even Spike. (Hey, remember them?)

Eric was born in fabulous Rochester NY — for no reason he's ever been able to figure out — and has lived in the greater Los Angeles area for so long he can't remember what real life looks like.

left: The author, full of hope, in the parking lot of Nickelodeon circa 2000.
right: The author, confused, in a photo studio nearly twenty
years later, wondering just what the hell happened.